D0182156

The First $20 Million Is Always the Hardest

"A sly, entertaining tribute to American can-do ingenuity. Ken Kesey would be proud."   —*Boston Herald*

"A rollicking good read that sheds a revealing light on the personalities and values of Silicon Valley."   —*Business Week*

"A wild ride . . . a wonderful read."   —*Houston Chronicle*

"Clever and irreverent."   —*Los Angeles Times*

"If Charles Dickens were alive, it's likely he would be writing about our computerized society. . . . Dickens being otherwise engaged, it is well that we have a satirist of the caliber of Po Bronson."   —*Cleveland Plain Dealer*

"Bravo! . . . Original and sparkling. This is a book for anyone who has a computer, or who wants to know about computers, and it will cure that itch to upgrade."   —*Baltimore Sun*

"Bronson perfectly captures the antic side of Silicon Valley's mad quest for money and fame. . . . He is raising the bar for successors trying to create the next killer novel."
                    —*San Francisco Chronicle*

"First-rate entertainment . . . marvelous twists and turns. . . . The book simply grabs you, smartly capturing its time and place."   —*San Jose Mercury News*

"A crafty, funny, and sympathetic depiction of a world that's high-tech to the max, but very human for all that."
                    —*Publishers Weekly* (starred review)

THE FIRST
$20 MILLION
IS ALWAYS
THE HARDEST

ALSO BY PO BRONSON

Bombardiers

PO BRONSON

THE FIRST $20 MILLION IS ALWAYS THE HARDEST

.....

A SILICON VALLEY NOVEL

Perennial

An Imprint of HarperCollins*Publishers*

This is a work of fiction. The characters, incidents, and dialogues are products of the author's imagination and are not to be construed as real. Any resemblance to living people is entirely coincidental. Where the names of actual companies are used, the situations, incidents, and dialogues concerning those companies are entirely fictional and are not intended to depict any actual events or change the entirely fictional character of the book.

A hardcover edition of this book was published in 1995 by Random House, Inc. A mass-market edition of this book was published in 1998 by Avon Books.

THE FIRST $20 MILLION IS ALWAYS THE HARDEST. Copyright © 1997 by Po Bronson. All rights reserved. Printed in the United States of America. No part of this book may be used or reproduced in any manner whatsoever without written permission except in the case of brief quotations embodied in critical articles and reviews. For information address HarperCollins Publishers Inc., 10 East 53rd Street, New York, NY 10022.

HarperCollins books may be purchased for educational, business, or sales promotional use. For information please write: Special Markets Department, HarperCollins Publishers Inc., 10 East 53rd Street, New York, NY 10022.

First Perennial edition published 2000

Designed by Victoria Wong

Library of Congress Cataloging-in-Publication Data has been applied for.

ISBN 0-380-81624-5

00 01 02 03 04 RRD 10 9 8 7 6 5 4 3 2 1

ACKNOWLEDGMENTS

The author wishes to thank the following people for their assistance with the manuscript: Nina Schuyler, Jon Karp, Jim Humes, Ethan Watters, Ethan Canin, Peter Ginsberg, Jess Taylor, and David Munro.

THE FIRST
$20 MILLION
IS ALWAYS
THE HARDEST

OMEGA LOGIC CORPORATION

EXIT INTERVIEW TRANSCRIPT

Note: This is an abridged transcript approved by the Legal Department for permanent storage in the employee's personnel file. A confidential unabridged transcript is retained by the Legal Department.

Employee: ANDY CASPAR
Most Recent Department: SALES & MARKETING
Interview Date: April 10, 1992
Departure Date: April 10, 1992

Reason for Departure
☐ Terminated
☒ Voluntary

INT: You may not take anything other than your personal belongings. Client records, your Rolodex, notebooks, any equipment issued to you, cellular phones, laptops, all backup diskettes—those must be turned over by this afternoon.

CASPAR: I turned them in yesterday. I gave you the form ten minutes ago.

INT: That's fine, I just need these statements on the tape.

CASPAR: Okay.

INT: And you understand that your memory of the information that you turned in, that information is also the property of Omega Logic, and you may not share that information with any future employers.

CASPAR: What would I share? It's all going to be obsolete soon anyway. Your prices, your technology. The customers will still be there but in three months all the contacts will have changed.

INT: If you could just acknowledge having heard these questions, this will go faster. Now, have you accepted a job offer from another employer?

CASPAR: No.

INT: Have you applied for positions at any other corporation or organization?

CASPER: No.

INT: Can you give us some idea of why you are choosing to leave?

CASPAR: Can you give me a good reason to stay?

INT: Your performance reviews were excellent.

CASPAR: So?

INT: Uh, presumably you were *good* at it, and would take pride in that.

CASPAR: I'm only twenty-six. If I'm already good at it, what challenge does that leave me for the rest of my life?

INT: Hmmm.

CASPAR: Let me ask you something. Does your job have any real honest-to-god challenge in it? Does it present you with problems you can't solve?

INT: This interview is not about me.

CASPAR: See? That's why I'm leaving. You can leave yourself out of it. But I can't. I can't live in just a small part of myself anymore.

INT: [pause] I think patience and stability are sometimes underrated.

CASPAR: Who are you trying to convince? Me, or yourself?

1

The Shiny Shoes

1995

Oh, God. No sooner had Francis Benoit started explaining to this reporter the difference between the ISA and PCI electrical standards when the reporter's head nods—customary cues that implied "Go on, I'm with you"—were replaced by this high-tempo bobbing and rocking motion that signaled that the reporter's brain had lost the train of thought and was spinning idly, frozen like a processor caught in an infinite loop.

He knew what she wanted. She wanted Francis to say something *familiar*, something *tangible*—something like "Imagine the motherboard is like a fruit tree"—to rescue her brain back into this time and place. But he wasn't going to say it for her. Forget it. He *hated* having to translate his work into dumbed-down metaphors for the shiny-shoe set—the meddlesome lawyers, media scribblers, and potential corporate sponsors who came through wanting to understand without doing the hard work of paying attention.

The reporter was from the *San Jose Mercury News,* and she'd been invited to chronicle the design of a next-generation chip for one of La Honda Research's sponsors, Omega Logic. Francis was the lead designer. The reporter's name was Nell Kirkham. She sat with her legs crossed and her head tilted back so her hair fell behind her shoulders. She didn't wear earrings or a necklace or rings, but only a tenth of the cost of the gold watch she was wearing was devoted to telling time. She didn't wear the kind of cheap makeup that needed reapplying after every meal. She was a woman who wanted it both ways: she wanted to be considered pretty but be taken seriously for her intellect. She wanted men to think she was beautiful, but not to come on to her. She would never flutter her eyes. She would never giggle or tell people they were smart or try to make them feel too special.

She said, "Now this *project,* this chip. Most projects have code names."

Francis wasn't going to let her go in that direction. "What's your question?"

"What's this project's code name?"

"The six eighty-six."

She looked disappointed. "Most code names . . . are . . . more *metaphorical* than that. More . . . *inspiring.*"

Francis had given it the name 686 specifically to avoid any metaphorical simplification. "And your question is . . . ?"

She sighed and put down her pen. "I don't just want my stories to be about how you're packing ten million transistors on a chip. I'm really interested in being able to write about the personal journey you go through. I want to know what this means to *you.*"

"Well, it won't be ten million transistors. We're getting the specs from Omega's fabrication team. It might be *six* million."

"Whatever!"

Francis pinched his forehead with the fingers of his right hand. He blew out some air. "Ms. Kirkham, with all respect, if Omega's plant in Singapore could put ten million transistors on a chip, we would produce a radically different circuit design, not need graphics accelerators, math coprocessors, et cetera. Ten million transistors, *Christ.* That would put half of Omega's competitors out of business."

"But you understand my point, right? I need to know what you *think* about the project. I want to write about how it makes you *feel.*"

Francis agonized over this. He'd spent the past ten years of his life devoted to designing more powerful computers. that time, computers didn't actually operate any faster users, since the software programs had grown so huge that it all the new hardware power just to maintain the status quo. Bigger software required faster hardware, which in turn stimulated demand for even bigger software. Omega was La Honda's biggest sponsor, and Omega was taking heat from Wall Street, *Chip or Die*. The truth was, Francis had a hard time seeing the point of yet another faster beast. He'd agreed to take the assignment very reluctantly. But he wasn't going to tell this story to a reporter who wouldn't even bother to understand his technology.

He said, "What do you mean, 'how I feel'?"

"Well, for instance . . . La Honda is a nonprofit research lab. Sponsors pay you to design things, and then you don't ever see any profit from that. You don't really even get the credit. So how does that make you *feel*?"

Ahhh. Reporters always got around to asking that. They couldn't understand that all Francis wanted to do was to work without intrusions, to create. They couldn't believe that he wasn't interested in being a billionaire.

"I feel fine," Francis said. "I get what I want from it."

"But you watch all these young guys with uncountable wealth on the cover of magazines . . ."

"What about 'em?"

"Jealous?"

"Naw . . ."

Despite all the roll-up-your-shirtsleeves myths and stereotypes, when you got right down to it, working in a corporate start-up meant you spent 80 percent of your time doing complete *bullshit*—chasing venture capital money, writing technical documentation, hiring people—and all of it involved *dumbing down* your work. And the meetings! It was inevitable that at some point the system of for-profit entrepreneurship rewarded engineers who were good at dumbing down their work. To participate in that game would be a waste of God-given talent, it would be a crime against Francis's very own nature.

When he didn't say anything more, she tried again. "Well, does it make you feel you have something to prove?"

"Mmmm. This feeling, this feeling of having something to prove—you know what it comes from? It comes from when somebody doesn't believe you, doesn't believe *in* you. And the only person in the past month who's questioned me, the only person who doubts me . . . is *you,* Ms. Kirkham. I *told* you. I'm happy with the way it works around here. You think all that matters is *money,* and *magazine covers?* Fine. But don't presume that's all that I think matters. Now, if you excuse me . . . I've got to go talk with Hank."

They were in Francis's office. He stood up, hands on hips. While she gathered her tape recorder and notepad into her shoulder bag, he walked to his doorway and stood holding the door open. There was nothing impatient in his body language but by merely being one step ahead of her, he kept her unsettled. She dropped a pen on the way out.

. . .

About the same time, an air-conditioned van was on its way from San Francisco, an hour north. In the van were a photographer and his camera crew, intent on shooting an ad for a new line of casual clothing, Lo-Tech Workware.

Some Italian conglomerate had built up sufficient internal consensus to approve their ad agency's recommendation: put unassuming clothes on semifamous titans of the American computer industry, take pictures, and print the pictures alongside the slogan "High-tech insiders wear Lo-Tech on the outside." Their problem was that these supposed titans might be downright physically grotesque. Their solution was to hire the renowned Italian fashion photographer Adriano Paschetta; these advertisements would present themselves as "art," avoiding the beauty question altogether. Paschetta was flown out to San Francisco, given first-class treatment for several days to prime his artistic temperament, and then put in an air-conditioned van for the trip down to Silicon Valley.

The producer had received by fax very specific directions, but still . . . They had found the turnoff for Old La Honda Road, passed over a little gangplank bridge, and ascended into an evergreen forest, where sword ferns straddled the one-lane road and neon velvet moss circled the tree trunks. Dirt driveways were marked only by clusters of mailboxes, sprouting like wild mush-rooms. Their instructions had warned them about the serpentine turns and the steep inclines, but about two miles up, the asphalt became all cracked and broken so the wheels of their van started a drumbeat *rump rump rump* which made the van's owner uneasy—he was in the rear seat, turned backward, trying to keep his lighting equipment from crashing into the van's walls; then the canopy of forest overhanging the road began scraping the metal roof, and naturally they started thinking they'd missed a turnoff, this couldn't be it, no way, something was wrong here, this couldn't be the way to the world-renowned La Honda Research Center.

Right about when their ears popped from the altitude, they caught up with this fat guy on a frail 50 cc pedal scooter, which was whining and bleeding a trail of oil-tainted blue smoke into the air. A plastic grocery bag dangled from the elbow of one arm; a diminutive Styrofoam helmet adorned his head. He was wearing cut-off shorts no bigger than a jock strap and a striped, elastic-ribbed T-shirt so small it cut indents into his shoulders where the sleeves ended.

There was no room to pass, and the fat guy wasn't about to pull his scooter over into somebody's driveway and lose all his momen-tum, so they had no choice but to roll along behind him for the next mile and stare at the pale smile of flesh between his shorts and shirt.

Adriano Paschetta hadn't been told much, but one of the things he'd been told, when he asked about the *location* of this shoot, was that the La Honda Research Center had originally been built as a school for the dumb, back in the early fifties, by some grand phil-anthropic matron who thought she could improve the intelligence of those society left behind by giving them a positive and encourag-ing environment of their own. And when the fat guy on the scooter pulled into the entrance of the research center, Paschetta wondered if maybe this was all a prank from the boys in New York, a wild goose chase, and that the La Honda Research Center wasn't some renowned science lab at all—it might still be a school for the dumb. Coming from New York, where power is expressed in huge build-ings rocketing skyward—where power is expressed, above all, in concrete and glass—well, they just expected more than a converted high school. Two three-story I-shaped buildings with sloped, Spanish tile roofs bordered a field of overgrown, trampled grass; cement pathways crisscrossed the field and led up into the trees behind the buildings. The buildings were brick, but resurfaced with a thin layer of terra-cotta or adobe, which had provided a porous surface for ivy to climb on. The flower beds separating the lawn from the buildings had blackberry bushes growing in them. Blackberries! Where the camera crew came from, the blackberry bush was considered an invasive *weed,* even in the heat of summer with berries popping up beside every thorn, yet here it was growing right in the flower beds, trimmed into orderly four-foot-high thickets. The surface of the parking lot suggested it had once been a pair of tennis courts; the angled stalls were full of skinny-wheeled Colts and four-speed Mazdas. The fat guy, who had leaned his scooter up against a bike rack in the parking lot without locking it, waddled along a pathway for several steps, the landing of each foot initiating a jiggle that tremored up and across the surface of his body. He reached into his grocery bag, dug around with his fist, and came out with a double-stick fruit Popsicle. With a thumb and forefinger he snipped a hole in the wrapper, then put his mouth around the end and exhaled sharply, inflating the wrapper. When his mouth came away it had the wrapper between his teeth. The thought then occurred to Adriano Paschetta that the whole notion implied by this marketing campaign was dangerous, and it might be a terrible and grave mistake to turn our culture over to a gang of brainiacs who cared not a whit about appearances.

They unpacked the van; it took all of them to move the gear indoors—lights, makeup kit, several camera bags, backdrops, and a rack of clothes to be worn by the titan, a man named Hank Menzinger, the executive director of the center. They'd never seen Hank Menzinger, didn't even know what he looked like, and as far as they could tell, *nobody* involved with the advertising campaign had seen whether or not he looked good in the clothes. Nobody'd even checked his *size,* for god's sake—the clothes might not fit! But according to the boys in New York, that was okay, that was *great* even, because the campaign was trying to be very unpretentious, it was trying to convey the message that "beauty is not just appearance." And so on. All they knew about Hank Menzinger was that he could be found in room 211, which was supposed to be upstairs in back, down a long hall.

So they hauled their gear up the stairs and down the hall and knocked on room 211 and a man inside said "Yup," and so they went in, banging their equipment on the doorframe. There was something wrong with the room; this was certainly *not* the office of any titan they'd ever seen. Where was the false fireplace, the leather-bound books, the regal oil painting of the officeholder? Where, above all, was the *secretary*? Instead, there were two sleek leather couches opposite each other, and on one of the couches sat a man. His head was tipped back to the ceiling. He had a shaved but stubbled head atop a lanky frame and looked pallid, as if he might have just been let out of the hospital after a long sickness. He was wearing a green T-shirt with a line of tiny white lettering across the chest, too small to read at a distance. His eyes were also green, and Adriano Paschetta mustered all of his artistic sensibilities to find inspiration in the very greenness of those eyes. Of course, they assumed this man was Hank Menzinger, and had no idea he was really Francis Benoit.

Francis Benoit had been waiting ten minutes for Hank Menzinger to finish his conference call in the inner room. Waiting was not one of Francis's strengths, and he wasn't going to let this crew of photographers or whatever they were keep him from giving Hank a piece of his mind. He took the crew in with his eyes and started stalling while his brain figured. . . .

"You're looking for Hank, huh? . . . Who are you guys, some photo crew, rack of clothes, huh . . . Wait—this for an ad?"

The producer introduced himself, and then introduced Adriano Paschetta. "The *photographer*," he added, after Paschetta's name failed to register even a raised eyebrow on Francis's face. "All the way from New York."

Francis went to the rack of clothes and shuffled through the hangers, quickly delivering his pronouncement on each article. "Yes, yes, no, no, *yeeesss*, no . . . Hey, wait, these shoes . . ." Francis turned to the producer. "These shoes are *shiny*."

"That's bad?" the producer asked.

"Yes, bad." He pulled the loafers out and set them on the carpet. "You know what shiny shoes mean, don't you?"

The producer's eyes squinted and his lips pursed. No words came out.

"Shiny shoes have to be continually *reshined*. Now tell me why I would buy a pair of shoes that have to be continually *reshined* when I could buy a pair—for no more money, mind you—that *don't* have to be reshined?"

The representative from the Italian conglomerate stepped forward to offer an explanation. "Well, we thought that the shine, the polish, conveyed a sort of *crisp* quality, sort of that high-tech, dust-free sheen."

Francis merely shook his head. "Crisp?" he said, drawing out the word. "*Crisp?* No, you see, this place is not about being crisp. Crisp is not a goal we aspire to. Using our time effectively is a goal we aspire to. Keeping our brains engaged at all times is a goal we aspire to. Shining our shoes is not on the list."

"Not on the list," the representative repeated. He seemed to make some decision. "Okay, no shoes. Thanks."

"It would have undermined your credibility," Francis added. "People in this town, they love to sniff out a fake."

"Thanks, thanks. Authenticity is important to us. Do you mind . . ." The representative's attention seemed to be fixed on the block of tiny white lettering on Francis's chest. The point size was so small the representative had to push his face within inches of Francis's sternum in order to read:

> WHEN ARE YOU GOING TO LEARN THAT A T-SHIRT IS NOT
> A FASHION STATEMENT, NOR A BILLBOARD FOR ADVERTISING,
> NOR A FORUM FOR YOUR POLITICAL IDEALISM, AND IS JUST
> A SWATCH OF DYED COTTON THAT KEEPS ME WARM ON COOL DAYS
> AND COOL ON WARM DAYS?

The representative said, "Ohh, that's good, that's excellent. Now *that's* authentic. Can we take a Polaroid? I don't want to forget the words. Tommy, get a Polaroid of this right here. You don't mind, do you buddy?"

You don't mind, do you buddy? Francis Benoit believed this intense media interest in the "culture" of silicon technology was just a cop-out, a way to try to portray the computer without actually trying to understand the computer itself, an unscientific methodology of falsely reporting the effects as causes. Cybersex, smart drugs, virtual reality—*Oh, please.* Francis couldn't give a flying fuck for any of it. And the last thing he wanted was for his T-shirt to become an icon. The last thing Francis wanted was to let some guys from New York use his *life's work* to help sell some T-shirts! *You don't mind, do you buddy?*

Francis put his palm over the type on his chest. "Hank Menzinger moved his office downstairs last week," he said. "Room 139. It's in the opposing wing of the building . . . the other end of the main lobby. Big red-haired guy. Can't miss him."

The producer waved his crew into action, and they all picked up their gear and filed back out into the hall, clanging and clicking. When they were gone, Francis Benoit sat back down on the couch, bent over, and began to untie the laces on his canvas sneakers. He pulled the sneakers off and tossed them in the trash can at the end of the couch. Then he stood up, slipped his feet into the shiny shoes left behind by the crew, and marched into Hank Menzinger's office.

. . .

In room 139 was a big red-haired guy who looked like one of those plots of land allowed to return to its natural habitat—he was cavemanish, his beard climbing all the way to his eyes and descending right into his flannel shirt. One of his front teeth was chipped. But as the camera crew eventually found out, he was not Hank Menzinger either.

"Who told you that I was?"

"Well, this guy in room 211, he seemed very helpful at the time. . . ." The producer's voice trailed off.

"Well, what did he look like?"

When the producer described the bald head and T-shirt copy, the big red-haired guy began to nod appreciatively. The big red-haired guy was named Ronny Banks, and he was the closest thing Francis Benoit had to a best friend. Ronny Banks had a master's degree in computer science or physics or electrical engineering like everybody else at La Honda, but it was well known that when push came to shove, Ronny Banks just didn't have "it"—"it" being the one commodity valued around here: brainpower. Ronny was more of a caddy than an engineer; the one reason Hank Menzinger had invited him back three times was that he kept Francis Benoit happy. Ronny was the one person who wasn't afraid of saying the wrong thing around Francis; Ronny was the one guy who could laugh it off after Francis ridiculed him. Ronny's sole purpose at La Honda was to play along with whatever pranks or riffs Francis was into at the time. So when the producer described Francis, Ronny knew exactly what was going on.

"Aww, that must have been Francis Benoit," Ronny explained. "He hates visitors to the center—they interrupt his thinking. He was just playing a little prank on you."

"Can you just then—won't you tell us where to find Hank Menzinger?" the producer asked.

"Oh, sure, sure. He's in the administration building, across the quad—that's the grass patch. First door on the right after you go in. I'll call ahead to make sure he's there."

"Would you do that?"

"Sure, I just said I would, didn't I?"

The men went out. Ronny Banks picked up the phone and dialed an extension. Tiny Curtis Reese answered the phone. Ronny could hear him slurping on a Popsicle.

"What are you doing right now, Tiny?"

"Compiling . . ."

"Lookit, you gotta go right now to the conference room in the south building. Take the tunnel—don't go across the quad. Right now, you hear me?"

"Awright." He hung up the phone. Tiny was a precise person, and if you told him to go somewhere *right now,* he assumed you meant *this very second.* He wouldn't even pause to ask why he was supposed to go to the conference room, or why he was supposed to take the tunnel. Tiny Curtis Reese didn't want to know, and he didn't want to ask, because it would only distract him from pondering the lines of code he'd written that morning. He could walk through the tunnel without being distracted as long as he kept one lone finger out at his side running along the wall to keep him from missing a turn, and he could sit in the conference room patiently as long as he didn't sit in one of those chairs that made the feeling disappear from his legs. He sat down at the conference table in one of the safe chairs and leaned forward to put his elbows on the tabletop when he noticed, almost immediately, that this table was several inches *higher* than his regular desk. And it felt good! He noticed that his back was straighter this way, and that his forearms lay flat. He pushed back the chair and leaned forward to his normal position—a position he knew exactly, because when he canted his back to the precise angle, a small pop always occurred somewhere in his vertebrae. So he felt for the pop, and then he shuffled forward to the table and straightened up and put his arms out. He repeated this several times, and that was how the camera crew found him when they came through the door.

The fat guy!

Adriano Paschetta gasped. The producer stopped in his tracks. The representative from the Italian conglomerate shuffled through his rack of garments, hunting for the largest item he'd brought, a terry cloth bathrobe embossed across the back with the phrase SPROCKETS & COGS, it was here somewhere. . . .

Tiny barely noticed them.

"Excuse us," the producer said, stepping forward.

Tiny said, "I've been waiting."

"We're very sorry we're late," the producer said. "We've had a little trouble finding you. You are Hank Menzinger, right?"

"No."

"You're not?"

"No."

The producer took a deep breath of relief.

Tiny said, "Hank Menzinger, room 211." Sometimes Tiny failed to use familiar components of speech, preferring an abbreviated English akin to the code he wrote. He would often repeat words rather than modify comments—to say a dish of food, for instance, was extremely hot, Tiny would say "hot hot hot." He especially did this with strangers.

"Is that in this building?"

"No." Chair forward, arms out.

"In the other building?"

"Yes." Chair backward, feeling for the pop.

The producer felt an urge to make Tiny suffer bodily injury. "Will you say anything other than *yes* or *no*?"

"No."

He took revenge on Tiny with an old schoolyard trick. "Is this your first time being stupid?"

"No, I mean yes . . . Wait . . . I'm not stupid."

The producer charged out of the room. The crew followed him, swearing and cursing. Adriano Paschetta stayed behind for a moment. He watched Tiny push his chair forward and backward. He'd been waiting all day for proper inspiration, he was looking for some distinct quality to capture on film, a quality that spoke to what La Honda was about. Suddenly Adriano Paschetta felt a surge of empathic energy rush through him, and he understood—he *got it*. He absolutely had to capture this—this *what?* This incredible level of *concentration*. This *focus*. He went up to Tiny.

"Excuse me, but, did you know . . . did you know that you are still wearing your bicycle helmet?"

Tiny put his hand on his head. Sure enough, the guy was right—he'd left his trusty Styrofoam helmet on his head this whole time. "What do you know . . . ?" he said. Then his hand went back down, and he fell back into his trancelike thoughts.

He didn't take it off!

Adriano Paschetta ran all the way to room 211.

. . .

This was the favorite kind of prank that Francis Benoit liked to play, because it was not just cruel, and it was not just revenge against the indignity of having to dumb down their work. This particular kind of prank stored a message, it taught a lesson—a lesson that would have to be learned by anyone who wanted to understand the way these computer engineers looked upon the rest of society. The name of the prank was "the infinite loop," a term borrowed from programming. An infinite loop is what causes computer programs to apparently stall or stop working. A program starts looking for a particular variable, the way the photo crew went looking for Hank Menzinger. It follows its instructions to go to a particular line of code, just as they'd gone to room 211. That line of code performs a function, such as steals their shoes, then orders the program to now go to another line of code, such as room 139. Still the program is looking for the variable, but at room 139, it is told to try yet another room. Francis Benoit knew that sooner or later somebody would set the crew straight and send them back to room 211, completing the loop. Were this a computer program, though, it wouldn't get frustrated or exasperated. It would just follow the orders stored in room 211—leave some shoes and go to room 139 again. It would continue to go around and around endlessly, *infinitely*. When a computer appears to stop responding to keystrokes, usually it is caught in one of these infinite loops, working just perfectly, following instructions one at a time—with no idea it's caught in a loop! It won't respond to keystrokes because it's not done with the last request; it still hasn't found Hank Menzinger, but it believes he's in the next room! This last part was important to the lesson. People can be caught in their own infinite loops *and have no idea they're caught in a loop*. Each step seems logical, while the illogic of it all evades them. As a necessary part of their work, the engineers at La Honda had trained themselves to spot infinite loops wherever they might be.

But they didn't have to look far. They had no farther to go than the Shell station at the bottom of the hill. Every morning, middle-aged men and women in hard-worsted suits stood beside their Lexus and Mercedes, filling up their tanks, quick to honk their horns, easily frustrated if forced to wait even a minute before handing over their credit cards—these were the people whose lives had fallen into infinite loops. Consumption as therapy: leasing the Mercedes was the reward they allowed themselves for having worked so hard for so many years . . . but the Mercedes cost a little more than they could afford, so they worked even harder . . . and on and on.

But it was not just individual people who had fallen into infinite loops. When the engineers at La Honda looked at the way society worked, sometimes all they could see was infinite loops. Just open the newspaper! Politicians ensure that taxes are always high enough to campaign for reelection on the pledge to cut taxes. Meanwhile, the public complains that it wants its politicians to "discuss the real issues," which the politicians would be perfectly willing to do as soon as the public would just stop caring about the first lady's haircut. The cure for this loop is with the educational system, but that happens to be caught in its own loop. Our failed educational systems guarantee that students will graduate uneducated, thereby creating an even greater demand for more failed educational systems. Education could get out of its rut if the entertainment industry would just clean up its act, and the entertainment executives would happily clean up their act if the public would just stop clamoring for more flesh-'n'-blood. But flesh-'n'-blood is the great pacifier, and we need it, particularly in hard times like these when taxes are so high. . . . From the researchers' point of view, up there in their little utopia, tucked in amidst eighty-seven acres of Bishop pine and Douglas fir overlooking Silicon Valley—a vantage point that they considered, without question, to be outside the "system"—society had some time ago entered into an infinite loop and stopped responding.

If the Lo-Tech producer stopped any one of these scientists on the footpaths around the center, and asked what he was *doing* with his time at La Honda, he would never get him to say what he really thought, what he really believed. Instead, he would get as narrow an answer as possible, such as "I'm trying to amplify you were you were wireless signals in the K-band spectrum," or "I'm testing the electrical storage capacity of heretofore unconsidered alloys." This was a way of talking about it by example only; it was just another way to lay a clue for an outsider. And if you got enough clues—if you had been duped into one of Francis Benoit's infinite-loop pranks, and you had hung out with the scientists for weeks on end—you would finally understand the very big picture of the La Honda Research Center. Their goal was bigger than any of them ever cared to state outright, for fear of coming across as *unrealistic.* Oh, you could say the computer is good for word processing or crunching data or interactive gaming, but you would have failed to see what those added up to. You could look at specific inventions that had come out of La Honda, such as the branch-prediction logic unit, or three-dimensional cubelets, or flash BIOS, or any number of computer languages—and totally miss the point. They all knew why they worked around the clock, week in and week out: they wanted to jolt society out of its infinite loop. Nothing less.

But it would take special men to pull this off. Not just anybody could jolt society out of its infinite loop. It took "ironmen." "Big iron" was industry slang for the fast, powerful computers invented at La Honda and elsewhere. *Ironmen*—they loved that word. No other word quite fit. Hank had given them that word. Every June, Hank Menzinger had to go to the four-drawer gunmetal file cabinet in the back of his office and comb through the La Honda personnel files to decide who was special enough to be one of them and who wasn't up to the task. And those that he decided were worthy he "reinvited" for another year. Reinvited! What a choice of words! Nobody was ever fired from La Honda—not one person in thirty years—but plenty had failed to be reinvited. Because to be fired implied that you had been employed, which itself was to imply a *commercial* quality that just didn't exist at La Honda. Scientists had worked at La Honda for years, and not one of them was paid a decent salary. Most of the live bodies around La Honda were graduate students on loan from nearby Stanford University, and there were plenty more where they came from. It didn't matter that they were paid a miserable wage, perhaps $35,000 a year if they were lucky, because La Honda was *not about money.* Money just didn't matter there. That form of currency was just not honored. Because what young people in America wanted more than anything else, in 1995, was a place to go during the day where their brain wasn't wasted. And there was no price you could put on that. For every kid at La Honda there were three at Stanford willing to take his place.

That they put in long hours went without saying—hell, just to get into the Stanford graduate program you had to have devoted most of your waking hours to your studies, and once you were at Stanford, it only got more intense. By the time you got to La Honda, there were no more hours in the day to give. So merely logging hours was not enough. Falling asleep at your desk, for instance, was not a sign of devotion. It was a sign you weren't taking care of your *instrument,* your *brain,* like failing to change the oil every four thousand miles. It was a sign of disrespect, of *desperation,* and in the front hallway of the south building there was a gallery of Polaroids of ironmen who had fallen asleep on their keyboards. That "I'm your slave, work me" tactic—which a newcomer at a commercial company might employ to climb a few rungs—just didn't cut it here. La Honda wasn't like the commercial sector. There were no semiannual performance reviews, no ten-rung salary ladder to climb, no job titles to garner, no business cards to hand out to friends. There was no marketing department to pass off your bloated code as sublime, no fancy software boxes you could put on your bookshelf and say "I did that," no sales figures to derive pride from. Oh, in a commercial company there were any number of ways to know where you stood in the grand competition. But at La Honda, there was only one: either you were reinvited or you weren't.

The process of reinvitation was torture on them. Throughout the year new people had been brought on as needed, so by May the number of ironmen had usually bloated to 110, maybe 120 people. Hank usually cut that by a fifth—but sometimes more, sometimes less, depending on the success of fund-raising and corporate sponsorships, which was a topic he kept very close to his chest (because it was not about money!). But he never told any of them how many he would reinvite. Instead he would occasionally post a list on the cork bulletin board in the foyer of the north building, right below the bronze bas relief of Monica Edmunds, the grand matron who built the place. On this list he might have scribbled ten names, all of them reinvited. Then, for a few days, nothing. The agony! You couldn't go look for a summer job, and it was too late even to sign up for summer classes at Stanford. Then another posting, ten or fifteen more names. The word of a posting spread through the buildings. The hopefuls rushed to the foyer. Oh, to be one of those with your name on the list! Officially, you played it cool: merely noted your name (Hey, there I am) and calmly strolled back to your lab. But inside you were positively beaming. The fuse to your ego had been lit, and you were soaring like a rocket. It was not uncommon for a young man, on the night he had been reinvited, to make the kind of moves in life that can only be done riding a bolt of confidence in one's own future—to propose marriage to his girl-friend or to make an offer on a condominium. Technological breakthroughs regularly came from young ironmen who had recently been reinvited, as if the fire in their brain had been fed pure oxygen.

When the number of names got to be around eighty, there was always the possibility that Hank would just say "That's it—that's the cutoff." Lobbying was considered unnecessary—the brightness

THE FIRST $20 MILLION IS ALWAYS THE HARDEST   21

of your mind was supposed to be self-evident, and if it didn't show, then you must not have it, so what was the point of arguing? You just had to wait. The names slowed to a trickle; undoubtably, some of the fellows and chairs were debating the merits of a particular student with Hank. And this was exactly why Francis Benoit had been waiting to see Hank Menzinger on the day in June 1995 when the photographer and his crew had popped into Hank's anteroom and Francis had managed to con them out of a pair of shiny Italian loafers.

. . .

Francis Benoit kicked back in an armchair across from Hank and put his feet up on Hank's desk, tipping over a jar of green pencils. He made no apology or effort to gather the pencils. Hank looked at Francis's shiny new shoes. They looked good, sharp. Hank wore a lambskin leather short coat that was as shiny as a Criscoed baking sheet; he had a broad back and a thick gut, a symbol that his ironmen interpreted as greatness of character rather than a weakness for sweets. His arms were thick and his hands so big that the center's janitors, who spoke mostly Spanish, had given him the nickname *Manos*. He had broad flat lips and long wiry hair that had once been red and a grin that made other men in its presence feel less alive. Hank Menzinger had taken over many a cocktail party with his sheer magnanimity. Students flocked to work for him. Reporters loved him. Companies gave him money. Hank Menzinger had once been an engineer, a good one, and had worked at Fairchild Semiconductor in the sixties, when that meant something. But at some point along the road, Hank realized that his greatest gift was not the power of his brain but the power of his personality. And that was nothing to be ashamed of, particularly if he applied his energy to the same goal he'd been applying his mind to—jolt society out of its infinite loop!

"Jolt" was Hank's word, too. Although it couldn't be logically refuted that the effect of technology was constant and gradual, Hank had trained the ironmen at La Honda to look at it from the point of view of world history, where decades are remembered as single moments. As a result, the prevailing belief was that at some point technology would turn the corner or get over the hump . . .

like breaking the sound barrier. It might be a single piece of technology, and it might be the pervasiveness of technology, but it was
most likely to be some combination. A certain amount of power, in
the hands of a certain number of people . . . The jolt would happen when 60 percent of American homes were hooked up to the
internet, or 90 percent, or 75 percent of the world, or when the
cost of a computer was less than that of a telephone, or when
technology allowed for a single world government, or *something*.
There was no topic more exciting. Nobody at La Honda assumed
his particular project during that year was going to be what put
society over the hump. From the point of view of history, that was
just too unlikely. Short of that, though, they dreamed of having a
front-row seat when history was made. La Honda was the front
row. However it happened, and whenever it happened, Hank
Menzinger had convinced them that it was mighty important that
they be at La Honda when it did.

Francis was looking out the window. His best friend, Ronny
Banks, still hadn't been reinvited. He said, "Some key people still
haven't been reinvited. So, naturally, those of us who count on
those key personnel are wondering what's going through Hank's
head . . . The count is eighty-five, it's been three days since you
added to it . . . four days . . . Naturally, we begin to wonder if
maybe you're not going to add to it at *all*."

As Hank listened, he leaned forward on his elbows, with his
hands flat against each other in a prayer position. When he spoke,
his hands parted, like the wings of a bird. "If you're asking whether
I'm going to invite any more people back, Francis, then my answer
is 'yes.' "

Francis didn't say anything. Typically he'd just let others talk, let
them fill the silence until they made a mistake.

Hank went on. "I have to be very selective this year, Francis.
Especially selective. You know already . . . I don't have to explain to you that the defense industry isn't as capable of sponsoring
research as it used to be. You know the position it puts me in,
Francis. I have to think about picking people who perform, people
who *produce*. I don't have *spare spots* to dole out."

Francis said, "You need people who've proved their worth."

"Exactly."

Francis nodded, as if with appreciation. "People who you can count on to get results."

"I'm glad you understand."

"And Ronny Banks . . . What has he done in the last year except inject red food coloring into the milk cartons in the cafeteria?"

"*Right.*"

Then Francis added, "And everybody else you are reinviting meets these criteria."

Hank stopped. "Well . . ."

"Do you have a list?"

"Tomorrow, Francis. The combination of people, the chemistry—it has to be right."

Francis said, "But there must be *some* names on it today?"

"Well, of course."

Francis waited him out. Eventually, Hank pulled a folder aside and brought up the list. He handed it to Francis, who read over the six names on it, going "yes, yes, yes" to each name as he considered the talent of the person. Then Francis got to a name, Caspar Andrews, and had to think about it for a second before he realized that Hank was talking about Andy Caspar. Andy Caspar was a pretty new guy, he'd been brought on only six weeks before, in late April, to test several software programs that had been written by others during the year. Testing was necessary but tedious, so much so that the engineers avoided the work if possible—testing just wasn't a way to demonstrate you had it, it wasn't a challenge to their prowess.

"Well, hell," Francis said. He brought his feet down and leaned forward onto the desk. "This kid Caspar here, he's just a tester! He hasn't proven himself!"

"Francis—"

"But you said you had no *spare spots* to dole out, and here you've got a mere *tester* on your list who's only been here six weeks! I think this spare spot right here ought to be put up for discussion. Spot number ninety-one, on the table." Francis slapped the list down on Hank's desk.

Hank shook his head. "Forget it. You do your job, I'll do mine."

Francis couldn't really believe the flak he was getting. Francis had agreed, somewhat hesitantly, to design another chip for

Omega, and he expected a little conciliation, a little pat on the back *at least*. A little "thank you" here—in the form of reinviting Ronny Banks—would go a long way.

"Uh-oh," Hank said.

"What?"

"You've gotten all quiet on me."

"So?"

"I can't read your thoughts, Francis, but I can tell when you're unhappy, and one of the signs is you clam up."

Francis despised being the subject of others' analysis. His privacy felt violated when they were wrong, but he was even more uncomfortable when they were right. Hank had been right.

As a way of reminding Hank of all that Francis had caved in on already, he said, "Nell Kirkham's going to divide the team! She's going to ask someone working on the memory module, 'Don't you think you deserve to work on the math unit?' Then she's going to ask someone working on the math unit, 'Don't you think you deserve to be working on the memory module?' "

Hank said, "Lloyd thinks having a journalist record the chip is an excellent idea." Lloyd was the CEO of Omega, and since Omega was one of La Honda's biggest sponsors, Lloyd also served as president of the board of regents of La Honda.

"Sure he likes the idea, he'll have every mutual fund manager from Newport Beach to London reading that Omega's new chip will burn rubber. His P/E will top twenty by Christmas, just in time for his board to vote a million-dollar bonus."

"Aww, cut us some slack, will you? You just hate anything that reminds you that you don't run this place. Sorry we didn't consult your majesty before bringing in Nell Kirkham."

"Oh, now hold on there—whoa. I don't want anything but to work in peace, so you can take your little power-struggle theory and put it back in its holster. . . . Lookit, this journalist, this *reporter* . . . Do I have time to teach a microelectronics lesson every day? That's *time,* that's *energy* that I don't devote to the chip."

Hank let a moment pass, then said, "What is this little display about, Francis?"

"I want Ronny Banks to be reinvited."

Hank Menzinger slid his chair back from the desk and turned to his gunmetal file cabinet. He pulled out Caspar's file. He knew this was going to happen. "A few years ago, Caspar worked at Omega Logic." Every year Lloyd Acheson looked over the list of reinvitees, and he swelled with pride if someone from Omega was amidst the brethren. Every year Hank Menzinger tried to make sure *somebody* who had worked at Omega was on the list at La Honda— even if they had only worked in Omega's marketing department, as Caspar had done.

. . .

Two floors below, in his office in the basement of the building, Andy Caspar was staring at something that had been carved into the well of one of his desk drawers by a previous occupant. It said:

> *What does it say about a man,*
> *that he spends his days at a gray desk*
> *in a windowless room?*

The ironmen were supposed to believe that work occurred in the mind, and that's where you really were, wasn't it? There was nothing dry or boring or dim about the mind. What did it matter where you sat? Sure, right. No amount of psychological justification was going to placate Andy into staying in the basement of La Honda for long.

Since he'd come to La Honda, he hadn't been given a decent chance to prove himself. He had been brought into a small, six-person team that was redesigning part of a chipset for digital satellites. They were all very anxious to finish because a new annual cycle was beginning, and this was the best time to sign up for new projects. Because the team was so small, they had a great deal of pride of ownership over their work, and they didn't want Andy to come in at the last minute and try to take credit. For the past six weeks, the team had been almost there, nearly there, or "one or two days away" from finishing. All of Andy's attempts to give input were rebuffed.

"How the hell can you possibly appreciate the intricacies of our problem?" they said to him. "You're just a *tester*."

So Andy resolved to himself, *If I'm just gonna be a tester, then I'm gonna be the best goddamn tester this place has ever seen.* He pored over their code for weaknesses, and then he exposed a weakness by putting that satellite chipset in a scenario where it froze up. Every day the team thought they were done, they had solved everything, time to hang up their hats. And every day Andy yanked them back to their desks with yet another wrinkle they had missed. He wrote programs that generated random scenarios for the chipset, so it was like having a whole *team* of testers in his office. Over the last six weeks, Andy had transformed himself from the peon the team looked down their noses at to the gremlin in the basement they feared.

Now Andy got a call from Hank Menzinger, requesting him to come by. Andy had to ask for the room number, since he'd never been there. He walked upstairs and entered Menzinger's office. Francis Benoit was also there. Menzinger pointed to a swivel armchair. Andy was amazed that Menzinger's office was so *cool*; it wasn't pretentious at all. He didn't have cheesy slogans on the walls. He had some bookcases, but not every book he'd ever read. He didn't have a humidifier. There was no CD player piping out ambient music. His desk wasn't anally organized. Andy couldn't believe it—here he was, sitting in the very same room with two of just about the hardest ironmen who ever existed.

Menzinger grinned and put Andy at ease instantly. "Listen, Andrews," Menzinger said to him. "As you know, I'm in the process of making reinvitations to personnel. To do this I usually consider the work accomplished over the past year. But in your case, I have to say—I have only my instinct to go on."

Benoit chipped in. "I want him to keep my friend Ronny Banks, but Hank here has been trying to convince me that we should keep you instead. Maybe you would care to help us."

Andy was caught off guard. What could he possibly say about himself that would earn their respect? What did they want? "Look, I'm not a conventional engineer," he started out, "I didn't even study engineering in college, but maybe that makes me . . . different." He was searching for an answer, but Francis Benoit leapt at it.

"Different? Now that's an interesting idea. How do you think it would make you different?"

"Well, I might approach a problem differently."

Francis baited him. "Are you saying you are different because you approach things differently, or you approach things differently because you are different?"

Now Andy wished he hadn't said anything. "Sometimes I think I see simpler solutions . . ." he offered.

"Ahhh, now we have something. You said before that you approach things differently, therefore you are different. Now you say that you have simpler solutions, so I am to conclude that you are *simple?*"

Andy looked to Hank Menzinger for help. He was still there, grinning away, as if all should be enjoying their merry selves right now!

"Perhaps Andrews would be a little more comfortable if you asked him some questions," Menzinger offered.

Yes, do that, Andy thought. But wait—*Andrews? With an "s"?* Menzinger had said "Andrews" again. Menzinger thought his name was Caspar Andrews! Menzinger was his supposed advocate in this debate, the one small chance he had at being reinvited, and Menzinger didn't even know his name!

"Uh, it's Andy . . ."

Francis said, "You used to work at Omega, huh? Did you ever sell the Falcon chip?" Francis had designed the Falcon.

"I left before the Falcon. I was selling the Eagle, the four eighty-six."

"Did you like it there?"

Should he tell the truth? Probably not. "Yeah, I guess."

"Then why did you leave?"

"Dunno. They don't really let marketing people become programmers. The usual career path is the other way around, programmers burn out after five years, move to marketing."

Francis said, "Why do you think they burn out so fast?"

This was a delicate question, but Andy couldn't avoid the truth, even if Omega was a big sponsor for La Honda. "In that environment, programmers have to make so many compromises . . . It's hard to keep the desire, the *will*, when half your work gets thrown out every year."

That brought a bit of a smile to Francis's mouth. Andy wondered if maybe he'd said something right.

Hank interrupted them. "Okay, Francis, we've got to come to some decision."

Francis said, "How about this: I will come up with one simple question. And if you get it right, I will give up my resistance and let Hank here have his way. If you get it wrong, then Ronny Banks is on my team another year. How about that?" Francis looked at the kid. He was square-shouldered and tall but didn't seem proud of it; he sat hunched over. The part in his hair was high on the crown of his head, with glossy curtains of locks hanging around his face. In truth, Francis had already agreed with Menzinger that they *had* to reinvite Andy Caspar—you had to please the sponsors, they were the source of money, you couldn't be impractical about this thing. But Francis just didn't want Andy to see his name on that list tomorrow and get stoned on the euphoria, thinking he's hot shit, calling his parents and bragging and all that. He didn't *deserve* that boost, not for just having some *marketing job* in the right company five years ago! Francis tried to think of the right question. . . . He looked around the room. On the wall above Andy was an old school clock. . . .

Andy waited in fear. He'd heard rumors about Francis Benoit's supposedly simple quizzes; he'd heard Francis liked to create huge grids composed of hundreds of oh-so-simple little mathematical questions and have ironmen race to see who could finish the grid first, testing them as though they were two microprocessors.

Francis's eyes were closed. When he opened them, he said "Okay. You have thirty seconds to answer this one question." He showed no emotion. "What time is it when the big hand is on the four and the little hand is on the eleven?"

What time is it when the big hand is on the four and the little hand is on the eleven? That was it? That's all? Well, hell, let's see, big hand on four is twenty, little hand on eleven, that's too easy, there must be some trick, what? Oh, shit—was the big hand the *hour* hand? It had been so long since Andy had looked at a clock that wasn't digital. Is the "big hand" the *long* hand, or is the "big hand" the *fat* hand? Back in school when he was a kid they used the phrases "big hand" and "little hand" all the time, but that was a long time ago, a real long time ago, and maybe he had the terms switched in his mind.

Then Andy realized that this kind of second-guessing was exactly what Francis wanted him to do. Something else was going on. Francis was playing some sort of joke on him. *Why?* This wasn't a test at all. The question was too easy.

Pretty soon Hank Menzinger had to laugh at the sheer beauty of Francis's work. *What time is it when the the big hand is on the four and the little hand is on the eleven?* Hank could see the clock right behind Caspar's head, saying 11:20 right then and there! Beautiful! And yet just looking at Caspar you could tell he was in turmoil, his head slightly bowed, his eyes ascending partly into his eyelids, desperately concentrating. Simpler solutions! Hah. The kid would remember this moment for a long time. He would learn the same lesson that old Monica Edmunds learned when her prized students left her school to assimilate into the mainstream, a lesson which eventually compelled the lady to board the windows, chain the doors, and donate the facility to Stanford: the brain worked at the speed of electricity, the speed of light, as long as you didn't feel the pressure, as long as nothing got in your way. But a man in a panic, he could get *anything* wrong. . . . Brains could be as sharp as quartz or as dull as Jell-O, depending on the way a man handled pressure.

Andy said, "This isn't a real test. What the hell's going on?"

"Oh, I assure you," Francis said. "If you get the answer correct, you will be reinvited. Or are you stalling, because you're having trouble with such a *simple* question?"

Andy tried to think ahead. Was he walking into some trap? They must have already decided to reinvite him, and now they were just fucking with him. Why? What had he done to be fucked with?

"Time's up," Francis said, looking at the clock on the wall to keep time. For a moment the tip of Francis's tongue slid out from between his closed lips. Then it was sliding around the inner surface of his cheeks, playfully. There was a glint of pleasure in Francis's eyes. He said, "What makes you think *you* can be an ironman?"

For a moment, Andy considered answering "midnight," or some such obviously incorrect answer, just to see what would happen. Then he decided not to risk it. "The time would be twenty minutes after eleven," he said. He stood up and walked to the door. As he went out, he heard Francis burst out in laughter at his prank.

. . .

The camera crew was crowded into the anteroom again, waiting for Hank a second time, and here a man came out of Hank's office. What a relief! He was young and tall with thick hair and good skin. The producer was ecstatic; after the hospital patient, the mountain man, and the whale-boy, the producer couldn't hide his excitement that Hank Menzinger turned out to be a good-looking guy. He stood up and thrust out his hand.

"Mr. Menzinger . . . hi, hi, *wow* . . . I can't *tell* you how much of a pleasure it is to meet you." The producer watched a big smile come over Mr. Menzinger's face. He even had great teeth! Those boys in New York had done their homework after all!

Andy instinctively shook this man's hand. He held on to it, shaking firmly and warmly, taking in their act, figuring out what was going on. He was tempted to go along with it. Naw, don't be stupid—why risk Hank's wrath? Then he remembered Francis's words: *What makes you think you can be an ironman?* Well, if Francis Benoit thought he was the only one with audacity around here, he would learn differently.

"So . . . where should we go?" Andy said. "My office—it's too small of course. There's a lab down one floor—a big room, plenty of outlets for your lights."

"That'll be fine," the producer said. "We'll just follow you down there."

Andy led them into the hall and—taking bold strides he thought appropriate for the executive director of La Honda—down one flight of stairs to the materials engineering lab on the second floor. He punched in a code to the security lock over the door, waited for the bolt to click, and then held the door open for his entourage to pass. Once inside, he pulled a shade down over the door's porthole, so nobody passing by would notice the camera flashes.

Finally having something to do, the crew broke into action. One man covered the lab's windows with dark cloth, blocking out natural light. Another man erected a scaffold and draped a white backdrop from its front. A third cranked down the telescopic legs of a tripod, mounted a reflex camera on the top, and plugged in an airbulb shutter-release cord. He then began playing with lenses, unscrewing them to insert filters. Done with the windows, the first man began popping flashes and testing light exposure.

"Don't forget to check batteries!" the producer called out. He took Andy by the arm and guided him to the rack of clothes. "We'll feed you clothes to change into as we go," he said. "But why don't you start with whatever looks comfortable? Go ahead, just pick some things off the rack and try them on."

Andy stood in front of the rack, browsing through its selection. The pickings weren't horrible. He slipped into a knit shirt and a pair of knee-length corduroys. He pulled his white socks up. Then he looked at the shoe selection, all sorts of shoes on pegs at the base of the rack. He turned back to the producer, who was across the room.

"Hey! Hey, um . . . these shoes . . . Don't you guys have any sneakers?"

2

Good Good Good

A few weeks later, Andy Caspar found a Post-it note on his monitor. "Please see me ASAP—Francis." He consulted a La Honda directory to locate Francis's office, then headed upstairs.

Like Hank's office, Francis's was actually two offices linked together, with one serving as the anteroom. The anteroom was barren. It did not have chairs to sit down in and waste away the day. It did not have decorations to distract. It did not even have carpet to muffle sound. The anteroom was more of an airlock, a zone to remove all your insecurities and hang them up on the lone chrome coat tree before going into Francis's office.

Francis leaned against his desk with his arms crossed. "Oh, good . . . Caspar, great, you're here. Take a seat, please."

Andy sat down. The only thing hanging on the wall of Francis's office was a large dry-erase board marked with diagrams. Books were stacked up into two-foot-high mesas around the room. There was a coffeemaker on the corner of Francis's desk, but no coffee mugs in sight. Maybe Francis drank straight from the urn. The desk legs were etched with scrapes. One window was open, letting in a breeze. Tree branches shielded the windows from direct light, but Andy noticed that the ceiling had been rigged with special full-spectrum incandescent light equipment.

Andy waited for Francis to say something. It was a while in coming.

Francis cleared his throat. His tongue wet his lips. "I suppose it is your intention to volunteer for the six eighty-six project, like everyone else around here?"

"I was thinking of it."

"As you probably know, there will be way more volunteers than the thirty spots on the team. But since you used to work at Omega, Hank has it in mind to put you on my team. He tried to convince me your knowledge might be helpful, but the truth is he's just trying to kiss Lloyd Acheson's ass." Francis began to scratch his chin casually. Then Andy saw that there was a small scar on Francis's chin, and he was scratching the scar. "What do you think of that? Do you think that's fair, leapfrogging the other ironmen?"

"You know, all I really want is to get out of testing. I just want to get on a project I can apply myself to."

"That's good, Caspar. Because if you do volunteer for the six eighty-six, let me tell you what the next year will be like—"

Andy jumped ahead. "You're going to make me a tester for the six eighty-six."

"Aha, you catch on fast. Yes, you would be a tester. Nothing but testing. There will be twenty-nine men giving you orders and making you their tester of first choice."

"Come on, you gotta give me a chance, this isn't fair. I'm sorry I took your buddy Ronny Banks's place, but once you get to *know* me . . . if you give me a *chance*—"

Francis let out a little chuckle, as if it were a cough. "Don't try to figure out *why* I'm doing what I'm doing. You'll only get it wrong."

Andy took a deep breath. "We started off on the wrong foot. What can I do to set us straight?"

"Hank can't put you on my team if you don't volunteer."

"Isn't that a little excessive?"

"Maybe. But let me make you an offer. I will give you another project to volunteer for. If you do, and you stick with it . . . then a year from now I will *guarantee* you a reinvitation for next year."

That didn't sound so bad. Andy didn't know what he'd done to rub Francis the wrong way, but at least Francis was giving him the signal *now,* rather than a month from now, when it would be too late to switch projects. In a small way, Andy appreciated Francis's being up front about it. And a guaranteed reinvitation? What could be better than that?

Andy said, "All right. I'm with you so far. What's the project?"

Francis slid a piece of paper across his desk to Andy. It was a list of potential projects. Francis leaned forward and circled a line at the bottom of the page. "A computer that will sell for only three hundred dollars."

"Three hundred!"

"You think it can't be done?"

"Well, a computer can be built for any price. It's just a question of how much it can do. Three hundred bucks, that's just a step up from a cellular phone."

"Maybe."

"I guess the point—I guess the object would be to see how much you could do for that limit."

"Exactly."

Andy thought about it. The 686 was to be a computer that could do just about anything. It gave the user a lot of power, a lot of options, a lot of freedom. The opposite was true for a really cheap computer. "Why this project? There's plenty of others. If you just want me off the six eighty-six, why don't you let me choose another?"

"I have my reasons. If you're smart, you will probably discover them soon enough."

"So that's my choice, huh? Be the little man on a big computer, or be a big man on the little computer?"

"But with a *guaranteed* reinvitation. Obviously, the word can't get out that I'm promising reinvitations a year in advance. This conversation we have just had, this deal I am offering you . . . it is just between us. If you tell anyone—if the word gets out—I will guarantee you that you will *not* be reinvited next year."

What the hell. It was a project. Work on it for a year, prove himself, get reinvited . . . move up to something better next year. Andy Caspar hadn't expected to suffer this kind of hierarchical bullshit at La Honda—it was one of the reasons he'd accepted the invitation in the first place, to get away from the favoritism and politics at Stanford. But that was perhaps a foolish thing to hope for. Once he got to work, once he delved into the project . . . all of this would fade away.

. . .

Hank Menzinger relaxed in his office. In the past few weeks Hank had managed to leap quite a few hurdles. He'd persuaded Francis to begin research on a new chip, a project that would bring La Honda nearly six million dollars over the next year, and he'd kept Francis from blowing his lid over not reinviting his best friend. It was quite a week. The best thing was, he didn't have to force anybody's hand; it all unfolded naturally, comfortably. People saw the sense in the situation and reacted accordingly, nothing more, nothing less.

Hank Menzinger was a mystic, a believer in transcendence. Oh, Hank was not one of those New Agers, oh, no—he had never starved himself intentionally and never sworn off women and never resolved to read the Bible. It had been a long time since he thought suffering was noble, though he still suspected luxury could be corrupting. He didn't despise movies that cost one hundred million dollars to make as much as he despised movies where actors failed to enunciate their lines. He admired the energy of youth but didn't miss those years. Despite his apparent power and status, Hank Menzinger was not immune to the fear that someday he would be irrelevant and unemployable, but today he did not feel that fear.

Hank was eating a sandwich when there was a knock on his door, and then that kid Caspar was standing in the doorway. Watching him, Hank had a strange, not quite déjà vu sensation, as if looking upon this scene from the eyes of a third person. When he spoke, he heard his own words echo in his head as if they were being spoken by someone else.

"Afternoon, Caspar. You want to take a seat?"

Caspar moved to a chair.

Hank smiled at him. "I'd offer you some of my sandwich, but it's smothered in horseradish. Good for the sinuses." That was a lie. Who cared about sinuses? The best thing about horseradish was it kept a sandwich from going bland after the first bite.

"Mr. Menzinger—"

"Hank."

"Uh, Hank, sir. It's about the—"

"No 'sir.' Just 'Hank.' "

"It's about the six eighty-six project."

"You're not here to try to squeeze one of your buddies onto the project, are you, because if you are, forget it. If I offered you one more spot, I'd have to do it for everybody."

"That's not it."

"You mind if I eat?" Hank took a big bite out of his sandwich.

"It's . . . well, okay, it's like this. I don't want to volunteer for the six eighty-six project."

Hank stopped chewing in surprise. Then he tried to spit out the food in his mouth, but figured ıt was just as fast to chew and swallow. It took him a while. "What the hell are you talking about, Caspar? Did I hear you say you *don't* want to volunteer for the six eighty-six project?"

"Yes."

"Why the hell not? This is the highest god-almightiest project we've ever had at La Honda and only a goddamn fool would fail to volunteer for it."

"Then I'm a goddamned fool."

"What's going on? Are you taking me on? Huh? You trying to get a rise out of me?"

"No, I just want off the six eighty-six."

"What do you mean, you don't want to volunteer? What do you think I brought you into this place for?"

The kid looked out the window. He didn't look happy. "I guess I wasn't aware of maybe all that would be involved."

"Well, nobody knows what's going to be involved. This is a brand-new chip, start at zero, work from the ground up."

"I don't wanna—"

"You're making a huge mistake, Caspar. Listen to me, Caspar, I know that you can darn well volunteer for whatever you want to volunteer for, but nobody has ever not volunteered for what I want them to volunteer for. What's going on? You don't like Francis? You got a gripe? What?"

The kid shook his head but wouldn't speak.

Hank didn't want anyone tampering with all he'd done to create momentum for the 686. He was about to launch into a long argument, the sheer length of which might compel Caspar to withdraw his request . . . but then Hank relaxed and thought about how good a week it had already been. What was the big harm in someone's quitting the 686 before it started? Just pick another warm body and get on with it. Hank didn't want to make too much of this. He said, "You're lucky, Caspar. On any other day I might take this a little more personally, and I might not back down so easily. But I don't feel like getting all hot and bothered today, so I'm going to let this slide. I suppose there's another project you'll volunteer for?"

Caspar said that there was.

"Which one is it?"

He was choking on his Adam's apple. "The three-hundred-dollar computer."

Hank couldn't believe it. "That? You wanna jump from the six eighty-six to *that*?" The idea of the three-hundred-dollar computer had been kicked around for a couple years, but it never seemed quite right for the bigger-and-faster mentality at La Honda.

"I think it's important. If we had a computer for three hundred dollars, then maybe a whole lot more people in this world would be using one. Schoolkids, for instance."

"*So?*"

"I want to give it a try."

Hank didn't see how he was going to find a sponsor for it; in fact, he feared he might be embarrassed trying to find a sponsor for it.

Hank said, "You know, there's no sponsor right now, so there's only a tiny budget . . . that'll only last a couple months. Then we'll have to try to get a sponsor based on what's been done so far."

"There's no sponsor?"

"No, of course not, not for this."

The kid was pinching his eyebrows with his fingers. "Well . . . who do I report to?"

"Report to?"

"Yeah, the team leader. Who's the team leader?"

Hank smiled. "Well, I guess *you* are."

"Me?"

"You're the only one who's volunteered for this so far."

"The only one? *By myself? Without a sponsor?*"

"What were you expecting?"

"I don't know . . . I don't know anything about being team leader. . . . How am I going to succeed without resources?"

Hank said, "Look, Caspar, I guess you got a little confused. You can have your spot on the six eighty-six back."

"No! Wait, no, I'm sorry . . . I just didn't . . . I just thought there would be *a team,* but . . ."

"We'll just forget you ever came in here."

"No, that's okay, sorry. By myself is fine. Forget the six eighty-six."

"Well, shit. All right, then. What can I do? I don't want to push people, and I'm not in the mood right now to waste an hour convincing you otherwise. So you're the main man on the three-hundred-dollar computer. I'll set you up with a lab. . . . You're lucky I'm in a good mood right now, Caspar, or I'd take you by the ear and give you a mouthful. . . . Ah, what the hell, no skin off my back . . . forget I said that. You do what you want, Caspar, that's what I always say. I'm not forcing you."

Andy's head was bowed. His hands grabbed fistfuls of hair. He stopped doing this and leaned back. "Can I ask something?"

"Ask away."

"Is there anything to stop me from recruiting a team?"

"Stop you? Not really. There's a couple dozen men available that weren't picked for the six eighty-six. If you can get them to volunteer for your project, go ahead. But I can't give you any more money—you'll be stretching the budget even thinner."

· · ·

Andy Caspar drove home in the afternoon. It was the first time he'd ever left La Honda before dark.

Andy lived a half a mile from the Stanford campus in an upstairs bedroom above an old lady who got mad and threatened to kick him out if he made too much noise. The house was ancient and it creaked; sometimes just walking around was considered too much noise. When he'd accepted the invitation to La Honda six weeks before, he'd had to give up his university-sponsored housing, and in the middle of the semester, this place was the only thing available.

There were two upstairs bedrooms, each with its own separate entrance in the rear of the house. In his room, Andy had rigged up a kitchenette out of a closet, with a half-height refrigerator and a chrome toaster oven and a single-coil hot plate. There were fig and crab apple trees outside his window. He shared a bathroom and a short hallway with the woman who lived in the other bedroom, Alisa, a graduate student in industrial design. On her desk—which he could see through the window as he went up and down the stairs—she always had some contraption made from Popsicle sticks or Styrofoam. As he came up the stairs on this afternoon, he saw her face through the crack in the shade. Her hands were busy. She smiled. She was wearing a paisley-print orange bandanna over her hair to keep it from dangling in her hazel eyes. He put his hand up to wave hello. He wanted to say something to her, to knock on her door and tell her his problems, but she had some music going softly and seemed occupied with her project.

Andy sat in his room, drinking a twenty-two-ounce beer and gnawing on a rope of pepperoni. He was beginning to figure it out: Francis had made him volunteer for the three-hundred-dollar computer *because* it had no sponsor money and no team leader and no game plan. It was a dead-end project, entirely likely to fail. It wasn't enough for Francis to kick him off the 686; Francis wanted him to further humiliate himself by failing.

And then there was the project itself . . . Francis had gotten him to volunteer for a project that would very likely be looked down upon by the other ironmen. The thing was, designing a computer for three hundred dollars might be just as much of an intellectual challenge as designing one to sell for five thousand dollars . . . but the project itself suggested something about the men who worked on it. Without a doubt, engineers always wanted to work on the biggest, fastest computer possible, just the way consumers would plop down five grand for a computer they often only used to write letters—because it was a symbol. A symbol of power, of intelligence, of being up-to-date. If computers were cool, then a bigger piece of hardware was a shortcut to being really cool.

And so what does it say about a man, Andy Caspar thought, *what does it say about a man, that he designs a computer that is simple and cheap?*

Andy remembered how right before he left Omega, the Falcon chip—the one that Francis Benoit had designed—was in development. The sales force would get demonstrations and technical literature. There was one older guy, mid-forties, a mutterer, combed his hair over his bald spot. A midlife crisis had taken everything from him but his job. He never called it the "Falcon." He called it the "Beast," and he was a fanatic. The Beast was going to save Omega, and it was going to save him. It was as if once the Beast shipped, he would become a beast—animal, voracious—and all these young women were going to think he was the sexiest thing in the valley. All that power on that chip was going to transfer over to him. He milked the Falcon for every bit of metaphor it could convey. And he was just a salesman! If that was the way salesmen looked upon their product, how would the very people who designed the thing feel about their project?

What does it say about a man, that he designs a computer that is simple and cheap? Andy could imagine how the other ironmen would answer that question. It says the guy is simple. It says the guy lacks the brains to do something better. If he wanted to recruit a team, he would have to overcome this bias.

He heard Alisa in the bathroom filling up her rice cooker with water. If he went right now to get a glass of water, he would bump into her. . . . If he just did it, right now, *now.*

She was bent over the sink, trying to wash her rice by pouring off the water and refilling the pot several times.

"If you want to get in here for a moment," she offered.

"Your bandanna's coming undone," he said, pointing to her head.

She said that she could feel that it was.

Andy went behind her and reknotted the bandanna. As he looked into her rice cooker, he could see that it wasn't rice she had in there—it was spaghetti, broken in half. "You're making spaghetti in a rice cooker?"

"It's an experiment."

He asked her why she was washing the noodles.

"I'm washing the noodles to get them to fit in the pot, so I can get the lid on. I don't know why I didn't just buy rotini or macaroni. I was at the store and had this inspiration, *make spaghetti in the rice cooker!*"

Andy laughed. There was a pause. Andy looked down at their feet. He said, "Uh oh, two people in the bathroom at the same time. We're probably giving old Mrs. Ferguson downstairs a fit. Not sure these old floorboards have been tested this way in years. She's probably recording this into her complaint log right now. Gettin' out the red pencil. June twenty-sixth, five forty-five P.M.: *Loud creak, followed by thudding.*"

Alisa started to laugh, then her brow furrowed with concern. "Does she really have a log?"

"No, I'm kidding."

"Thank god."

Andy said, "So, how have you been lately?"

"Working on my final project," she said.

He asked what her project was.

"It's an overnight travel bag for the modern businessman," she said with some verve, as if it were a slogan she had practiced.

Andy nodded with admiration. "Compartment for your running shoes, toiletry case that snaps in place, reinforced plastic sleeve for your ties—that sort of thing?"

"I just wanted to make something out of polyurethane, actually, don't really know why I picked a travel bag . . . but, hey—compartment . . . toiletry case . . . that's brilliant. You mind if I use those? What was that again about ties that you said?"

"No, please, by all means . . . A *sleeve* for the ties."

"I'm going to go write that down before I forget." She carried her pot of spaghetti into her room, leaving the door slightly ajar.

Andy turned and strolled back toward his room. Her voice cut him off.

"Hey, will you do me a favor?" she said.

He turned around. She was standing in her doorway holding a hunk of Parmesan and a grater. "Okay, this is embarrassing, but I have this strange inability to use a grater. Cheese, carrots—I can't do it. For some reason I only make the cheese break off in my hand. Potato peelers, too. Can't do it. Please?" She held out the cheese and grater.

He took them and followed her into her room. "Umm—?"

"Just on the desk," she said, pushing some magazines aside.

He began to grate the cheese. "You really can't do this?"

"Please don't make me show you. It's embarrassing." She put her hand over her eyes. "So, I've never seen you home so early. What's going on?"

"Ahh . . . it's a long story. But there's a guy at La Honda who has it out for me, and I don't really know why. The upshot of it all is that I got bumped over to this other project."

"That's when I usually quit."

"I can't go back to school," Andy explained. "When I took the invitation to La Honda in April, I forfeited my semester work and scholarship."

Alisa leaned her back against the doorjamb to her room. "I'd ask what the project is, but it would probably go right over my head."

"No, you see, that's the thing—this is the one project that doesn't go over people's heads. And that's why . . . Well, it just doesn't seem like a *challenge* like the other projects. It's this simple computer, supposed to be able to sell for just three hundred bucks."

"Three hundred dollars? Can that be done?"

"Well, theoretically, if you make the software simple enough so it needs less expensive hardware. Then you use an online connection, store all your data on the internet. The computer wouldn't have any data drives. But you see, it doesn't do anything *new,* it just does it cheaper."

Alisa put one foot up on her door. It was hard not to look at her leg. "I don't know," she said. "That sounds like a pretty cool project to me. I mean, three hundred bucks . . . you could put one on every school desk for that. And if it was simpler, well, maybe more people would buy one. Don't you guys think about that kind of benefit?"

"Only a little . . . Our idealism is a mile wide and an inch deep. But you're right—we don't think much about what ordinary people want in a computer. We just think about what *we'd* want. Cool new things . . ."

"Let me tell you something about cool, from a designer's perspective. If you're any good, you can make anything cool. You know, some guys put on a wool cap and look silly, but other guys—it's *stylish*."

"That's good. I'm going to design the 'wool cap' of computers."

"Well, I'd buy one."

"Thanks." He'd grated half the cheese. "This is probably enough, huh?"

"Yeah, that's enough for cheese fondue, actually."

"Which is yet another potential use for the rice cooker!"

She laughed. Andy went back to his room and flopped down on his bed. Immediately he began to feel anxious about the day's events—jaggy, in the veins. He tried to calm down by staying perfectly still, but he didn't last long—he wasn't the kind of person who could sit still when he was being pressured. He rolled onto the floor and started doing push-ups. He'd done push-ups already that morning, as he did every morning, but now he did more. His way of doing them was to do a set of ten, then a set of nine, then eight, and on down to one. This way, he always made it to the end, because as he got more sapped and his will to keep pushing weakened, the challenge at hand—the next set—was proportional to his will.

As he pumped them off, he found himself thinking about Alisa making spaghetti in her rice cooker. She didn't have a hot plate or a refrigerator, but that didn't stop her from making the most of what she did have. This encouraged him—he knew it's what he must do, he knew it was what he *would* do. If life dealt him a three-hundred-dollar computer project, then he would make the best of it.

. . .

When Tiny Curtis Reese received an e-mail from Andy Caspar inviting him to come to lunch "re: volunteering for the 'VWPC,' " Tiny was wary.

He had recently received a photocopy of his evaluation for the last year, in which his team leader had reported that Tiny was "a bulldozer who pushed through any task set in front of him." It was meant as praise, but nevertheless—*bulldozer!* Tiny was deeply hurt when he read the evaluation. He thought he'd done the right thing in accepting without complaint the tasks given him, working through the problems on his own without asking for help, and not bragging about his successes. But what was the lasting impression he'd left on his boss? That he was a bulldozer! What the hell did that suggest? A machine with no creativity! An order-taker! Tiny's team had designed several gallium-arsenide chips, which are used in digital wireless telephones and, more important, very cutting edge. It was the kind of project that made other engineers go "Wow!" But a bulldozer shoveled *dirt,* a bulldozer was low tech, a bulldozer needs someone else to be the *driver.*

His boss was a bit of a joker, and the phrase might have been used ironically, but nevertheless—it had made its way into Tiny's *permanent* file. When Hank read through the file, looking over the volunteers for the 686, did he recognize that the phrase was used satirically? Francis Benoit didn't like order-takers, he liked ironmen with balls. Tiny couldn't help but suspect this was one of the reasons he wasn't chosen for the 686.

And so Tiny resolved to himself that he wouldn't join a project unless the leader understood him, valued who he was. Team leaders were given some access to Hank's files. If Andy Caspar thought he was going to get another bulldozer, a machine to carry out his orders, then forget it.

Two other guys had also been invited to lunch, Salman Fard and Darrell Lincoln. Tiny went down the hall to see if either of them had any idea what this VWPC project was about. He found Salman in his office.

Salman looked like an Arab version of John Lennon circa 1966—bangs slightly curling down his forehead, half-moon eyebrows, slightly hooked nose, and a drooping mustache that cut off the corners of his mouth. His hair was so black and so glossy that it looked wet. He wore pegged khaki pants that ended just below his calves, and he was nervously tugging at the top of his athletic socks. His sneakers had little nubby black cleats; if a football game suddenly broke out, he would be the only one prepared.

Recently, Salman had been getting headaches from staring at a monitor. To remedy the problem, he Scotch-taped a folded-down paper napkin over his left eye. Bands of tape ran across his forehead and down his cheek. Then, as a joke, he'd squirted a touch of iodine onto the napkin.

"Christ, what happened to you?" Tiny asked, wincing.

"Aww, my girlfriend and I had an argument."

"And she hit you in the eye?"

"She's a little passionate."

"Jeez. What were you fighting about?"

Salman said, "I accused her of not being as passionate as her little sister."

"Hell, I'd hate to get in a fight with her little sister."

"Well, that's what started the whole thing."

Tiny was incredulous. "You got in a fight with her sister?"

"Yeah. She kicked me in the balls."

"Kicked you in the balls! What were you fighting about?"

"I accused her of living with us only to perpetuate a jealous rivalry with her older sister."

"Holy shit. They sound like a pair."

"Yup. You ought to come over for dinner sometime and meet them. The most beautiful couple of ladies in the whole world."

Salman didn't know why he told lies about his girlfriend. They just popped out. In truth, his girlfriend was a mousy sweetheart who taught sixth-grade English to Catholic-school girls. He loved her dearly and wouldn't have her any different, but for some reason he wanted the ironmen to think he dated a hysterical sexual adventuress who had nothing better to do all day than shop for a new purse. Most of the guys didn't even have a girlfriend—the long work hours made keeping one nearly impossible—yet Salman felt somehow that wasn't enough, he had to lord it over them. It just slipped out! "God, are my balls sore," he would say to someone, as they waited in line for lunch in the cafeteria, pushing their orange trays toward the steam-heated food. Salman despised his own flirtation with normality. But he knew in his heart he *wasn't* normal, and he wanted to make sure everybody knew just how not-normal he was, even if he had to tell some white lies to get the real truth of his individuality across. He wasn't middle-of-the-road, he wasn't plain vanilla, he wasn't just a statistic. In the domain of La Honda, brainpower was the commodity universally desired, but the commodity most scarce was regular sex. Salman had talked his way into being the envy of the ironmen.

Tiny asked, "What's 'VWPC'?"

"Dunno," Salman said.

"Maybe 'Virtual Workstation Personal Computer.' You think that could be it? Workstations—you ever work on one?"

"Mmmm . . ."

"You did?"

"Me? Oh. No."

"They *rock*."

"Mmmm . . ." Salman agreed.

"But what's a *virtual* workstation?" Tiny asked.

"Good question."

"You got any ideas?"

"Me? Huh . . . uh . . . it's gotta be a personal computer that's every bit as righteous as a workstation computer."

"Andy Caspar is an *x* to me," Tiny explained. "I've never met him. Have you?"

"Me?"

"Yeah. You met him?"

Salman shrugged. "Sure. You know, in the lunchroom and all."

"What's Darrell think?" Tiny asked. "Have you talked to him?" Tiny knew that Salman and Darrell were friends.

Salman shook his head. "I could call him. Should I?" Salman picked up his telephone and dialed Darrell's extension. Darrell's office was up one floor. Salman got him on his speakerphone. "Hey, Darrell, I'm here with Tiny. We're talking about this memo. Why don't you come down?"

Darrell said, "Why don't you guys come up here?"

Salman sighed. "Just come down, man."

"I'm in the middle of something."

"But there's two of us down here."

Tiny tapped Salman on the shoulder. "Let's just go up," he whispered.

Salman rolled his eyes. "Don't go anywhere," he said to Darrell, then disconnected the line. "You can't give in to him, Tiny. He *always* does that." They headed out the door.

"Does what?"

"Aww, he makes minor moments into challenges to his status. He doesn't want to come downstairs because he doesn't want us thinking that we can order him around."

"I don't think that," Tiny said.

Salman shook his head with frustration. "Of *course* not. But he's got a hair-trigger personality. Last year, we were on the same project together . . . There were twelve of us, and we rotated the duties of making backup copies of all our work. Every day, it was somebody's turn. But Darrell hated doing it. It was beneath him. He thought we should hire an undergraduate assistant to do it. It took one hour every twelve days, but he griped about it as if it took him half the day. If you were still on your computer when he came to back it up, he started counting aloud the seconds until you logged off."

Tiny said, "Nice friend."

"I dunno. He's . . . you know . . . Maybe I gave you the wrong impression. He gets mad but he never holds it against me."

They reached Darrell's office. Darrell looked like a study in alternative fabrics: he wore sport sandals with neoprene straps, nylon jogging pants, a fleece baseball cap, and a casual coat made out of gray shag carpet. As usual, around his neck hung a set of Walkman headphones, with the cord dangling down to his belly button. He was small and wiry.

Darrell had a couple cans of cold soda waiting for them. He popped them open himself, wiped the condensation from the sides with a napkin, and offered the sodas with the line, "See? We wouldn't be having these in *your* office."

Salman didn't say anything. He wanted the soda, but Darrell had only offered the sodas as a way of winning the argument. If Salman drank the soda, it would be giving in. He held it in his hand. It was cool and wet. It was only a few seconds before he took a big slug.

"What do we know about this Andy Caspar guy?" Tiny asked.

Salman said, "He was one of the last guys reinvited."

Darrell objected to inferring anything from that. "He was a tester on the satellite chipset, right? If he got reinvited after just being a tester . . . maybe he's sharp."

Salman said, "Not sharp enough to get picked for the six eighty-six."

"You weren't picked for the six eighty-six, either," Darrell reminded him.

"I got screwed."

"Screwed? How?"

"It was politics."

"Politics?"

"Mmmm."

Darrell didn't believe him for a second. Salman was just rambling. He didn't have a legitimate complaint. Darrell finally said, "You know, we *could* just ask Andy what 'VW' means."

"Mmmm . . ." Salman concurred.

"Volkswagen," Tiny said without thinking, "a cheap, simple, mass-produced computer."

His words stayed in their minds.

"Nawww," Darrell said. "We're ironmen. We don't do *simple*."

"Right," Salman said. "That couldn't— No way. I don't see it. Do you, Tiny?"

Tiny didn't say anything. That spooked Darrell, who rambled on. "Logically, now, okay? *A,* we all want to be reinvited next year. *B,* in order to be reinvited, we must prove that we have the right stuff. *C,* to prove we have the right stuff, we must tackle problems which can only be solved if you have the right stuff. *D,* a simple computer can be built by people with simple stuff. Which leads to *E:* nobody would ask us to volunteer for a simple computer. Right? That's only *logical,* right?"

"It is to me," Salman said.

Tiny nodded, then said, "Unless somebody important thinks we don't have the right stuff."

Darrell groaned. "Did you *have* to say that, Tiny?"

"I wasn't—I was just examining the *logic*."

. . .

"Oh shit," Salman said, as the three young men came out of the building at noon. Parked beside the south building was a car he hadn't seen before, a vintage orange Volkswagen Bug with chrome saucer hubcaps and sheepskin covers over the front seats. Andy Caspar was leaning casually against the bubble hood of the VW. When he stood up at their approach, he was a foot taller than the car. There wasn't any beanpole quality to him at all; he wore an alligator shirt hanging out over his khakis, but both were so faded that the look wasn't preppy. His arms and shoulders weren't flabby or bony. A red baseball cap shielded his eyes from the sun. His face was slightly freckled. People with freckles never have bad skin.

Andy shook their hands.

"Shotgun," Darrell said.

"Tiny's the biggest," Salman said. "Let him have the front seat."

"Sorry. Should have called it."

They climbed into the car. Tiny sat behind Darrell. Tiny's knees pushed through the seat, gouging Darrell's back.

"Cut it out, Tiny."

"I'm not doing anything. You should have taken the backseat."

It took them a while to settle down. Andy didn't say much until they had dropped off the ridge and pulled onto the 280 freeway headed north. Interstate 280 was the most beautiful metropolitan-area freeway in the country. The 280 freeway did not have eight lanes squeezed into room for five, it did not have billboards, it was not lined with hotels, and it did not have a gas station at every exit. The only businesses off the side of the road were golf courses.

"Okay," Andy said. He rolled his window down an inch. "My guess is you already know why I've asked you here, but let me make my pitch anyway, okay?"

Darrell and Tiny nodded. Salman stared out the window at a woman in a Mercedes two lanes over.

"Okay. Darrell—how fast are we going?"

Darrell glanced at the speedometer. "Fifty-five."

"And that Mercedes over there, how fast is *it* going?"

"Fifty-five."

"The speed limit," Andy said. "She could go twice as fast as me if it weren't for the speed limit."

"What's your point?" Darrell said.

"For most computers today, the internet connection is the speed limit." Andy repeated what they already knew but hadn't quite thought about in this context before: at that time, June 1995, the biggest rage was to connect to the internet via modem, and from there gain access to far more information for the computer than could be conventionally stored on your hard disk. You couldn't help but imagine that a few years ahead most computers would be connected to the internet for several hours a day. The problem was, that connection was *slow*. It was doubling in speed every year, but it was still far slower than the rest of the computer, particularly a microprocessor like the 686. A computer can only work as fast as its slowest link. Just as a Volkswagen performs almost as well as a Mercedes on a freeway, a cheap processor would work as well as a 686 when the data coming into it was regulated by the modem. Similarly, the second-hottest use of computers, after connecting to the internet, was to play CD-ROMs. But CD-ROMs were also extremely slow, and the microprocessor was never taxed by the load, not even by the most outrageous full-motion video being read off the fastest CD-ROM. So the two coolest uses of the computer, there in summer 1995, didn't require high-end processors. Yet people bought them anyway. "Power is going to waste," Andy said, echoing what they had been taught was the ultimate sin—to waste their own brainpower. "You see, for the average person, they don't need all that power."

Well that may be just fine and dandy for the average person, but as far as the ironmen sitting in the car were concerned, they didn't build computers for *average* people. They didn't relate to average people. They couldn't imagine what went through the mind of an average person. Brilliant minds design brilliant products. But *average minds,* well, hell—they designed Water Piks.

They didn't try to argue, though. To argue the point was to imply that the issue was up for debate, which it wasn't.

Mostly they just shut up and let Andy drive and talk. "This is a 1971 model. That's *1971,* I'm saying. It lasts forever. Look, why don't more people buy computers? Why do people put off buying one? It's because they're afraid, and what are they afraid of? They're afraid that five months after they take the damn thing out of the box, it will be obsolete. The next version of the software will require more RAM, more processor speed, or a bigger hard disk.

It's a rat race, and you never catch up. *More, more.* Look at this car, is what I'm saying. *Look* at it. Simple. It can't do everything, there's no antilock brakes or power steering or fuel injection. It's slow on the hills, worthless in the snow. But you pay only for what you get, and it still works perfectly *twenty-four years* after it was built."

Now the ironmen had always believed in the principle that what made them special was their raw brainpower, not their acquired knowledge. Anybody could study a subject, learn the details, develop expertise. The way they usually talked about it was that their brainpower was *indivisible and transferable.* It didn't matter what project you worked on so long as it challenged your mind. A true ironman could prove himself equally as adept at designing a digital satellite router as network software. Hank had instilled this doctrine specifically to prevent the ironmen from worrying about falling behind—if you've got the treasured commodity, you can always catch up. But the whole hubbub around the 686 project undermined this. Quite abruptly, the project you were on mattered, and dearly. Under these new rules, a little fear of falling behind was hard to keep from blooming into an all-out paranoia.

And as they saw it, driving along that afternoon, if they worked on Andy's VWPC they would only fall that much more behind everyone else. The VWPC was not cutting edge, it was not cool, it would never make another ironman go "Wow." At best it would look and act the same as any plain vanilla box-o-wires. At the end of the year, even if the toy was a roaring success, where would they be? *I'll be a year behind, that's what!*

"Hey, look at Tiny," Salman said.

The two in front glanced back. Tiny was stiff as a statue. His arms were suspended unnaturally. His head was dipped down slightly, the mouth open. He was breathing but his eyes weren't moving.

"Don't touch him," Darrell said.

"Why not?" Salman said. His instinct was to jar Tiny.

Darrell said, "You're not supposed to wake sleepwalkers."

"Who says he's sleepwalking?"

"Well what do *you* think it is?"

"Maybe he's having a seizure or something."

"Here, I'll roll down the window, put some wind on him." Darrell did that, and soon Tiny's eyes blinked, and then he was back.

Salman said, "Wow, man, you sure had us scared. You passed out or something."

Tiny explained that it wasn't an uncommon occurrence. "I feel just fine, though."

"What is it?" Andy asked. "What causes it?"

"I've got a bad back, cuts off my nerves," Tiny said. "Things go haywire."

Salman reached forward and popped Darrell on the shoulder. "You shoulda let him have the front seat, man."

"How the hell was I supposed to know?"

Tiny hadn't told them the truth. He *did* have a bad back, and it did make his legs go numb. But that wasn't the cause of the seizures. His bad back was just another symptom. The seizures didn't normally scare him—he'd suffered them off and on for three years. There was a medical explanation—*petit mal epilepsis*—but Tiny wasn't much of a believer in medical explanations. It didn't explain how he had *gotten* the condition in the first place. Even the doctors said stress was a factor, so Tiny didn't blame anything but himself. He believed the *epilepsis* was just a manifestation of some fault in his mental approach to life. Somewhere, way down deep in the biochemistry of his body, at the level where thoughts were chemicals, his system had a bug. His chemical thoughts were being misread by their receptors, causing some sort of short-term uptake blockage, gridlock at the mind-body connection. Conscious thoughts couldn't get through, and then simple physical instructions like "move the right hand" couldn't get through. Tiny believed that if he could just think properly—if he had the right healthy attitude—he could avoid the *epilepsis*.

• • •

Andy eventually drove them to the Peninsula Creamery in downtown Palo Alto, though there were a hundred faster ways to get there than detouring onto the freeway. They took a booth and ordered quickly.

The Peninsula Creamery was not one of those chichi diners

where all the waitresses were young artists and the specialty of the menu was a twenty-two-dollar flaming cabbage, though there was an oyster bar across the street that catered to that crowd—a crowd that at lunch was composed mostly of software salesmen schmoozing purchasing agents. Through the Creamery's big plate-glass window, the guys could see them at their sidewalk tables, wearing prescription sunglasses and tossing back shots of French water, sans gas. The Creamery was the ironmen's type of place. *Practical.* Beside every booth was a chrome coat rack. All the forks were the same size and had the same number of tines, four. Everything on the menu was tried and tested. Nobody came around scraping crumbs off the tabletop while you were eating. They didn't play music in the bathrooms, and nobody had ever paid attention to the lighting, except to make sure there was some.

"No talking until the food comes," Darrell said, a bit perturbed by it all.

"Why? Why can't I talk?" Andy said.

"Okay, you can talk all you want," Darrell said. "But I won't listen."

"Why? Am I offending you?"

"Don't ask me. I'm not listening."

"Why not?"

Darrell didn't say anything.

"Christ, Darrell, I'm trying to make an important point here. I'm not going to shut up so you can eat your french fries in peace. Schoolkids can't afford a computer, few people outside of America can afford a computer."

Darrell slammed down the ketchup bottle on the table. The cap blew off and a dollop of sauce landed on his cheek. He swore. "They don't make the Volkswagen Bug anymore, hate to tell you, buddy."

"*Bullshit,* Darrell. What do you think they drive in the rest of the world, Hondas with dual air bags? They build Bugs at VW plants in Manaus, Brazil, and in Puebla, Mexico—same design for fifteen years. You know what a brand-new Volkswagen costs in Brazil? Two grand! A fifth the cost of what the cheapest car costs here."

"Two grand?" Tiny said, with interest. He didn't know that. Tiny had never traveled anywhere. *A new car, for two grand?* For the first time it occurred to him that maybe somebody really could build a computer for cheap, if they had enough volume. Not him, but somebody. As he thought about this, he stuffed fries into his mouth like an assembly-line worker, one right after another.

Andy went on. "You know why they build two-thousand-dollar cars in Brazil? It's because they can't afford ten-thousand-dollar cars. So you think they can afford three-thousand-dollar computers? You have to think about the jolt, here."

"Mmmm . . . I'm trying not to think about it," Salman said.

"What did Hank say? 'A certain amount of power, in the hands of a certain number of people.' Well we've spent all our time at La Honda working on the first part, trying to increase the power. But maybe we should think seriously for once about the 'certain number of people' part of the equation. If we're truly serious about our mission, then we have an obligation, I'm saying. If we're going to pay more than lip service to our stated motivations of democracy and populism, this nut has to be cracked."

Darrell felt that Andy had him all wrong. It would take more than a speech to win Darrell over. Words were comparatively cheap. Darrell wasn't devoid of opinions on weighty matters; he wasn't politically immobile. He knew all about the toxic hazards of chip manufacturing and the human rights violations of the countries where chip plants are located. He did not wear the same pair of pants five days in a row. Darrell was not a geek anymore, and he hated when people assumed he was. He did not still, at the age of twenty-seven, have a favorite shirt and a favorite color. He didn't have a nickname for his car. Darrell was not a dreamer. He did not wish to travel to places he knew he would never be able to visit, and he didn't want a cushy job because he knew cushy jobs didn't exist. His only enemy was hypocrisy and the only virtue he thought worth praising was authenticity.

Darrell shot back. "Listen to yourself, Andy. We don't disagree with your ideals. We just don't see why we're the ones to do this project. It's an exercise in *economics*. Three hundred dollars of economics. I didn't study economics. Tiny didn't study economics. If we did, we'd be in Hoover Tower, not La Honda. La Honda is not about money, man. We don't worry what it's going to *cost*. All that matters is what it can *do*. Then we turn over our project to some profit seekers who can worry how to get the cost down. You want me to corrupt that tradition? No, thank you."

Salman let out a little cough into his fist.

Darrell said, "Turn your head when you cough, *please*."

"I'm not sick. I just had a little something in my throat."

"So what? You still should turn your head."

"And cough toward the other table?" Salman shot back.

Darrell just shook his head.

They gave up talking for a while and went to work on their food. Andy had been careful not to recruit anybody older than him, since an older guy might resent working for someone who was only twenty-nine. Other than that, Andy had picked each of these guys because of their computing specialty. But it wasn't going to be enough to just tell Salman, for instance, "I need a good graphical-interface guy, and you're the best available." He was going to have to really push their buttons. Take Darrell—Andy had assumed that Darrell, like most engineers, loved the Socratic argument, loved to debate his way to the truth. Darrell seemed to like arguing, but once he was engaged in a fight he was so intent on winning the argument that he stopped listening. Andy was going to have to win him over without provoking Darrell's fighting instinct.

Andy was also worried about Tiny. The guy almost never spoke. He gave no clues. Most engineers don't have any trouble speaking up, but Tiny was like a kid trained not to speak unless spoken to. Or someone accustomed to taking orders. Maybe he was waiting to be asked for his opinion.

Tiny stared out the window. A pack of ties came out of the oyster bar, patting their stomachs and reaching for their sunglasses. They paused on the curb, said something to one another, then crossed the street in the direction of the Creamery. They came in the back door and slid into a booth behind Tiny. Tiny glanced over his shoulder. There were five of them. One of the guys told the others about how this was a legendary place, then he started on some bullshit lie about how Steve Wozniak had drawn his original vision of the Apple on a napkin from the Creamery, and the napkin now hung in the Smithsonian. Tiny couldn't tell if the audience for the story knew they were being had. Then the waitress came, and they kept calling her "Flo" even though her name was Linda, and then one guy wanted to know if he could have wheat germ in his milkshake.

As he was listening, Tiny was thinking, *That's the other life for an engineer.* They were lucky to be at La Honda at all. Maybe they were being too critical of Andy's project. *A certain amount of power, in the hands of a certain number of people*—it's what they always talked about. Besides, building the damn thing might not be so easy; the three-hundred-dollar limit was so tight that conventional software couldn't run on a computer like that. They would have to write an entire new library of software—not a small job. And they would have to do it with only four people. . . . By the time lunch was over, Tiny had thought about it long enough to be intrigued. But then, on the way home—the shortest way—he was riding in the front seat and out of curiosity opened the glove compartment and he found the car registration and saw that the VW wasn't registered to Andy Caspar, it was registered to an Alisa Jennings.

Tiny passed the registration back to Salman, who said, "Hey, you—you don't own this car!"

"I never said I owned it."

"You let us *think* you owned it."

Darrell grabbed the registration. "Well shit, what kind of car *do* you drive, Andy?"

"Eighty-four Lincoln. It's a piece of shit, though."

"What, a Mark Four?"

"Uh-huh."

"That's a V-eight!"

Andy nodded.

Darrell said, "Ahh, fuck you, man, you yuppie gas-guzzling hypocrite. Nothing's worse than a hypocrite, man. Nothing."

"But I never said I owned it!"

There was about a minute of uncomfortable silence. Salman tried to smooth it over. "Hey, you guys remember the joke about if Microsoft built cars?"

Nobody said anything. Finally, Darrell said, "Well?"

Salman said, "What?"

"*Well,* what *about* if Microsoft made cars?"

"Yeah—you remember the punchline?" Salman asked.

"So what is it, for god's sake?"

"I don't remember. I'm *asking*. I think it was funny."

Darrell shut his eyes and pursed his lips. "Sometimes, Salman
. . . you—*Jesus*." He shook his head.

"What? What'd I do?"

Andy let the silence hang there for a moment. Then he said, "If
Microsoft made cars . . . we'd all have to switch to Microsoft
Gas."

"That's it!" Salman said. "That's it!"

To which Darrell said, "Do you see me laughing?"

. . .

When they got back to La Honda, Andy asked them to come up to
his lab, which was on the hill a quarter mile above the main buildings. Andy also asked Darrell to help carry a box of stuff he had
stored under the hood of the VW. Tiny and Salman walked ahead.

The pathway was covered with umber redwood sprigs and pale
lemon laurel leaves. When the wind gusted, needles of Douglas fir
rained down on their shoulders. At this time of year the tree trunks
were covered with pale green fungus, and the branches dripped a
wispy, cotton-candyish lichen. There weren't many bugs. It wasn't
more than ninety degrees out.

To Darrell, Andy said quietly, "So I need to know if you're the
person I assumed you were."

"What does that mean?" There was only a little defensiveness in
his voice.

"I'm gonna be honest with you. I'm new around here, don't
know many guys. Hank gave me a little access to the employee
files. And I asked you today because of something I saw in your
file."

"Huh."

"I looked at your financial disclosure form." To avoid any conflicts of interest, the ironmen had to reveal where they stored their
money, if they had any. Darrell had some, not a lot, maybe twenty
grand. "All your money's in Apple stock. I looked at that, and I
asked myself, What kind of man would keep his life savings in the
stock of a company for which the death knell rings every couple
years? That man would be one with a lot of faith despite the odds.

With a lot of idealism. Someone who thinks superior technology will rise to the top despite an inferior business model. So I want to know—is that you? Do you have a lot of faith? Do you have ideals?"

Who wouldn't answer yes to that question?

"Yeah, I still have my ideals," Darrell said.

"And you're not intimidated by very long odds?"

"No, I'm not intimidated by that."

Andy nodded his head appreciatively. He didn't say anything more.

The lab was just an aluminum-sided single-room trailer, about sixty feet by fifteen, with a baffled roof to dissipate heat. The punch-code lock on the shabby aluminum door wouldn't stop anyone serious about breaking in. Small sliding-glass windows with bug screens at each end provided the only natural light. The walls were neither wood nor wood paneling, but wallpaper printed to look like wood paneling.

There were four desks with chairs, and when the guys went to sit down, it was easy for them to imagine working at the desks. It was a natural reaction to test how well the drawers slid in and out and to rub their palms over the desktops. Andy began unpacking the stuff from the box.

To get their respect, Andy said, "You know, I had a chance to work on the six eighty-six."

"You did?" Darrell said. This had clearly caught him off guard.

Andy nodded. "Hank wanted me to volunteer, but I never did."

Salman asked Andy, "How come you didn't want to work on the six eighty-six?"

"I don't know. . . . Well, I guess . . . well, I didn't want to be just one of thirty guys taking orders from Francis, stuck in some hierarchy. That's not me, that's not my style. You probably wanted to be on the six eighty-six, huh?"

"Me?"

"Yeah."

"Well, *sure.*" Of course Salman wanted on the 686, it was the highest-status project at La Honda.

"So is that your style, to be just one of thirty guys?"

Salman had never thought about it that way. "Well . . ."

"Taking orders from some subteam leader who is in turn taking orders from Francis Benoit, who is in turn taking orders from some product manager at Omega? That *appeals* to you?"

"Well . . ."

"Let me ask you something," Andy said. "At the end of the year, when the six eighty-six is done, other engineers around the country will know about it, and who do you think they will give credit to? Do you think they'll give credit to all those thirty guys?"

"I guess not," Salman admitted.

"We don't get much money for being here," Andy said. "And I'm not talking about fame here. I'm just talking about the respect of other engineers—our ilk. I would like to work on a project so that if it succeeds, I get some respect."

"And on this project . . . you think it'll be different?"

Andy nodded. "I'm sure you guys are asking yourselves, 'Who is this new guy who wants me to work for him?' Am I right? You don't know me from Adam, right? . . . Let me put it this way. On every other project you could volunteer for, you will have to subjugate yourself to some team leader. But not on this project. I'll communicate with Hank and handle the money, but I'll never put myself above you."

Andy gave Salman a big grin. He'd been waiting for the right moment to say all that. Salman was easy; the guy was always telling macho lies about his girlfriend, which suggested he would join the project as long as he could see that it was somehow a way to prove his manhood. Andy reached into his box and pulled out a quart-sized glass jar, medicine-brown in color. He set it down in sight of Salman.

"What's that?" Salman asked.

Andy slid the bottle across the desk. Salman took it in his hands and stared at the label, which said "Bolasterone." Below that, it said, "5 mg. For oral usage only." Below that, but not in very small print, it gave a long warning: "Warning! This pharmaceutical product should be taken under the supervision of a qualified medical doctor only. Limit intake. If patient begins to see blood in urine or have any pain in the kidney area, see your doctor immediately."

Salman's eyes grew wide. "What is it?" He handed the bottle
back to Andy.

"Anabolic steroids."

"Where did you get them?"

"They're made in Mexico. My brother goes down there a lot,
sends me a jar now and then."

"What does it do? Does it give you muscles?"

Andy had him going. "It would, if I worked out a lot. But since I
don't, it just makes you mean and angry. Keeps up your stamina,
your *fight*."

"Wow. Is it safe?"

Andy unscrewed the cap on the bottle. "Sure, if you keep it to
two pills a day." With that, he poured out five white pills into
his hand, shook them, and threw them into his mouth. He
chewed them. They were really vitamin C, ascorbic acid, and the
sourness made his face wrench, which took the Cheshire-cat grin
off his face. He was afraid the grin would give away his little
prank. He'd got the empty bottle from a friend who was a phar-
macist.

Andy held the bottle out toward Salman. "You want some?"

Salman's head shrank back into his body, like a turtle. "No
way."

"Darrell? Tiny?"

They grimaced and shook their heads. "Do you always take
those?" Darrell asked.

"Naw. Only in crunch time. But there's gonna be a lot of crunch
time around here." Andy couldn't hold it in anymore. He started
laughing.

"What's so funny?" Salman asked.

"Sorry. . . . I'm not very good at deception." He gave another
chuckle. "Any you guys want some vitamin C?" He held the bottle
forward again.

Salman leaned forward and gave the bottle a sniff. He put his
hand in and came out with a few. He sniffed them, put his tongue
on one.

. . .

Andy took a deep breath. "So what do you guys think? About the project, huh?" He wanted them to answer together. If one volunteered they'd probably all follow. "Salman?"

"Me?"

"Yeah. What do you think?"

"I dunno. I'm thinking." He turned to Darrell. "What do you think, man?"

Darrell's arms were crossed. From this defiant position he managed to shrug his shoulders, as if to suggest "I'll go along but I'm still wary."

Andy turned to Tiny. He didn't want to ask a question that Tiny could answer no to. "Tiny, let me ask your advice. Let me pick your brain for just a moment. You've been here a few years, been on a few projects. If you joined this project, how would we start? What would be the first thing we would need to understand before we started?"

This caught Tiny off guard. He'd been given a lot of orders from team leaders before, and he'd also been given a lot of intellectual freedom, but he'd never been asked for advice.

They all turned to Tiny. He was sitting with his chin in his hands, his elbows jackknifed on the tabletop. On each wrist he wore two athletic wristbands, darkened with sweat. As he spoke he looked down and away, toward the floor. "I've been thinking . . . and I can see that there's not just one way to design a computer that would sell for under three hundred dollars. There's a whole set of quite different possibilities . . . so, well, it wouldn't be like we'd just be assembling a train set . . ."

He paused and licked his lips. "It's true that anybody worth their salt could design one, but they might design it the *wrong* way. And then, it would be just another brilliant idea that failed because of poor engineering. If someone else did this, and they did it badly, it would ruin the opportunity for better machines to come later."

Tiny put his hands down on the table. "So it's important, *really important,* that the first VWPC be good good good."

Tiny had drawn a line between *our* VWPC and any old cheapie computer made by *them,* meaning anyone else. Theirs would be a screwup, a face-plant, a botched job. Ours would be elegant, brilliant, righteous, and worthy. To get right down to it, theirs would prove that they didn't have the brainpower, and ours would prove that *we* did. *It's important that it be good good good!* Not just anybody could build the VWPC!

3

The Grids

The methodology of computer engineering is to break a problem into smaller and smaller parts, until each part is easily solvable. It was the way computers worked—they broke words and pictures and sounds into long strings of ones and zeros. And it was the way engineers traditionally tackled huge projects, such as designing the circuitry to connect four million transistors on a new chip or writing a new software program that had two hundred thousand lines of code—they broke the problem into units, and each unit into functions, and each function into steps, and each step into sequences, and each sequence into an itsy-bitsy task that could be completed before lunch.

Francis Benoit had a way of teaching his team the importance of breaking down their project into manageable tasks. He had written a simple computer program, which printed out a large grid of boxes. In each box it placed a randomly generated mathematical problem. These were not the kind of math problems you had to use calculus to solve. They were simple addition, subtraction, multiplication, and division—very much like the operations a computer chip performs millions of times every second. 6×9; $96 - 47$; $45 + 12$. The kind of problems every sixth-grader can whiz through. On the grid there might be ten columns and twenty rows, two hundred problems in all. The trick was, the problems were interdependent. $6 \times 9 = A$. $A - 47 = B$. $B + 12 = C$. These variables of A, B, C went through the whole alphabet and the Greek alphabet and every character the computer could print, so eventually some of the boxes contained problems like $K \div \beta = \rho$. Not only were they interdependent, but they were randomly scattered throughout the grid. You could stare at the page for a minute and not even be able to tell in which order to perform the calculations. You couldn't tell which variable was the final variable: maybe it was K, or maybe it was β, or maybe ρ. In order to solve the grid, you had to just start with numerical problems and work your way in to defining some of the variables, then on to other variables, until you eventually worked down to the final variable. If there were two hundred problems, you had to solve every single one of them accurately in order for the final variable to be accurately solved. A single mistake would throw off the whole thing.

So far, this might have been like any other math test the ironmen had received in junior high. They had excelled on tests like this their whole lives. They *enjoyed* proving themselves against a test. They loved to sit in a big auditorium with two hundred other test-takers and crunch through the exam in half the allotted time, put their pencils down, zip up their backpacks, throw their answer sheets into the cardboard box on the stage, and walk up the aisle toward the exit, eliciting jealous turns of head at every row. But Francis Benoit added a wrinkle: his grids were a one-on-one competition. They were a race. The first one to finish wins. Francis would take his new team members and make them pair off and go against each other. Well, this was nothing like an auditorium full of English majors. There was no time limit to scoff at. They were going up against other ironmen . . . and the first to finish wins . . . and whoever wins proves himself to Francis. The pressure was incredible! Francis put one of his grids down in front of an ironman, and suddenly simple little calculations could stump the brain. 11×13 . . . *What time is it when the little hand is on the eleven and the big hand is on the four?* If they got even one little problem wrong in the whole series, the end result would be off. So the ironmen fought off the desire to backtrack and to check their work. They tried to convince themselves to trust their brains, to

$\varepsilon \times N = \chi$	$3 \times I = J$	$25 - F = L$	$W + \Psi = \Re$	$O \times P = R$
$\Phi \times \Gamma = \varsigma$	$\chi - \Psi = C$	$153 \div 9 = G$	$L + 28 = M$	$64 \div 16 = \Omega$
$B - 13 = N$	$J \div 69 = V$	$\Phi \times K = \Gamma$	$\Xi + \Phi = \Psi$	$(\Sigma - U) \div 29 = \Phi$
$P + K = U$	$8 + D = E$	$15 + A = I$	$(I \div \Im) \times 7 = \varepsilon$	$46 - 23 = D$
$7 - 18 = H$	$27 \div 9 = W$	$3 \times 8 = B$	$G + 9 = Q$	$A + \Re = \Im$
$4 \times 21 = F$	$486 \div 81 = \Sigma$	$(\Gamma - J) \div 73 = \Pi$	$43 - 22 = P$	$O \times G = Z$
$V + 6 = \Theta$	$2 + 6 = A$	$81 \div 9 = O$	$210 \div 15 = K$	$139 - M = T$
$208 \div 52 = \vartheta$	$24 + X = Y$	$84 \div 12 = S$	$\Omega - \Theta = \Xi$	$W - H = X$

trust their accuracy . . . but suddenly a fraction or a decimal point would appear in a solution, and they would doubt themselves—"a decimal point! Maybe I made a mistake several steps ago." And they would look across the desk at the opposing ironman, a guy who had whizzed through just as many tests during his life as the rest of them, cranking away there, pencil to paper . . . oh, the agony! Under this pressure Francis Benoit could reduce these brainiacs to humiliated, sweating wrecks incapable of knowing their own names.

Being smart was not enough. The general consensus around La Honda was that plain old smarts were not very rare. Smarts and fifty cents would buy a cup of coffee. Smarts and *confidence,* though—that was the explosive mixture. A fortress of confidence was the proper image to project. Bravado. In those halls there was so much bravado and machismo bumping into each other that if you lit a match the whole place might explode. Francis's simple grids were designed to find out who really had confidence and who didn't.

The ironmen had developed some guidelines about the grids which had been passed down year to year. Twenty percent of the time the ironman who thought he had won in fact had come up with the wrong answer. Decimals and fractions might carry through several calculations, but they usually disappeared before the final variable. Several of the ironmen coded their own computer programs to generate their own grids to practice upon, but Francis countered by just generating larger grids—four hundred problems, which would take half an hour to work through. Or he would surprise them with a grid of only thirty problems, a sprint. *Anybody* could win a sprint! . . . just like that, all the pressure and fear came back, and along with them the humiliation.

But there was one last touch. Every time Francis started a new project with a new team, he would make everybody on the team perform one grid in competition, just to get a feel for what a grid was like. He did this for all thirty members of the 686 team. He set them up in lab A and passed around grids and waited until fifteen pairings were completed. Then he flat out announced to the team members that they were free to challenge him as the team leader— they only had to beat him on the grid. If anyone thought that he was better prepared to make the overall design decisions on the 686—if he wanted to be the one who cut the 686 into batches, chunks, fragments, and tasks—then he should challenge him. He, Francis Benoit, wasn't *imposing* himself as leader. He wasn't the autocrat. He maintained that he was the leader because he had the smarts and confidence to do the job—nothing more and nothing less. And he meant what he said. As he made the announcement, a half dozen ironmen would get it in their heads that they were going to challenge Francis. This would be their big break; they could leapfrog the whole ranking system and become famous as the inventor of the 686. It was almost as if Francis were saying, "If you're a true ironman, then you would challenge me." They thought they were receiving a sermon about how ironmen always questioned authority. *He wants us to challenge him!* Then Francis mentioned the catch: If Francis was going to gamble his position as team leader, then whoever challenged him had to gamble too. If they lost in their challenge, they had to give up their spot on the 686 team. Well, when he said this, a little air went out of all those egos around the room. No way was anybody going to risk his spot on the team. Francis would ask for challengers, and they would all look around the room to see if anybody stepped forward, and they'd try to avoid one another's eyes—No, not me, are you crazy?

Then Francis said, "Not one person here thinks he can make better design decisions than I?"

Well, maybe some of them did. But they weren't confident enough about their abilities to go up against Francis on a grid. They'd heard Francis was fast, that he never broke under pressure.

Then Francis chuckled, and the real fun began. He would slowly repeat his offer, but each time he would progressively lower the ante. Now they could have his spot as team leader, and if they lost they could still be on the 686 team, but they would have to be the designated *tester*. The ironmen heard this new offer, and they asked themselves if they were willing to risk being a lowly tester for the next nine months, and their answer was no, they weren't. They'd already convinced themselves that they couldn't beat him, so betting would be in vain. Then Francis repeated the offer again: If you lose you have to write the manual—a tiresome project that would take about a month. He'd get no takers. He'd lower the offer again and again, until if you lost you merely had to come to his house and clean out his rain gutters. No takers! The lower the ante, the less confident the ironmen grew of their ability to take Francis on. They'd see that they weren't even confident enough to risk an afternoon cleaning gutters! So Francis kept going, until *finally* someone had to challenge him.

"All right then," Francis said, speaking to the 686 team. "One last time. I can't make the bet any smaller than this. If you challenge me and win, then you get to be the leader of the six eighty-six team. But if you lose, then you have to buy me a Pepsi."

A Pepsi! The ironmen were held in awe of Francis's confidence in his own abilities—he was risking practically his entire life, to win what? *A twelve-ounce can of Pepsi!* What balls!

One kid, Link Smith, couldn't take it anymore. He could see how Francis was humiliating all of them, knew exactly how he was doing it—and yet that didn't help Link very much, because he felt pretty darn humiliated anyway. If nobody challenged Francis, then the ridicule would never end. Francis would lord it over them for months. Link had breezed through his first grid, and so what the hell? He stepped forward. He coughed into his fist to clear his throat. "All right, I'll do it." Link wore leather wristbands, a ribbed tank top, and trousers with a satin tuxedo stripe down the sides of the legs.

"Hooray for Link Smith!" Francis boomed, laughing. When his face scrunched up, the skin of his chin folded not around the natural cleft but a half inch to the side, around the scar. "Let's everybody give him a hand, why don't we?" They all started applauding, including Francis. He was making this into a circus.

"Let's get going," Link said. He wanted to get it over with more than he wanted to win. Link didn't admire Francis, and he didn't like Francis, but he still wanted to *be* Francis. They all did. And why? Because he was in control of himself. Because he didn't have to give respect to others in order to be respected by them. Francis was a little over forty, an age when other men begin to crave fame and fortune. In the eyes of the ironmen, Francis had avoided those seductions, stuck to what he loved and did well, and ended up with the best of both worlds. His name was known by his peers. He'd put enough money in the right IPOs to never wonder whether he could afford a vacation. He had been true to himself.

Francis turned to him. "Well, where's your ante?"

"My ante?"

"The Pepsi. I don't want you to skip out on the bet."

So Link had to walk across the quad and into the lounge and put some quarters in the vending machine, the whole time thinking how he was going to get his ass whipped for sure. When he came back, Francis examined the Pepsi can for a moment, then went to his computer and clicked on a command that made two identical new grids grind out of the old dot-matrix printer in the corner. He took a seat on one of the stools across from Link, with the Pepsi can between them, and someone from the audience ran over to the dot matrix printer to rip off the grids. These were set down in front of the two contestants.

Link glanced down at the seven rows and eighteen columns of boxes and went to work. He dropped his head and began to crank, when all of a sudden he heard a *pfffrst!*

He looked up. Francis had just popped the top on the Pepsi! He was taking a swig, enjoying himself. . . . Well, it was just too much. Francis was so sure that his challenger would lose that Link began to believe it himself, and pretty soon Link felt the urge to check his work . . . and then it was all over, Link broke down, incapable of trusting his calculations. He began to hear his own voice in his head, hear the numbers get called out and echo around in there, and he tried to remind himself that he was not supposed to *listen* to the numbers: idiot, *I'm supposed to multiply them.* Pretty soon he couldn't choose which box to calculate next—this one looks easy; no, wait, this one here . . . at which point he just tried to look busy, when really he was just waiting for Francis to end his misery.

. . .

Up the hill, the VWPC team was also breaking apart its project into smaller jobs. Tiny took responsibility for the hardware, the box, as well as any special microcoding that needed to be burned into the chips. Salman appointed himself in charge of the middleware, which included the operating system and the network/internet connection. Darrell took the software; he would write as many application programs as time allowed, and these programs had to be *small*—so they wouldn't demand much memory when stored in the VWPC, and so they could be downloaded over the internet very quickly. Andy would be a sort of rover, doubling up on whatever area was giving them the most trouble, and he would be the team leader—though at that point none of them had any notion of what being the team leader involved. They soon found out. Every word that came out of Andy's mouth and every line of e-mail he circulated and every gesture he presented was calculated to keep his team in a state of fear without pushing them into a state of hopelessness. He let them know the budget was very tight, that it wouldn't last long, but he never actually showed them the figures—creating fear through uncertainty. They could last about three months without a sponsor, but he didn't tell his team that—the knowledge that they had only ninety days to rig a prototype would have been debilitating. Instead, he broke it down into weekly goals. He would say, "We've got until Sunday to figure out what parts we're going to use. From now until Sunday, don't think about anything else."

Andy laid down only two rules for the team to live by. First, the VWPC had to be built so it could sell in stores for three hundred dollars. There was nothing magical about that figure, no technological reason for sticking to that price. But conventional wisdom suggested that for a consumer item to reach a critical mass of homes (as the team hoped for their box), it couldn't cost more than other small home appliances—TVs, microwaves, stereos. Several video game consoles had been introduced the previous year, and the two consoles priced around four hundred dollars were poor sellers, despite offering superior technology. Darrell Lincoln was a huge video game fan, and when anyone questioned Andy's three-hundred-dollar rule, Darrell quickly piped in with an anecdote about the graveyard of discontinued devices.

Andy's second rule was that the hardware for the VWPC had to be chosen from parts already available for sale. There was not enough money in the project's budget to manufacture and test original chips.

These rules forced them to quickly make some very hard decisions. Andy started them off by making a retail-price list of all the parts in a conventional desktop computer:

motherboard	$125
central processor	$400 to $750
CMOS chip	$15
ROM BIOS software (flash)	$10
dynamic RAM $40 per MB, approx.	$300 to $600
static RAM (motherboard cache)	$50
chipset	$50
case	$15
power supply	$10
expansion slots	$75
hard disk	$110
floppy disk	$25
controller card	$45
modem	$75
video card	$50
video RAM	$80
graphics accelerator	$50
monitor	$200 to $400
keyboard	$30
mouse	$30
DOS operating system	$20
Windows interface	$40
bundled software	$200

These parts added up to a computer that would sell for around $2,000 without any peripherals such as a CD-ROM player, scanner, or printer. When the team looked at this list, a wave of despair swept over them. The generally accepted plan for a $300 computer was that it wouldn't have any long-term storage, such as a hard disk; instead, all the software and personal files would be stored at a remote server on the internet, which the VWPC would access. But according to Andy's list, cutting out the storage parts—hard disk, floppy disk, and controller card—only saved $180. They weren't even much below $2,000 yet!

"This is hopeless," Salman said, rubbing his temples. "There's no way this can be done."

"Stop thinking about the big picture!" Andy said. "Just work on one part at a time."

"If I tell myself to stop thinking about the big picture, then that's *still* a way of thinking about it."

"Resist it."

"I can't *help* it."

So Andy broke it down further. "All right, Salman. Fuck the weekly plan. You've got until nine o'clock tonight to figure out what our options are for central processors."

Salman said, "Or else what?"

"What do you *mean,* 'Or else what?' You've got to get it done by tonight, that's it."

"That's not how you do it. You have to threaten the stick. You know, the carrot and the stick. What's the stick?"

"You wanta be the team leader?" Andy asked.

"Jeez, I'm just telling you how it's done," Salman said.

"I never figured I was going to have to hold your fucking hand on a daily basis."

"You don't have to hold my hand. Just show me the carrot and the stick, that's all."

Andy was getting irritated. "If you don't get it done by nine, then you have to spend the night here until you *do* get it done, how's that?"

Salman shook his head. "Not enough. I'm already figuring on spending two nights a week here, minimum."

Andy went away to think about it for a few minutes, and then he came back with a plan. He made Salman call his girlfriend and tell her to meet him for dinner at MacArthur Park, a very nice restaurant, at eight-thirty. Andy stood by Salman's side while he made the call. It was very uncomfortable for Salman because Andy overheard how his voice softened when he talked to his sweetie pie.

"Boy, she's gonna be pissed if I'm late," Salman said when he got off the phone.

"That's what I'm counting on," Andy said.

So Salman started calling chip manufacturers and having product specifications faxed over. A new Falcon operating at a clock speed of 133MHz cost about $720, but Salman was amazed at how quickly the prices dropped off. Just last year's Omega chip, the Eagle 486DX2, could now be purchased for $150, though Omega was about to stop manufacturing that chip. Other manufacturers' early-edition chips were even cheaper, as low as $50 in some cases. Just a few years ago these had been state-of-the-art, and at the time they'd had plenty of processing power to drive the graphics demanded by the software. But since then, software had bloated in size, and the old chips couldn't even draw the screen anymore. Within a few hours Salman realized the problem really wasn't the cost of the processor—it was the complexity of the software. If they could get their VWPC to run simple software, then an old chip would handle the job. So he picked the best chips for $50, $75, and $100, then corralled Darrell to talk about the software. They made up a chart of how complex the software could be with the different chips.

He gave the chart to Andy at 7:30. "Let's do this every day," Salman said, holding his arms above his head. "Hey, tell me the truth. Do I stink?"

"I'm not going to smell you," Andy said.

"I have to decide whether to take a shower."

"Why don't you just take one?"

"Because she likes it when I'm a bit stinky. But not *too* stinky."

"Well, why don't you take a quick shower, then, like, run up and down the stairs a few times."

"Hey, that's good!" Salman hustled out the door.

Andy had spent the day tackling the second biggest item on the list, dynamic RAM, or DRAM, the short-term-memory storage. Everything else in computers was getting cheaper, but not RAM. RAM used to be a small factor in the cost of a computer, but an economic quirk had turned RAM into a huge stumbling block: a fire in the plant of the world's largest manufacturer had driven prices way up and the supply could not meet the ever-increasing demand.

Andy's solution was really quite sneaky, and it exploited the way RAM is plugged into the computer. On most personal computers, there are four sockets for RAM. A customer who has eight megabytes of RAM usually has four chips of two megabytes each.

In order to upgrade to twelve megabytes, the customer can't just install a new four-megabyte chip, because there aren't any more sockets available. They have to take out two old chips, subtracting four megabytes, and plug in two new chips of four megabytes each, adding eight, for a net gain of four megabytes. Well, Andy made a few phones calls to the repair shops in Silicon Valley who performed these upgrades for customers, and he was told that, by golly, all these old two-megabyte chips *were just lying around in boxes!* The shops had so many they didn't know what to do with them. They were perfectly good chips, solid-state engineering that would never break down. So Andy called some RAM manufacturers, and he found the same thing—old one-megabyte and two-megabyte chips could be had for as little as ten dollars a megabyte, one fourth the regular price! That gave the team a little leeway with the software. As long as they were willing to adapt to older chips, the VWPC could have four to eight megabytes. This little bit of knowledge gave the team a big boost; suddenly their goal didn't seem so unattainable.

Tiny and Darrell attacked the third big-ticket item on the parts list, the whole video display system, which included the monitor, video card, video RAM, and graphics accelerator—a nearly five-hundred-dollar combination. The team quickly had to make a decision whether to put their limited amount of money into the monitor itself or into the subsystem that processed all the graphics. Andy insisted that there was no money for both. In order to afford either, they were going to have to use a monitor with a very small screen, perhaps only 8.5 inches diagonally, a bit smaller than the screens on most laptop computers—"but the same size as the original Macintosh screen," he quickly added. Andy figured an 8.5-inch high-resolution monitor without the video subsystem would cost about eighty-five dollars, while an 8.5-inch low-resolution monitor driven by a video subsystem would cost ninety-five dollars.

This really involved a fundamental choice between whether the VWPC would be used only to read text or also to play video. The display of text, such as the articles people read on the World Wide Web, requires a high-resolution monitor to draw letterforms' delicate serifs and strokes. But in order to play video games or run animation on the VWPC, the screen would have to redraw *entirely* as often as thirty times a second. A new image has to be calculated and processed and delivered to the screen constantly. That takes a good subsystem.

Tiny Curtis Reese didn't watch television, and though he loved strategical computer games he had no interest in the shoot-'em-ups that were popular with kids. Tiny read books obsessively, particularly paperback thrillers by Alistair MacLean and Frederick Forsythe, and so it wasn't a surprise he lobbied for the text. But he also made a compelling argument: all of the team members believed that the best use of the VWPC would be in schools. Most schools had a computer lab, where students would go one hour a day to learn about computers. But they weren't really *using* the computer as a tool to study their other subjects. Ideally, every desk would have a VWPC on it. Then, students could plug into a network to get their history lesson, and in the next hour plug into another network to get their math quiz. Textbooks would be moved online and would be very cheap to access since they didn't have to be printed. Tiny made the point that if the most important use of the VWPC was in schools, then text was the obvious priority.

Darrell started laughing out loud.

"What's so funny?" Tiny said.

"You—you hypocrite."

"What?"

"Admit it, Tiny, we're all slaves to images. I am, Andy is, you are."

"I'm not," Tiny said.

"You can't live in this decade and *not* be. Images are like air pollution—they're not something we make a choice about."

"We're making a choice here."

Darrell guffawed. "Come on, man. If the VWPC isn't a device to transmit images, we're just letting the television rule. We can't resign that turf so easily."

"Images destroy the imagination," Tiny said.

"*Some* images do, and some *don't*. The VWPC is a chance to broadcast images that spark the imagination."

"For example?"

Darrell sighed. "I don't *have* an example. All the images society has invented were for the television or movie reel."

Andy interrupted. "So, Darrell, you want us to build the VWPC so it can broadcast a whole new library of inspirational images that haven't even been created yet?"

"Uh, yeah."

"Well, we've got only a few months' worth of money in our budget. Do you think this library of inspirational images that society will create will be available, say, by *October*?"

Quietly, "Probably not."

That seemed to put an end to the argument. They all returned to their desks and tried to get back into their work.

But Darrell wasn't quite willing to give up. He nodded acquiescently whenever the topic came up, but he stewed privately. The other team members could tell he wasn't completely on board, and they kept needling him. They knew Darrell was a voracious shoot-'em-up enthusiast who spent many sleepless nights mastering the newest add-on levels in his favorite games, and they assumed he couldn't separate his work from his play. Video games, they correctly pointed out, were already a booming industry; there was no dearth of affordable game players and games. The world didn't need another device to play games upon.

But Darrell's reasoning was slightly more subtle; he recognized that almost *all* computer geeks got their first look at a computer through some kind of computer game. Darrell believed that games transformed the box from a work tool to a plaything, and thereby burned a positive association into the hard wiring of a future geek's brain. Games taught people to *love* their computers, and once in love they continued to explore the other features and uses available. They became curious. By contrast, most ordinary people in office buildings first use a computer as a word processor. They aren't very curious to explore what else can be done with the thing. Curiosity, Darrell insisted, was the all-important key that unlocked the many doors the computer could take you to. Only curiosity would drive those young students in schools to stay an extra hour at the end of the day and explore the internet. Darrell feared that if students just used their VWPCs as study tools, VWPCs would get about as positive an image as textbooks—heavy tomes we want to burn to a charred crisp right after final exams.

After ten days of arguing and thinking through the details, the team was looking at a new price chart:

motherboard	$75
central processor	$50
CMOS chip	$15
ROM BIOS software (flash)	we write
dynamic RAM $10 per MB, approx.	$40
static RAM (motherboard cache)	luxury item
chipset	$20
case	$15
power supply	$10
expansion slots	????
hard disk	nix
floppy disk	nope
controller card	good-bye
modem	$75
display system (video or text?)	$85 to $95
keyboard (w/mouseball)	$20
new operating system	we write
application software	we write

That totaled $405 to $415, without any expansion slots. Well, that wasn't too bad. Andy also figured in some general rules about the economies of scale in manufacturing, which suggested that for every doubling in the *unit volume* of hardware built, your costs went down 25 percent. The manufacturing stage was a long way off for this team—more accurately, it wasn't even in their game plan. Their goal was to build just a few of these VWPCs, and then to license the package to several multinational conglomerates who could afford to manufacture and assemble in massive quantities. Andy made what he thought was a reasonable assumption: if a computer company like Omega Logic could sell a quarter million $2,500 computers a year, then it was fair to guess that another company could sell at least a half million VWPCs at only $300 a pop. Thus, a doubling of volume, and in turn the 25 percent reduction in cost—a little paperwork and $410 magically became $302.50.

$302.50! They were there! They had made a ton of compromises; there was no capacity for sound, and maybe not for video, and so far it couldn't even connect to a printer. But they were enough in range to see the project wasn't futile, which was probably more important.

"See, look at that," Andy said, showing Salman how he had magically transformed four hundred dollars into three hundred dollars. "We did it. You thought it was impossible."

Salman looked at his math. "Yeah, now all we have to do is write an entirely new operating system and an entire new suite of software."

"Will you stop looking at it that way?"

"Sorry, I had a religious upbringing: I've been trained to fear the future."

. . .

Francis Benoit was gazing out his office window when he saw Lloyd Acheson crossing the quad from the parking lot. Francis couldn't figure why the president was here—there wasn't a board meeting scheduled, and what could be so important that it couldn't be taken care of with a phone call?

Lloyd had carefully coiffed long blondish hair—the kind of color pinewood is when they call it blond, which isn't much color at all. The gray hair expected from a man of his age wasn't peppered in; instead, it had taken over its own separate but equal patch above one temple, coming down in a swoop. He wore a gray suit but Rockport shoes, made for walking. He had tiny little crimp marks around the eyes, rather than deep creases. He didn't carry any extra weight. His efforts at casualness were, however, betrayed by the slightly pained expression on his face, as if someone had just described to him a gruesome medical procedure involving long needles.

Francis was watching Lloyd's stride for a hitch or a limp. There was a legend about Lloyd Acheson that never failed to make it into any profile of the man: when he was in his mid-twenties and just another Silicon Valley engineer chasing secretaries, he and two friends went rock climbing for a week at Pinnacles National Monument, about a two-hour drive south. There was an accident on a climb. One of his friends died, the other was critically injured. Lloyd walked five miles to find help, at which point he collapsed. When he got to the hospital, they found that both his legs were broken—he had walked five miles with two broken legs. After the accident, Lloyd became a pit bull, a man with a singular purpose: to succeed. That was the legend anyway, or one version of it. Francis had never trusted it. It wasn't just that Francis found it hard to believe. It was *too* perfect; it was the kind of story you make up to demonstrate how tough you are. Francis also thought that anybody who broke both his legs—if they were real breaks, and not just stress fractures—would have a limp.

Francis didn't see any limp. In fact, Lloyd had a real jock's swagger, shoulders rolling and dipping. He entered the north building, probably on his way to see Hank.

Francis got up from his chair.

. . .

Lloyd Acheson didn't pay many surprise visits to La Honda. When he poked his head into Hank's office, Hank's first thought was: *He's been fired from Omega.* His second thought: *Omega's been bought by AMD and they want to kill the 686.*

Hank said, "Don't say you were just in the neighborhood."

"Relax . . . Sit down . . . At ease, buddy." Lloyd fell into a chair. His suit coat scrunched up around his neck as he tucked his hands behind his head.

Making it look like he was just closing down whatever he had running on his computer, Hank flipped between screens to check Omega's stock price. A third of La Honda's annuity trust was invested in Omega Logic stock. Last month it dropped 8 percent of its value, but on this day it hadn't moved since morning.

Hank tried again. "You got a meeting with Francis?"

"What is it with you engineers?" Lloyd said, playfully. "The most impatient breed of people I ever met. . . . You're all like children of alcoholics, terrible fear of the unknown. You hate not knowing what's going to be said."

"I'm paid to think ahead."

He got a chuckle out of that. "Don't use that as an excuse. It's in your personality, Hank."

"This business keeps us edgy."

"Hah, *business*. You used to get a grimace on your face during the pause between Johnny Carson's setup line and his punchline. You hated that moment when you couldn't anticipate the joke."

"Lay off, will you? . . . What am I supposed to think, your surprising me like this?"

"You're not *supposed* to think anything. You're supposed to wait for me to tell you what I came here to tell you."

"And that is?"

"Jeez, *easy* . . . How's that reporter working out? I like her columns."

Hank said, "You don't think they're avoiding the technical stuff too much?"

"Hey, I'm getting ten column inches every Wednesday, what have I got to complain about?"

"Francis isn't happy. Says it's humiliating."

Lloyd gazed out the window. "He's just trying to make you feel guilty, so you will cave in on something else he wants. Don't let him con you."

Hank always felt one half step slower than Lloyd. Hank didn't think that Lloyd was any smarter than he was—that wasn't it. It was the same feeling Hank got around people who had spent a lot of time in Manhattan—they were superverbal, there was no natural hesitation between thought and voice. So Hank had long ago gotten used to Lloyd's capacity to outmaneuver him in an argument, and Hank had learned not to feel inferior about it. He just wished Lloyd didn't have to do it every goddamn time they met.

Hank wanted to get to the point. So he said, "Well, I've got a meeting downstairs. So if that's all . . ."

"All right. Sit back down there, cowboy. I'll get to the point. I got your budget memo." The board had to review and approve any final budget. "I saw a line item, 'SubthreeCPC.' Unsponsored. Went looking for the description, found it in some old project lists."

"And?"

"Hank, are you outta your mind?"

"Not sure it can be done, myself, but what the hell do I know?"

"Are we on the same page, Hank? It goes against everything we're about. It's an *exercise in economics,* not a science project."

"Hey, I don't disagree. But some guys volunteered. Maybe they see something in it, I don't know."

"There's hundreds of projects to choose from. Why not choose those that keep your sponsors still sponsoring your work? Nobody in the country will want to sponsor a three-hundred-dollar computer. They'd be the laughingstock."

"What, do you think I'm looking forward to having to find a sponsor for it? But . . . it's the way this place works, huh?"

"Hank."

"What?"

"Hank, you're not getting my point. Did you think about this project at all? Let's say they design this thing, and people hear about it. What's that going to do to the reputation of La Honda, huh? It's a piece of plastic, Hank. When people think La Honda they think big iron, not plastic."

"It's just a tiny minor project—"

"Hank, don't you see? It's the opposite end of the spectrum from what La Honda does. La Honda designs the computers that keep the margins high in our business. This, this piece of plastic . . . I have to say, Hank, from the point of view of one sponsor—I'm wearing my Omega cap, now, not my La Honda cap—from my point of view, I don't like it when I hear you're going to build a product that would undercut my business. I don't like it at all."

A third voice interrupted them. "Ahhh, the dreaded *Omega* cap." Francis was standing in the doorway. It was unclear how much he'd heard. "Lloyd, you give us money to design your chips. You're happy so long as you get your chip. Sponsors don't give a fuck about what else we're up to."

"Don't be *naïve,* Francis."

"What's the big deal?"

"We're going to have a reporter snooping around here. Pretty soon she's going to include the project in her column. Now how do you think that's going to make me look? I'll be sitting in some congressman's office in Washington with the heads of LSI and Motorola, and we'll be arguing how we need Asian import tariffs relaxed, when in will walk some staffer with this article which suggests that—of all people—*Lloyd Acheson* is the person trying to turn this industry over to the Japanese mass producers. And the guy from Motorola and the guy from LSI will look at me with a face like 'What the hell are you thinking? You're gonna kill the golden goose.' I can see it all happening. You could seriously damage La Honda's reputation—believe me, it doesn't take much. If potential sponsors start to think you're in the plastics business, pretty soon the sponsorships dry up."

Francis countered, "Have you been smoking dope?"

"What? Huh? What do you mean?"

"You heard me. *Have you been smoking dope?*"

"No—why? What—?"

"Because you're paranoid, man. All that stuff about sponsors drying up, it's not going to happen just because a few engineers have a go at some garage tinkering. You're way too hung up on your public image, you know that?"

"Lookit, Francis, you may not be happy about it, but I'm the president of the board, and one of the reasons is because I understand the significance of maintaining our mission. Our *mission*, Francis. La Honda has a charter and a mission and the duty to uphold that mission. And nowhere in all that is there anything to suggest we should start making plastic toys. If I let the project proceed, I would be neglecting my duty. You hear me? Huh?"

Francis still leaned against the doorframe. "What the hell do you expect Hank to do? He's already got volunteers working on the project. You can't just yank them off. Christ, the rest of the ironmen will revolt when they hear about it."

"Well that's our problem, when you get right down to it."

Francis added, "This isn't some programming division at Omega. You can't just march in here and order people around."

This got Lloyd mad. "I'm not ordering anybody around! Who said I was ordering anybody around? I came in here today to talk about a solution. Talk it over with Hank here."

The two men were quiet for a moment, staring at each other. Hank took the chance to jump in. "So what should I do?"

"Leave 'em alone," Francis said quickly.

Lloyd shook his head. "Hank, whoever it is on this project, go to them and ask them, for the good of La Honda, to step down. What has it been, three weeks? That's nothing. Put 'em on another project, I don't care."

Hank thought about it. He tried to avoid the gaze of either of the men. He knew better than to tell them what he was going to do, or it would just spark another round of bickering. "Okay," he said. "I've taken both of your inputs, I've heard it, I've considered it carefully, and I'm going to have a talk with the team. Thank you for your input. Now, if that is all . . . Francis? Did you have something you came in here to talk to me about?"

"It can wait."

That was odd, thought Hank, as Francis spun around and disappeared. It's never waited before.

. . .

Tiny had begun to research motherboards, the main circuit board that everything else connects to. There were some ninety different motherboard manufacturers; a third of those were American companies. Tiny just started calling salespeople and asking them to list what they had to offer. Tiny had never had a knack for talking with strangers, and so his calls were something like a series of blunt commands. Without any introduction whatsoever, he asked the salesman to describe *every* motherboard they sold, and Tiny just listened, waiting until he heard the salesman describe a configuration that interested him. Then he'd chirp, "Yes, two of those FedEx. Continue." These were corporate salesmen who were used to selling boards in hundred-unit lots. Once the salesman heard that Tiny only wanted two motherboards, he conveniently got a call on the other line and asked to call Tiny back.

"How's it going on those motherboards, Tiny?" Andy asked him, walking by.

"Good."

"Why aren't you on the phone?"

"I'm waiting for them to call me back."

"How long have you been waiting?"

"Three days."

"Three days! Oh, no. Why don't you call them again?"

"They said they would call me back."

Andy groaned. He peppered Tiny with enough questions to figure out what had happened. "Okay, it's time for a lesson in telephone etiquette." Andy walked back to his desk, picked up his
phone, and dialed Tiny's extension.

"Hello?" Tiny said, picking up his receiver.

"Tiny, it's me, Andy. Okay, when you call somebody, you have
to be nice to them, you have to *encourage* them. Like this: 'Hi, my
name's Curtis Reese, I'm calling from La Honda Research Center
in California, and we're looking for a motherboard under a hundred dollars with a thirty-two-bit bus and limited architecture.
We're designing a prototype now but our eventual initial order for
manufacturing will be at least ten thousand units." Andy went on
like that for a while. "Okay, now you try it."

Tiny repeated it back to him, word for word, even down to the
"umms" and "ahhs." But he repeated it without any inflection, as
if reading back a script of gibberish.

"Well, that's pretty good."

So they got on the phone together, and Tiny made a call, and he
did just fine. He ordered some test boards and spec sheets to play
around with. Nothing jumped out at him about these boards. Most
of them were still too complicated—they were built to run with
more expensive computers, so their architecture and chipset were
designed to accommodate a hard disk and a printer and usually
much more. These features would just go to waste in the VWPC.
Then, just by chance, Tiny got some e-mail from a friend in Florida
who was moving back to Silicon Valley and looking for work. In
Florida, he had been programming the interface for a joint-venture
experiment in interactive TV, a once-touted but ultimately disap-
pointing attempt to offer movies on-demand to consumers. The
joint venture had been funded by the phone company and a couple
of media companies. In order to make a TV interactive, they had
built prototype "set-top boxes," much like cable boxes, which
plugged into cable lines and could send information as well as
receive it. Willing to look anywhere, Tiny asked him about the
motherboards in their set-top boxes. His friend had no idea, but
put him in touch with the manufacturer, a company in Manchester,
England. They made specialty motherboards for personal digital
assistants and cartridge-based game machines. Tiny spent the night

on the sleeping porch in the south building, and got up early the next morning to make the call to Manchester. He worked his way through several salespeople, insisting that he speak to the most informed salesman of the bunch. The company had designed several different motherboards for set-top boxes, but they weren't going to mass produce them because the future of the joint venture was in doubt. Meanwhile, they had quite a few spares that weren't being used. These motherboards had the right kind of architecture: they had been designed to work with a television, so they had a video subsystem right on the motherboard (rather than as a plug-in card), and a digital-sound subsystem, and an architecture designed to plug into a cable outlet which could be modified for a modem. The set-top boxes had been priced preliminarily at $300, so these motherboards cost only $125. Though $50 over their budget, it seemed worth the trade-off: they got some video power, as well as some sound. More important, they would have a motherboard designed as if with their uses in mind—nothing would be wasted.

Best of all, these set-top boxes had one spare expansion slot. The team could configure the slot to accept a printer, or a scanner, or a camcorder—really anything, even a *video game machine!*

"Tell Darrell, will you?" Tiny said to Andy, after explaining that the motherboard would accommodate a video game machine.

"Why don't you tell him?" Andy asked.

Tiny sighed. "*Because,* if it comes from *me,* then it will be like I gave in to our argument."

"What argument?"

"Text versus video. Don't you remember?"

"But that was over a week ago! You're *still* arguing?"

Tiny bit his lip. "No. But it was never resolved, which is more important."

"But you don't have to choose, Tiny. That's the beauty of the motherboard you found."

"I know, I know. . . . But if I *did* have to choose, I'd still choose text."

"You really want me to tell him?" Andy asked.

"Coming from you, it won't look like I gave in."

"It's like the Mideast peace talks with you guys!" Andy said, but he went over to tell Darrell.

He stood over Darrell's desk. Darrell had his face scrunched up close to the screen, as if by getting closer he could figure out the problem he was working on. "Hey, just so you know, we got a motherboard that has a port for a game player," Andy said.

"We did?" Darrell said. He fell back into his seat and put his hands behind his head. There was a big smile on his face. "So Tiny came around after all, huh?"

. . .

There was a quick rap on the hollow door to the trailer, and then Hank Menzinger walked in.

Hank stood with his arms clasped behind his back. "Hey, Caspar . . . guys. Tiny."

Andy said, "Come for an update?"

Salman asked, "You want us to get out for a minute?"

Hank said, "No, stay, you should all hear this."

"Hear what?" Andy asked. "You got a sponsor?"

"That's what I want to talk to you about, Caspar. Occasionally, the board advises us against pursuing some projects. This is standard, you see—some of the board members have tips on competitive research, that sort of thing."

"So?"

Hank shrugged. "I'm just letting you know. I'm giving you advance warning. I'm taking a little heat about your project."

"Heat? What for? Why?"

"It's not unusual, Caspar. There are so many competing interests in Silicon Valley that some heat from the board is common. Sometimes it's petty bickering that goes away . . . sometimes a project conflicts with a board member's corporate agenda . . . sometimes it's legitimate concern for what La Honda should be devoting itself to. It's hard to anticipate and it's hard to tell what's really behind it."

Darrell chipped in. "But it was on the project list. Doesn't that mean it was approved?"

Hank explained. "Your project's been on the list for years. Years ago nobody had an objection. Now, though, they do."

"You don't give in to your board, do you?" Darrell said.

"Give in? No, it's not like that. I can take plenty of heat. But our board must approve all sponsorships. It's not always a rubber-stamp vote. It's not unusual for battles to occur."

Andy never expected a sponsor to come easily. "But you'll still look for a sponsor when we're ready, won't you?"

"Of course, of course. But you might want to consider what it will feel like if you put three months' work into a project and then suddenly have to drop it. How hard that will be."

"But maybe in two months . . . We're making headway. When the board sees what we've done . . . the objections will go away."

"Maybe. But Lloyd Acheson doesn't change his mind very often."

"*Lloyd Acheson* is against our project?" Salman blurted.

"He doesn't like it."

Andy said, "I still don't understand. . . . Why would Lloyd be pissed off by this project? Why doesn't he like it?"

"He has his reasons."

"Such as?"

Hank put his hand over his mouth for a moment; his eyes shifted off to the side. He was thinking what to say. "Think about it for a second. . . . Omega pays us to design their next-generation chip to compete with Intel, and then he finds out that some of his money is funding the very kind of project that could undermine the need for big iron on a desktop. If you were in his shoes, would you be happy about that?"

"What the hell are you talking about?" Andy said. "We're not taking anybody on. We're not trying to *undermine* Omega. This is ridiculous."

"Don't call Lloyd Acheson ridiculous."

"But we're just four guys in a trailer, for god's sake. How the hell are we going to *undermine* Omega?"

Hank put his hands out, palms down, trying to get Andy to relax. "It's not that you will. Of *course* not. It's about the *appearance* of conflict. It's about what La Honda stands for and is committed to."

Andy tried another angle. "Did you talk to Francis about this? What did he say?"

"Francis knows how sensitive Lloyd is to appearances and alliances. Francis doesn't like it, nor do I. We're very concerned about sponsors exerting too much control over La Honda. But Lloyd is our *president*."

It was occurring to Andy how devious Francis's revenge on him was. Not only did he kick him off the 686, not only did he push him onto a project that had no sponsor and was likely to fail . . . but it was a project that would earn him the ire of the president of the board of regents. Again, Andy couldn't understand why in the world Francis was making him go through this. But what could Andy do?

And then it clicked for Andy. *Francis knows how sensitive Lloyd is to appearances and alliances.* Maybe this didn't have anything to do with Andy, not really. Maybe this was all about something between Francis and Lloyd. And Andy was just one of Francis's pawns.

Andy said, "Are you ordering us off the project?"

"No, of course not. I'm just explaining to you the reality of the situation. It's up to you guys to decide what to do with it."

"You expect us to abandon a project just to restore proper *appearances*?"

"It doesn't matter what project you work on, you know? All that matters is that your brain is engaged, that you're challenged by your work. Now, why don't you volunteer for one of the other projects? They could use a bunch of bright guys like you. Let me know, huh?"

Hank walked out, his footfalls sending vibrations through the carpet into the sheet-metal floor.

• • •

Andy turned to his team. "Did you guys understand what just happened?"

Darrell said, "Yeah. If we were counting on Hank to get us a sponsor, forget it."

Andy nodded. "No way is he going to order us off the project, that would be too much. But he's going to make less than a token effort at luring a sponsor. When we complain, he's going to show us some letters he didn't actually mail, and present his appointment book full of meetings he never had, and tell us, 'Sorry boys, nobody was interested.' "

Tiny asked, "How much . . . money do we have left in the budget?"

Darrell asked, "Do you think he will take that money away?"

Andy said, "Maybe fifty, sixty days' worth. He won't take that away; it's not worth the *political* consequences. He's got to make it look like he gave us a fair effort."

"Fuck," Darrell said. "We were just *getting* somewhere."

"Now we're going to be a month behind on whatever project we join," Salman muttered.

Andy said, "So you don't believe in the VWPC."

"Of course I *believe* . . ." Salman answered. "But *our chances*. The odds were long enough already."

"But maybe Lloyd's opposition will fade."

Salman said, "You want me to take that chance? We're talking about *Lloyd Acheson*. If we piss him off this year, forget being reinvited next year."

Andy said, "You're willing to just walk away from our project? You don't feel like there's anything of *you* at stake here? This is your *work*, your *craft*, your *life*."

Salman looked down at the floor, ashamed.

Andy tried again. "Anything can happen in sixty days. *Anything*." He turned to Darrell. "What about you? Do you feel like he does?" Andy knew what the answer would be. Darrell was such a fighter that in the past ten minutes his devotion to the VWPC had probably doubled. Andy wanted Salman to hear this.

Darrell said, "Who the fuck is that guy to tell us what we can and can't do?"

Tiny said, "Right. Right, right, right."

"La Honda is about *volunteering*," Darrell added. "They don't force us to do shit. Maybe Hank can keep me off the six eighty-six project, but if so, what right does he have to tell me what other project I work on?"

Tiny concurred. "No right. None."

Salman pulled his head up. "I'm not like you guys. I try to pretend I'm tough, but it's an act. Darrell, you *like* fighting. Tiny, you can pull yourself into a shell like a turtle. And Andy, you can be cavalier about pissing off Lloyd Acheson because if you lose your job here you can go run a bank or something. But La Honda's my *life*. I don't fit in elsewhere."

Andy picked up a chair and carried it over beside Salman's desk. He sat down. "I'm not being cavalier. I'm dead serious about what I'm doing here. Before you give in to Lloyd Acheson's whisper of pressure, I think I should tell you what I know about Omega Logic. Maybe it will make you think differently. Remember, I used to work at Omega. In ninety-one, ninety-two. One of the reasons I went back to school—and one of the reasons I'm here—is that I hated what I saw when I worked at Omega. Chips that cost us fifty dollars we'd sell for five hundred. Magazine reviewers weren't testing the same machines we were selling in stores. We'd sell Eagle four eighty-sixes; and consumers would look on the box and see the Omega brand name and say, 'Okay, top of the line.' But only the processor was new. We'd build on eight-bit bus motherboards that couldn't be upgraded. Junk! Stuff you wouldn't wish upon your enemy. We'd install last year's version of the software. The failure rate for Eagle chips off the manufacturing line in Singapore was fifteen percent higher than the industry average, and they were making up the losses with cheapo parts. Give away an antistatic coating for the monitor for free to every buyer. But the monitor *always* has an antistatic coating, the damn thing comes off the assembly line with it. Yet we'd make a big deal of giving it away for free. Two years of demos at trade shows, glad-handing and schmoozing die-hard users. And you know what? They loved us. We'd host an open-bar cocktail party at the Tonga room, and the joint would be packed. The diehards loved us because compared to Intel we were the little guy. They thought Intel was trying to take over the world. They thought we were like communist guerrillas trying to overthrow the dictator, when we were just gouging profits off their idealism. We didn't deserve their adoration, not one bit. I was lying through my teeth five days a week. Power, power, power, man—you need more power! You're not a man unless you upgrade! I'm still sick of it. So when I hear Lloyd Acheson doesn't like my project . . . when I hear he's worried about how it will *appear* if his money supports a project that is an alternative to what *he* wants consumers to buy . . . I feel it's time to take a stand. I feel it's time to say 'enough.' I'm a human being, goddamnit. I've come to believe in this project. I don't get many chances in life to believe in something, and I'm not going to throw this away—not for Lloyd, not for La Honda, not for Hank, not for anybody."

Salman picked at the elastic top of his socks as he listened. He thought of himself as a person who took the moral path through life. Now, after what Andy had said, Salman wasn't going to be able to cave in without losing his self-respect. "I don't know . . ."

Andy added, "It's just *politics,* man. It'll work itself out."

"This is hard for me!"

Andy gave him a moment. Then he said, "Let me ask you this, Salman. What does it say about a man that he would cower to a company that betrays the diehards?"

"I'm not cowering! I'm thinking!"

"We've got sixty days. I'll find my own sponsor if I have to. Give it sixty days."

"Okay! Okay! Leave me alone now, will you? Will you just give me some time alone?"

4

A Gift Item

Simply having four years at La Honda on his resume could have landed Ronny Banks a job in the research department of just about any company in Silicon Valley. But Ronny Banks didn't want a job, not a *real* job; he'd picked up Francis's deep scorn for locking yourself up inside some company. He'd never worked very hard at La Honda, and he didn't want to start now. Instead, he called up one of Omega Logic's competitors—another chip manufacturer, Xircuit—and offered his services as a "consultant": in exchange for $50,000, Ronny offered to bring Xircuit up to speed on the latest advancements Francis Benoit was likely to build into Omega's next chip. Xircuit was a notorious copycat firm—they did very little R&D, instead imitating the design of other chips on the market, but their prices were 30 percent cheaper. To them, fifty grand was a bargain for what Ronny offered. They scheduled a meeting. It may have been morally repugnant, but Ronny had checked with a contracts lawyer and found that this trade was perfectly legal. Most employees who leave Silicon Valley firms are bound by noncompete clauses in their nondisclosure agreements, but La Honda Research Center wasn't a "business" in the traditional sense—it didn't *sell* anything. According to Ronny's lawyer, if La Honda wasn't a commercial entity, then it couldn't enforce a noncompete. Ronny had his lawyer write up this opinion, and he took it to the meeting with him. What a loophole! Ronny should have quit La Honda years ago. All this time, making a little cash had been only a few phone calls away.

But when Ronny arrived for his meeting with Xircuit, a team of lawyers met him in the lobby and took him into a conference room on the first floor. They wouldn't give him access to the rest of the building. Apparently, they had already contacted La Honda's general counsel about the procedures for hiring an unnamed ex-employee, and La Honda had covered their ass just fine, thank you very much. La Honda's standard position, as Xircuit interpreted for him, was that Ronny had merely soaked up La Honda's intellectual property during his four years, and that the "property" still belonged to them. If Ronny consulted for Xircuit, that would be tantamount to stealing trade secrets.

"Well, that means I can't work for anybody," Ronny complained.

Not quite. Xircuit's lawyers explained that Hank Menzinger could sign a waiver releasing the intellectual property rights. According to La Honda's counsel, Menzinger signed these waivers all the time, particularly for the young kids. La Honda didn't want to handicap anybody. The whole rigamarole was just a formality—but necessary. Xircuit told him to come back after he'd met with Hank Menzinger.

. . .

"Well, it's good to see you so soon again, Ronny," Hank said, leaning over his desk to shake Ronny's hand warmly. "How's the job search going?" Hank sat back down and began to play with a pencil.

Well, that was quick to the point. Hank obviously knows why I'm here. "I've got a few good leads, but I'm having a little legal problem, if you know what I mean."

Hank nodded his head and pursed his lips in a gesture of empathy. "I sure do," he said. "I've been divorced a few times myself."

"No, that's not it." *Maybe he meant it as a joke.* "Your lawyers tell me—they say that I can't work out there in the same area as I did here."

"Well, that's right, Ronny. But you're an ironman. Remember—
indivisible and transferable. You can work the same magic on software as you did on circuits. Oh, wait. . . . Now that's right. You
never actually worked any magic while you were here, did you,
Ronny? Hold on . . . I'm remembering something. Yes, that's
right—one Monday morning about two years ago, I opened the
door to this office and saw that my carpet had magically been
replaced with wall-to-wall Kentucky bluegrass sod."

Ronny chuckled nervously. It had been a hell of a stunt. It had
been Francis's idea, of course, but Ronny had pulled it off.

Hank continued. "You did a heck of a job on that. I'm sure
there's some firms in the valley who could use your talents . . . as
a gardener. I've noticed a lot of brown lawns at the office parks.
Must be a real shortage of capable handymen."

"It wasn't my idea," Ronny offered.

"I didn't expect it was."

"You know, I really wanted to apologize to you at the time, but
Francis wouldn't let me."

"I'm sure he wouldn't. Francis thinks men should stand by their
decisions. I'm sure he pointed out to you that if you were *truly*
sorry, you wouldn't have done it in the first place."

"He did! That's exactly what he said." Ronny had a glimmer of
hope—maybe Hank was just making him sweat it out. "Hey,
Hank, you know, I heard this thing from my lawyer—she said that
you can sign these waiver forms."

Hank made a grunting noise and scratched at one ear with the
pencil.

Ronny added, "She said it was kind of customary."

"Well . . . I can't sign one for you unless I know who you're
going to work for, can I?"

"You want me to tell you who I'm going to work for?"

Hank nodded his head. He was playing with the pencil again,
bored.

"And then you're going to give me the waiver?"

"That's the way it usually works."

Ronny thought about it. It seemed as if they had a deal.
"Xircuit."

"You're going to work for one of Omega's competitors?"

Ronny laughed nervously and said, "I sure am." Well, of course he was! This was all a formality, wasn't it? Ronny wasn't ashamed to take what he had coming to him.

"You want me to sign a form saying it's perfectly okay if you sell out our biggest sponsor?"

He chuckled again. "Yup." He looked around the office. Why wasn't Hank just giving him the damn piece of paper?

"Well, that doesn't sound very smart of me, does it? Sign a form like that? Do you think I'm not very smart, Ronny?"

For some reason his nerves were getting to him, and Ronny couldn't suppress his grin. "Uh, no, Hank. You're a smart guy."

"Are you laughing at me, Ronny?"

"No, it's just—I'm tense. You know, I *need* this form so I can work. I need it. So just tell me what you want from me and let's get it over with, okay?"

Hank spun slowly side to side in his swivel chair. "I don't want anything from you, Ronny."

"Oh. Okay. I guess that's it then." *Is he going to give me the form?* Ronny leaned forward, making a move to get out of his chair, watching Hank to see if Hank got out a piece of paper. Ronny stood up, patting his pants pockets.

"I'll see you around, Ronny." Hank was cool.

"Sure, sure. See you around." Ronny took a step toward the door. Maybe Hank was going to *mail* the waiver to him or right to Xircuit's legal department. Ronny wished he'd bothered to get the details from his lawyer.

"I'll look for your yard work in those office parks."

Ronny was at the door. He turned around abruptly. "You're not going to give me the waiver, are you, Hank?"

Hank chuckled. "That's very perceptive of you, Ronny."

Ronny went out into the anteroom, closing the door behind him. He stood there, breathing hard, his hands on his hips. He *had* to have that waiver. There was no way he was going to take a regular job. He had to convince Hank. Francis had been his best friend for four years, but where was Francis when Ronny needed him? Ronny had stopped by Francis's office just ten minutes ago, asked Francis to put in a good word with Hank about this waiver, and Francis had turned him down. *Wouldn't even put in a good word with*

Hank! Was that asking too much, for an old friend? "What's in it for me?" Francis had said.

Ronny turned around and knocked on Hank's door, opening it at the same time.

"Well, hello there, Ronny. Forget the way to the parking lot? It's in the other direction."

Ronny sucked his lower lip. "I want to offer you some information."

"Oh?"

"I know something that will interest you, big-time."

"I think our lawns here are in just fine shape, Ronny. But thanks, anyway. We've got a back-to-nature theme going, and brown is in."

Ronny clenched his teeth and ignored Hank's ribbing. "You've had a lot of trouble around here lately. That kid Caspar, the three-hundred-dollar computer, Lloyd Acheson."

Hank's entire face dropped. He stopped swiveling and leaned forward on his desk. He stared right at Ronny, then got up and took two quick strides to his door, shutting it. "You know something I don't know?"

Suddenly the whole secret came tumbling out. "Well you know the whole thing about the three-hundred-dollar computer," Ronny said eagerly. "After you guys ordered Francis to design a new chip, and then brought a reporter in to cover his project, and then to top it all off you picked that Caspar kid over me. Boy, was Francis mad! He cooked up the prank of a lifetime. A real beauty."

Hank was kind of bent over by his door, his arms crossing his chest, each hand gripping the opposite elbow. "So what'd Francis do?"

"Jeez, he engineered the whole thing. He went to your mama's boy, Caspar, and convinced him that life would be so miserable for him on the six eighty-six that he'd rather die than work for Francis. Then Francis ordered him to volunteer for the cheapie box, knowing how much it would piss you and Lloyd off." God, it was great to let the secret out. It was taking a piss after holding it in for hours, it just felt so good not to have it inside him anymore. "Francis promised Caspar a reinvite next year if he went along with it.

You have to admire the plan, the beauty of it, don't you? Of all the ironmen, he picks your boy Caspar, Lloyd's little brownnoser, the kid who took my place just because he worked at Omega. Boy, I would have loved to see Lloyd's face when he found out! Nobody pushes Francis Benoit around, hah!"

Hank was nodding silently to himself. His eyes had gone to jelly. His forehead was shiny with perspiration. His lower lip twitched.

Ronny said, "You know Francis and his pranks . . . always trying to teach lessons."

"Sure, sure . . ." Hank said, but he didn't look so sure. "How do you know all this?"

"Heck, he told me all about it just ten minutes ago when I stopped by his office. I went to ask him to put in a good word with you. About the waiver. He blew me off. He was working his own way to get even. Doesn't do *me* any good, of course."

Hank said, "And this is his way of getting even?"

"I'll bet it got your goat, huh? That's the whole plan, see. Francis doesn't give a shit about the cheapie box. He figures that without a sponsor, the project will die on the vine of its own accord. In the meantime, he just wants you two to bend over."

"Bend over?"

"Yeah, you know . . . it's revenge, see? He wants the white flag."

"Oh." Hank was silent.

Ronny watched him struggle to soak in all this news. Surely, though, that would be enough to get the waiver. He'd just sold out his best friend, what more could Hank want? "So, hey, Hank?"

"What?"

"About that waiver . . ."

"What about it?"

"You know, come on, I thought we had a deal."

Hank considered this. He took a deep breath and walked back to his desk and sat down. "What was the *deal,* Ronny?"

"You know. I'd tell you about Francis, you'd sign the waiver."

Hank looked confused. "Did I say that?"

"You didn't *say* it, exactly. But that's what I was thinking when I told you."

"Maybe you jumped to a conclusion. . . . Let me think about it, Ronny. It may be that I need your assistance in this matter again, before it's all over."

"Don't think too long about it. You know, it's harmless stuff I'd be telling Xircuit. I'm a real idiot, when it comes right down to it. I can't tell them anything you should be worried about."

Ronny left, feeling vacant and guilty. First he'd tried to sell out La Honda, then he'd given up his best friend. But he needed the money! He wouldn't last two days on a real job. Ronny slipped out the back entrance, took the fire escape down to the ground, and sneaked around the back side of the north building to his car, thinking nobody had seen him go.

· · ·

The door had been locked all day, and the DO NOT DISTURB light had been switched on as well. Lloyd Acheson's secretary first thought that her boss must have an emergency board meeting that wasn't on his schedule. So she called some of the secretaries of the other board members, none of whom could find a meeting with Mr. Acheson on their bosses' agendas. So then she began to think it must be a personal matter, and she checked her phone log for any incoming calls from doctors or psychiatrists. There must be something wrong with Mrs. Acheson. . . . At about two in the afternoon, Lloyd Acheson's secretary finally broke down and called Mrs. Acheson and had to ask her if everything was all right. This piqued Mrs. Acheson's curiosity, and Lloyd's secretary explained the whole thing—how he'd marched in that morning, told her to hold all calls and cancel all meetings, and then locked the door. Perhaps there was a merger in the works or a hostile tender offer? The secretary called downstairs to the media relations department and asked them if there were any rumors going around . . . and of course that piqued their interest, because they assumed she was calling on behalf of Lloyd to find out if there had been any leaks . . . and pretty soon the whole media relations department had heard the story about how their CEO had locked himself up all day, canceled a lunch and two meetings. The time was right for a deal, wasn't it? The stock price had been depressed for months, and columnists had begun to wonder if Omega Logic could continue chasing the market leaders year after year. It wasn't long before the rumor zipped through the whole firm, posted in e-mail traveling between employees and from employees to their spouses at home, and by five o'clock reporters were calling asking "Is something going down over there?" because they had been watching the financial wire services all afternoon looking for a confirmation of the rumor that the CEO was in deep negotiations with somebody and their deadlines were in just a few minutes, so if Omega was going to make an announcement then by god do it right now. By six o'clock there was a small crowd of Omega employees milling about in the entryway to Lloyd's office. They were checking their watches and using the phone on the coffee table to call their spouses and say they'd be home late. They just had to hang out to see what was going on.

At six-thirty the door finally opened, and Lloyd emerged, grabbing his right wrist with his left hand and massaging the joint. His sleeves were rolled up past the elbows. He took one look at the crowd gathered in the entryway and said, "I can't talk about it," which only lathered them up more.

"Are we being laid off?" one of them blurted out.

"Of course not," he responded, irritated. "What's going on here?"

"You've been there *all day*," his secretary explained.

"Well I'm here *every* day. This is *my office*."

He asked his secretary to follow him into his room. There, on his marble desk, were about ten piles of handwritten checks on Lloyd Acheson's bank account. They were for tiny amounts—$1.32, $0.87, $1.09. Lloyd reached for his suit coat and slipped it on. He told her that he wanted her to mail out each of the checks in its own envelope. He wrote down the address to mail them to, a foundation in San Francisco. "But each in its own envelope," he insisted. Despite her protests and questions, he would tell her no more. She'd worked for Lloyd for thirteen years and had never seen such strange behavior. She began to look through the checks. They were all made out to the First Amendment Foundation. They were all for less than a dollar fifty. She started counting the checks, then gave up and just examined the numerical series—checks 1027 through 2026. One thousand of them! Outside the door to his office were a dozen people who would be demanding to know what her boss had been doing all day, and what was she going to tell them? That Lloyd Acheson had just spent the last eight hours writing one thousand checks to the First Amendment Foundation, each for about a dollar?

. . .

Andy was lying on his back on his bed, staring at the ceiling. He couldn't stop thinking about the meeting he had the next day. He was going to try to get a sponsor. His mind kept thinking about what he should say during the meeting, but Andy knew he was at his best when improvising—he didn't want to have any lines rehearsed.

But they kept entering his head. *For a fraction of the cost, you get almost all the performance.*

No, more concrete: *It's 90 percent of the features for only 20 percent of the money.*

He had to stop thinking about it. He wanted to go in loose and cool. It was important never to let people smell desperation. And how was he going to smell tomorrow if he was ragged from lack of sleep and he couldn't respond intelligently to criticisms?

Alisa knocked on his door. It was a quarter to ten.

He turned on his bed lamp and told her to come in.

She was wearing a tan leather coat and shorts. The coat was longer than the shorts.

"Do you always sleep in your clothes?" she said.

Andy looked down at himself. "Aww, did I forget to take them off again?" He looked up with a straight face. "Actually, these are prototype antiwrinkle garments from L.L. Bean. As a long-standing customer, I'm getting five bucks a night to participate in their beta-phase experiments."

"You're not serious!"

"Did you know that *gullible*'s not in the dictionary?"

She made a face, then added, "The scary thing is, that joke's worked on me more than once before."

There was a pause. Andy said, "So what's going on?"

"Nothing. I just felt like being social."

"I could use the distraction. Hey, I forgot to give this to you yesterday—"

"Give me what?"

Andy grabbed a brown grocery bag off his bookshelf. "I got this for you." He handed it to her.

She said, "Oh, a paper bag. Thanks, I always wanted one of these."

"Very funny."

She held the paper bag up to her chest like she was trying on clothes. She sashayed her hips. "It's a little small . . . but I *love* the material. Very . . . *organic*."

He laughed. "Come on, look inside."

"I'm just getting even, Mister L.L. Bean beta-tester."

"It's an FM car radio."

She looked down in the bag. "Thanks, Andy. This is too nice."

He said, "When you loaned it to me, I noticed your 1971 car has a 1971 radio. I'll install it for you."

"Wow, *FM*. You don't know how many times I've gone to a party and someone has said, 'Did you catch that piece on National Public Radio today?' and I'm like the *only* person in the room who didn't."

"Well, I was thinking music, actually. I know you always have your stereo on in your room, albeit at low volume. I figured you would want the same in your car."

She blushed, caught without a joke. There was a moment when he thought she might give him a kiss on the cheek, but they were standing too far apart for that to happen easily.

He bailed her out. "Come on, I'll go install it." He had a tool kit in his closet-kitchen.

The night was cool. The camphor smell of eucalyptus was pungent. Alisa's VW was parked in the gravel driveway. He opened the passenger door and slithered in backward until he had his head below the dashboard. She sat in the driver's seat, holding a flashlight under the dashboard to illuminate his work. She handed him tools as he asked.

"Needle-nose pliers . . . Are you getting some design work?" he said.

She said, "A little. *Very* little. I'm no good at presenting my projects. I can't take the criticism. There are these designers up in San Francisco, they have this, like *Star Trek* shield around them. I don't know how they get it. My shields are always, like, at ten percent strength." Her voice changed to a baritone Scottish accent. "She cannot take 'nother hit, Cap'n!"

Andy laughed. "It's hard to sell stuff you care about. It's a hell of a lot easier when you don't care."

"That's the truth. The irony is, then you get hired only for projects you don't really care about."

He passed her out some half-inch hexagonal nuts. He asked her to stick a screwdriver under the bolt heads and pry them out. When she did that, the old AM radio came free. He handed it to her and took the FM radio in return.

He said, "When I was at Omega, I'd practice a demo repeatedly, anticipate every technical glitch possible, and then we'd get to the customer site and try to set up and find that the extension cord didn't reach from the table to the outlet across the room. The demo of some five-thousand-dollar next-generation computer, brought back to earth for lack of a twenty-five-foot extension cord. I learned not to care. The thing was, then I could sell . . . sell hard. Because I didn't care . . . because it was all a game."

Alisa said, "I would *kill* to have what you have, that ability. I'd be rich by now."

"Hah . . . If I could only tell you how *guilty* it makes me feel. When I do it, I feel like I'm *betraying* my integrity. I think: true engineers can't shift into marketing mode, so who am I? I'm not a true engineer. . . . Wire cutters."

"You're *protecting* your work; what's so bad about that?"

Andy paused. "Will you write that down on a piece of paper for me and tape it up beside the bathroom mirror?"

"Not by the mirror. Then I'd have to read it. How about I wrap it around your toothpaste tube?"

"Uhh, not there."

"Why not?"

"Uhh . . . I've been out of toothpaste for two weeks. Needle-nose pliers again."

"You've been using mine!?" She socked him softly on the shoulder.

Soon the radio was in place. He asked her to try it. She turned the left knob. Nothing happened.

"It's the left knob, correct?" she said.

"Usually. Try pressing it in, sometimes that turns it on."

But that didn't work either. Andy slithered out of the car and then poked his head in. "Well, I see the problem."

"What?"

"I put it in upside down." He turned the right knob, and the music pumped from the speakers in the doors. He adjusted the balance with the left knob. "I'll flip it. This will take just a second."

"No, leave it," Alisa said. "I like it. It's original."

They sat there listening for a while.

Alisa said, "So what am I distracting you from?"

Andy sighed. "Thanks for reminding me. I had almost put it out of my mind."

"Sorry."

She waited until the end of the song, then she said, "So what is it?"

"I'm trying to pitch to a sponsor for our project tomorrow."

She said, "Well, there's only one piece of advice I can give you."

"What's that?"

"Bring an extension cord."

. . .

Francis Benoit was in his office when he got a phone call from a friend in San Francisco, a lawyer who ran a foundation that protected the rights to free expression online. Francis assumed the call was to ask for another donation—something Francis was always happy to give, particularly if a case had reached the courts. Francis gave the foundation about twenty thousand dollars a year, but he declined to sit on their board—he didn't like doing anything half-assed, and his experience with boards was you had a couple meetings a year where the same old priorities were reprioritized and the same old weak resolutions were unanimously resolved.

"Well, you've really done it this time," his friend said.

"What are you talking about?"

"I've received some donations lately, and it seems they all come at your recommendation."

"I try to spread the good word," Francis said.

"We received some donations from Lloyd Acheson; he referenced your name on the bottom of his checks."

"Really?" Francis, to his knowledge, had never spoken with Lloyd Acheson about the First Amendment Foundation. "How much did he give?"

"A thousand dollars."

"Not bad, for a start. I'll have to call him and thank him."

"It's going to take us all week to process the checks."

"What do you mean?"

"He sent a thousand checks."

"A thousand checks! Each for a dollar?"

"No. A different amount on each one. We have to enter them into the computer by hand. It's probably going to cost more than a thousand dollars of my bookkeeper's time to deposit the thousand dollars' worth."

Francis laughed. The donation to Francis's favorite charity could only mean one thing: Ronny had told Hank. Of course he would—Francis never would have told Ronny if he had intended to keep it a secret forever.

With these donations, Lloyd had tipped his hat to Francis. But not quite, not without a twist. Break down the thousand dollars into a thousand checks! Touché! Brilliant! Writing out a thousand checks was the kind of stunt only an engineer would think of and only another engineer could appreciate. By evoking this principle, "break it down," Lloyd Acheson was poking fun at engineers, but he was also reminding Francis that he had once been an engineer, too.

So the prank was over. It was fun while it lasted. Now Francis just had to wait for the project's money to run out, and then he would take a look at where their work stood.

Francis's resentment of Lloyd Acheson was rooted far deeper than a little frustration over a reporter and Ronny's not being re-invited. This went all the way back to the Falcon chip. Two million Falcon desktop computers had been sold at over three grand a pop, and from the point of view of Wall Street it was an unqualified success. But in order to make the Falcon fast, Francis had added a crucial feature. He had taken advantage of a procedure called parallel processing: the Falcon was actually two redesigned 486 chips side by side. Special software would divide any operation into two parts and give each chip one half the problem. It was the old divide-and-conquer approach, *but it required the proper software.* When Francis designed the Falcon, Lloyd Acheson had promised him that Omega would install such software.

But then some muckety-mucks had a meeting and made a decision that any software running on the Falcon had to be able to run on old Omega computers as well—computers that didn't use parallel processing. They installed a new software upgrade, but it didn't support parallel processing. What did all this mean? For most of those two million customers, one of the two chips was being wasted! Literally, it never even felt an electrical signal. It waited, dormant as a bear in hibernation. Yet people had paid for them. People were being ripped off, and they had no idea. As far as they knew, they had bought the top of the line. Their Falcons were still fast, since even that one active 486 chip was faster than the previous design. There were also numerous other advancements in the Falcon that kept customers happy: the motherboard circuitry was far more efficient, and little memory closets, called caches, were used on every card and chip. But the net result was that the standard Falcon sold by Omega was only a little more than half as fast as Francis had designed it. Half as fast. Imagine buying a new Porsche and finding out it only goes forty miles per hour! The real tragedy was this same dynamic was true for most of Omega's competitors. They were selling computers with chips inside that weren't being fully utilized. They were all afraid to sell software that wouldn't run on older machines. It was a *marketing* decision—and that said it all. These were *marketing* companies now, not really computer companies. Years ago, in the seventies and even through the mid-eighties, the chip companies actually built their own chips in their own labs, and software companies wrote their own software, et cetera. But in the nineties, much of what the public thought of as computer companies were just shell companies with dominant sales forces and advertising budgets. Most of their CEOs were middle-aged guys with MBAs and a few years under their belt building toothpaste market share for Procter & Gamble. They grew by acquiring outright all the shares of new start-ups. They paid others to design the heavy iron.

Then they had dumbed down his chip.

The ultimate indignity.

He wouldn't give Omega the same chance on the 686.

. . .

The Interstate 280 freeway ran north-south not twenty feet away from the front door of ModNet in San Jose, and as the team from La Honda stood outside the front door, the roar of twelve lanes of cars seemed a vicious sound, an aggressive attack on their ears. ModNet provided an internet connection to fifty thousand monthly subscribers—it was a sort of phone company for your computer, and it had tripled in size every six months since its start-up two years prior. This five-story building wouldn't hold them for long. Salman took one look at the dark hexagonal exterior windows and labeled it in his mind a beehive. What he saw and heard inside confirmed his impression—so much buzzing energy in everyone's rapid strides and to-the-point conversations. While trying to talk to the receptionist, Andy had been interrupted three times by couriers. Finally she called upstairs and confirmed their appointment. A security guard appeared, handed them temporary passes, and ushered them into another lobby, where they sat down on couches and watched the flow of bees pouring out of the elevators.

Salman said, "Will Hank take their money?"

Andy said, "If he doesn't, then a certain journalist is going to find out about it."

After five minutes that seemed like ten, an old friend of Andy's materialized and whisked them upstairs to a corner conference room. In the center of the table sat a half dozen cans of iced tea, drops of condensation drooling down the sides. Outside, the air was brown and hazy.

Andy's friend Donny Williamson had worked with him at Omega. Since then he'd held marketing jobs at several firms before coming to ModNet as employee number forty-three. He was now a vice president for marketing and wore knit ties. He was the kind of guy you love to hate, just for being so clean and healthy and doing so well in the world. He had no long hair, no facial hair. His fingernails were perfect little white half moons, and he had no crackly hangnails whatsoever. Groomed and trimmed. Declawed, if you will. He was the kind of guy who carried his extra weight on his back, rather than his gut, so no matter how old he got he would never look flabby. Despite all this despicable vitality, it was impossible to hate him, because he seemed genuinely happy, a mutant quality that was oddly endearing. He called Andy "Drew." Andy called him "Willy." Willy made sure everyone got an iced tea and one of his business cards, printed on heavy stock.

For the demonstration, obviously Andy didn't have a working prototype, but he'd rigged a 1986-edition Macintosh SE with a 1995-edition modem connection to make his point: the Macintosh had an extinct processor and a meager hard drive and a dinky gray-scale screen, but it was perfectly able to connect to the internet and function nearly as well as modern heavy iron. Andy had previously loaded up ModNet's internet software onto the Macintosh. He booted the program, and they all watched as the familiar ModNet interface displayed perfectly. Then Andy cruised a few demanding web sites, and as far as anybody in the room could tell, this old Mac was as fast as anything they had back home.

Then Andy disconnected from the internet and booted an old word processor, circa 1985, Macwrite 1.5. The display popped up nearly instantly; Andy demonstrated a few of the familiar features, just to prove that word processors weren't all that unsophisticated back in 1986. The Macwrite 1.5 application was only 144 kilobytes, less than one hundredth the size of the word processors installed on their hard disks back home. One *hundredth!* For one *hundredth* the size, they had a word processor that seemed perfectly capable for writing letters and long documents. It would download over a modem in ten seconds and boot in five. Oh, it didn't have its own built-in thesaurus, and it couldn't print mailing labels, but 90 percent of the time, this little program was sufficient. Nobody else on the team had seen Andy's demonstration before, and they all got a rush out of it. It reminded them what they were all about. They thought it was a good sign when Willy reached for the keyboard to compose a few lines on the word processor himself.

Andy detailed their work to date. He summed it all up with a phrase that echoed the demonstration: "Maybe it's not every bit as good as a PC. But it's ninety percent of the features for only twenty percent of the money." Andy had figured that an internet provider like ModNet had a vested interest in seeing the VWPC succeed, since it was the kind of device that might bring the "other 50 percent" to the internet—"the other 50 percent" being all those stubborn Americans who had never bought a computer despite having purchased cars, VCRs, and refrigerators. The "other 50 percent" was a sort of holy grail for the computer industry, a market they'd been unable to tap despite a blitzkrieg of hype. The conventional wisdom was that the other 50 percent would jump in en masse, all at once, and whoever led them—whoever instigated the jumping—would go down in history as big as Jesus Christ. The relevant point was that when the other 50 percent jumped online, a whole heck of a lot of them would come to ModNet.

"Maybe so, maybe so." Willy nodded. "But—maybe you don't understand, Drew. ModNet—we're already tripling in size every six months. Tripling, see? So—well, it takes every bit of our resources just to hang in there, to invest in a backbone to meet the demand we *already* have." He had a habit of raising his eyebrows after he said anything, as if he'd asked a question. It probably helped him in the world of business—he could appear to be merely raising questions when he was really confronting people.

Andy was ready for him. "That's *now*. That's *today*. Two years from now, though, your market will be competitive, margins dropping just as your shareholders start demanding they see those rolled-over profits. For then, you've got to have a strategy. Not now. *Then*."

"Okay, you have a point. Point taken. But what you're talking about, this VWPC—can I be direct with you guys? I don't get it. Why would I throw away the computer I already have and buy something *less* powerful? I don't get it."

"It's not for *you*. Think of students. Think of your mother."

Willy started to shake his head side to side harshly. "I'm a marketing guy, okay? I look at how we would market this. And I don't see it. What's *cool* about it? There's nothing *cool* that's going to get early adopters. The whole system of marketing in this industry, it's broken into stages. If you pass the first stage, you get to move on to the next. First stage is early adopters, users who will buy your gizmo or thingamajig for any price, just to play with it. Just to see what they can do with it. But it's got to be *cool*, it's got to seem out of the future. If they like it, they spread the word, and you lower your price and go after the early majority. But that takes big bucks—advertising, bundling, retailer co-ops. You don't get the bucks unless it's proven in stage one. Nobody gets the big bucks when the gun goes off. What you've got here, this VWPC, it's for the late majority and the laggers. We don't have a clue how to market to them."

Tiny had listened with interest. Tiny noticed Willy was wearing a black diver's watch that doubled as a compass, which might come in handy if he ever got lost in the maze of cubicles coming back from the bathroom. "Maybe you can't market to them because you've never had anything to sell them."

Andy tried to blunt Tiny's criticism. "What about a sales force?" Most computerware in corporations and schools had been pushed in by large national sales forces working on commission.

"At three hundred bucks, the margins are too thin. A salesman gets two, three percent. That's ten bucks. It doesn't pay for the parking and gas to make the sales call. This is the computer industry, guys. What you've got here, this VWPC—okay I'm not going to say it's not a computer, because it is, *technologically*. But from a marketing point of view, it's *not*."

"Not a computer?" This from Darrell.

"From a marketing point of view, I'm only saying."

"If it's not a computer, then what would you call it?"

Willy paused. "Maybe a gift item."

"A *gift* item?"

"Yeah. I could see people who have used computers for years buy these for their parents, just to get them online."

Tiny winced.

Darrell continued in a biting tone. "Sort of the way a tricycle gets people prepared for the road bike."

Willy shrugged. "Exactly like that. A starter computer."

Andy could see Darrell was about to blow his top. "Willy, we had hoped . . . we had thought . . . if you weren't interested in sponsoring us, maybe you would know someone who was."

Willy bit his lower lip. There wasn't much to bite. "I'll think about it. But honestly? No. Everybody in this industry . . . we have too much at stake in the way the industry already works."

On their way out of the building, Darrell walked past a box of diskettes offering "90-days free" access to the internet. In an effort to save trees, the cardboard diskette packaging was minimal, no more than a slipcase. The diskettes were about the same size, Darrell realized, as his coat pockets. He took enough to last him about five years.

• • •

The team couldn't brush off the "gift item" appraisal very easily. It was damn near impossible not to let it haunt them. Who had they been trying to impress all these years, if not their peers? They'd never been through an initial public offering that made them wealthy, and their names had never appeared in the *Mercury News,* so what had each of them been after this whole time if not the admiration of equals—if not at that moment, then down the road when another engineer would meet one of them and say, "Wow! *You* were the guy who did *that!*" and he'd be able to cough into his fist and give a modest little nod. That was what it was all about, wasn't it? Donny Williamson was the first peer outside La Honda they had shown their idea to, and they had gone into that meeting fresh with the thought, *Lloyd Acheson is scared of us.* They were expecting to knock the guy's socks off.

Instead, what had been his reaction? "A gift item."

Is this what they had been working so hard toward? Is this what they had challenged Hank's authority for? The "tricycle" of computers? The team began to discuss adding back in some of the conventional features of the personal computer. They wanted to make it more "like a computer."

Darrell vowed that the first software application he'd write would be a database, since that traditional business application would demonstrate the VWPC's number-crunching power. Salman started to feel self-conscious about the way the VWPC turned on and booted up. The way Tiny had been designing the system, the screen would be blank until the computer dialed into a server and downloaded an interface. This took about thirty-five seconds over the standard 1995 modem. Even with a faster download, they only projected being able to get the picture on the screen in twenty-five seconds, since most of the time was used dialing the server and negotiating the beeping handshake. Salman feared that if the screen picture didn't come up right away—within a few seconds—users would get the immediate impression that the VWPC was *slow*. Even though the screen display had nothing to do with the processor power, users would still draw that conclusion. For whatever reason, consumers had always judged computer power by how fast they loaded up software—how long they had to wait between clicking on "WordPerfect" and actually getting the WordPerfect screen. This was actually less a function of the processor than of the seek times of the hard disk; a slow hard disk could make any computer seem slow to the user. Nevertheless, they blamed the processor, and often made the mistake of trying to fix the problem by buying a new five-hundred-dollar processor rather than a new one-hundred-dollar hard disk.

Salman became fixated on this issue. "When you turn the damn thing on, it has to snap to attention," he kept muttering.

"It's a marketing issue," Andy scoffed, when Salman wanted to talk about alternatives. Andy was right—the VWPC wouldn't be any slower or faster by having the screen displayed immediately. All Salman was concerned about was users' misguided impressions.

"But it's their *first* impression," Salman argued. He eventually persuaded Tiny to consider the problem by pointing out that a PC took about fifteen seconds to show a "C\" prompt, and even more to display Windows. If they could get the VWPC to "snap to attention," users might mistakenly assume that the VWPC was actually *faster* than a PC. "Why not?" Salman said. "If it can work against us, then it can work for us as well."

Tiny came up with the possibility of never turning the computer all the way off. It would always draw a little power, say 0.3 volts, from the power outlet. The screen image would still be stored in RAM, and the voltage would keep RAM awake. When the user flipped the computer on, the image could jump out of RAM and get right back up there on the screen instantly. If the user ever unplugged the computer from the wall outlet, then the image would be lost with the voltage, but that would only happen now and then.

"I like that idea," Andy said, when Tiny briefed him.

Salman, though, had a different opinion. "The *first* time someone plugs it in and turns it on, it'll still be slow. It'll still have to dial up and establish a connection and download the screen. I'm worried about that first impression."

"Listen to yourself," Andy said. "You sound like you're going out on a blind date."

"Hey, I don't need a date to get my rocks clocked. That's you, buddy."

Andy paused, trying to see how the topic of conversation had so quickly switched from the screen display to their love connections. "What does that have to do with anything?"

"I—I don't know . . . sorry. It just comes out."

Andy gave Salman one day to think through a new solution, or they would stick with Tiny's "sleeping RAM" concept.

"Why don't we just code the graphical display onto the CMOS chip?" Salman suggested to Tiny. The CMOS chip runs the ship for that first thirty-five seconds after the computer is turned on, before the internet connection takes over.

"No room on the chip," Tiny said.

"Or a bigger chip?"

"Money, money, money, money."

Salman went to Andy, who said, "The motherboard we're using already has a CMOS chip on it. If we bought another chip, we'd be buying two and throwing away one. That's ridiculous."

So Salman went back to Andy and asked, "How much room on the chip *do* we have?"

"Almost none. I could give you maybe two lines of text. I can't even display a little icon, like the Mac smiley face."

So Salman spent that night brainstorming what the VWPC should say to first-time users, to make a good first impression. He began to see that this was part of a bigger problem: since it had no hard disk, the computer would be downloading a *lot,* and whenever it was downloading it would be inoperable. Darrell had promised to write simple programs that would download to the VWPC just as fast as big software suites uploaded off a PC's hard disk—the waiting time was supposed to be no different. But Salman was nervous. He kept thinking about the criticism—"a gift item."

The concept Salman came up with was to give their VWPC a personality. Whenever it was primarily occupied with downloading, it would display some banter across the screen. Text used up almost no memory; the first thing to download would be enough text to scroll across the screen at a reader's pace until the download was completed. And what would the text be? This was the great beauty of Salman's idea. Since the download was coming off a server, rather than a hard disk, the server would be regularly maintained and updated by a system administrator—eventually this would be a big company. So every morning, the system administrator could put in new text to download first and scroll along that day. For instance, news headlines, sports scores, jokes, stock prices, or SAT vocabulary builders—really anything. But the information would be of unlimited supply. Users could click on their choice of category when they logged on for the first time, and they could change their category whenever they wanted. It would be like those electronic ticker tape machines. As Salman envisioned it, the VWPC would *never* appear to stop working. It wouldn't resort to merely displaying an hourglass, as Windows did, and it wouldn't just show a picture of a gas tank filling up, as other software did. It would scroll news! Most important, it would do something that an ordinary PC could never do: it would use the central network to its advantage. This was a perceptual breakthrough for Salman—their project was no longer just a dumbed-down PC; in some ways, it would be even smarter, even better.

"Hey, Andy, can we have a meeting?" Salman asked him, wanting to explain the idea he had.

"A meeting?"

"Mmmm."

"What for? We're all already *here,* right now. You got something to talk about, just say it."

"I really wanted . . . can we schedule?"

"Now's not as good a time as any?" Andy asked.

"Come on," Darrell said, overhearing. "Just say it."

"Uh, no, that's okay. I don't want it to fall on deaf ears."

"We're not deaf," Andy said.

Salman shook his head. "Okay, I might have said it, but now I can't."

"Why the hell not?" Darrell said.

"You have to be *ready* to hear it."

"Hear *what*?"

Salman bowed his head. "See? Just forget it. There's all this tension now. I need us at peace. Receptive."

It took another day for Salman to get it out, but when Salman finally explained his idea to the team, they became ecstatic, practically euphoric. Darrell got shivers down his back. Salman's idea would be so simple to program, so simple to execute. It wasn't a technological issue at all, and that was what was so great about it. It was the kind of simple thing they could do merely by adopting the central-server model. For the first time, the VWPC wasn't just about money, it wasn't just about reproducing the PC at a different price point. It wasn't a cheap substitute. In the minds of the team, their project started to take on its own identity, separate and distinct from the PC. *Maybe Lloyd Acheson was right to be scared— we might undermine the PC after all!*

· · ·

Near the end of the month, Hank Menzinger got a call from La Honda's stockbroker, Quentin Black, who worked for a firm in San Francisco. During the spring, Hank had pledged La Honda's holdings of Omega stock as collateral against a loan from the brokerage firm. Hank had intended to pay back the loan as soon as he received the sponsorship funds from Omega for the 686 project— in fact, needing the money so badly, Hank had taken out the loan even *before* Francis had agreed to the 686. Hank wasn't any good with money; he couldn't keep his wits about him when a transaction was on the table. Quentin gave explanations as if they were just theories. "The word on the street is . . ." he might say. Or, "If you subscribe to the theory that the masses drive the market . . ." he would use as a lead-in. He never quite told Hank what *he* believed. He gave his "opinion" and his "thinking" and his "feeling," but never straight out his "advice." On the one hand, Hank knew he was never being fed false promises. On the other hand, Hank was always worrying.

One of the special percs of being the executive director of La Honda was that Hank Menzinger was commonly dealt in on the "friends list" of all the initial public offerings coming out of Quentin's firm. Being on the friends list allowed Hank to buy small amounts of stock at the opening trade price, or often just below it. Two out of three stock offerings surged up in the first day of trading, as the public fought for ownership of the shares, and Hank got to sell his shares 90 days after he bought them, often for a sizable profit. Over the years, the profits from this IPO trading had funded as many projects as had been funded by legitimate sponsors, but in the spring Quentin Black had given Hank a chance to buy *more* than just a few shares. It was a company that made virtual reality equipment—goggles and chairs and capsules—for sale to amusement parks. Quentin Black had given Hank the opportunity to put several million dollars into the deal, rather than the customary hundred-thousand-dollar slice, and Hank took Quentin's offer, went for the big one—he liquidated La Honda's position in money market funds and invested the cash in the IPO. Hank envisioned a future where La Honda would no longer be captive to its sponsors, and the beauty of that vision was so appealing he couldn't help himself. This IPO, though, just didn't have the demand, didn't have the market interest, and the shares that opened at 12 ended the week at 11, and by the end of the month were at 8. "Nature of the beast," Quentin Black had said, by way of explanation. The shares were now at 7½; Hank was afraid to sell and book the loss—the board would see the transaction, learn about the loss, and have his head. He wanted to cover it up. So Hank had used his shares of Omega as collateral, taking out a loan to cover his ass, and now Quentin Black had him on the phone.

"It's the end of the month, Hank. I just got a call from my credit department. We're going to have to do a margin call."

Hank didn't understand what Quentin was talking about, and said so.

"Omega's down six percent this month," Quentin said. "We're uncovered."

"What do you mean, 'uncovered'?"

"You're borrowing more than your collateral. You've got to make a principal payment to reduce the loan."

"But I thought we just made a payment two days ago."

"That was an interest payment. This is a principal payment."

"How much do we have to pay?"

"You have to bring the two in line. The collateral drops six percent, you've got to pay back six percent of the loan."

"But that's over two hundred thousand dollars! I don't have that kind of money lying around!"

"Sell some of your other stocks," Quentin advised him.

If Hank sold La Honda's other stocks, it would show up on the portfolio report that went to the board each month. So far he'd been able to move money around enough to keep the board from finding out about the loss, and he'd hoped to make the profits back on more IPOs, though this was proving to be impossible, at only ten thousand dollars a trick. "What else can we do?"

"That's really it, Hank. Call me back, okay? I got my credit department on my ass, jerk won't leave me alone."

Hank called Lloyd Acheson immediately, but Lloyd was in Geneva for some conference. Switzerland, of all places! Why the hell did he have to go to Geneva to run a goddamn computer company? Omega's sponsorship money hadn't come in yet. When Hank got it, he could pay back the loan in full and try to replenish the lost cash reserves.

Hank asked Lloyd's secretary if Lloyd was checking his e-mail or calling in for messages, and he begged her to have Lloyd give him a call, at home or at work, any time of day or night—it was an emergency.

. . .

About that time and halfway across the world, Lloyd Acheson was walking in the rain on the golf course outside the hotel Omega had chosen this year to schmooze its European distribution channel. Lloyd had arrived just that morning, and his body clock told him "Man, we're supposed to be *asleep* right now." But sleep wasn't an option. Lloyd had been hoping for some sunshine; he hoped a little sun on the face would raise his serotonin levels and fight off the jet lag. Instead, by the time he got to the hotel, a rainstorm had taken over the sky. For twenty minutes, Lloyd stood in his hotel room staring out his window with his bag of golf clubs slung over his shoulder—golf clubs he had brought almost entirely for this very moment, this bit of rehab—when he realized he was totally zoned out. This wouldn't do. He had to wake up! So he resolved to walk the course. He would carry his bag to give himself more of a workout.

Coming down the fairway toward him was a greenkeeper. He pulled up beside Lloyd.

"Just out for a walk," Lloyd said. "I'm not playing."

The greenkeeper nodded and drove on.

Elsewhere in the city, a convention was going on. This afternoon, he would sit on a panel. Tomorrow, he would give a speech. And if he could just get his body to adjust, it would be no problem.

Later, around seven that evening, Lloyd lay submerged in a hot bath, his nostrils a quarter inch above water. The long flight had dried out his sinuses and throat, made him feel sick. Downstairs, the schmoozing had begun. The twenty-eight people in Europe most vital to Omega had been invited for the evening. They were from the sales channel, mostly—resellers, distributors, buyers. And they hadn't taken time out of their schedule to have some free drinks or a nice meal. They were here for one reason: to see Lloyd. The annual encounter, where they could look the Man in the eye and judge for themselves whether he still had "it"—that combination of wit and savvy that had guided Omega on the journey from a twenty-million-dollar company into an eight-hundred-million-dollar company. They wanted to see that he hadn't burned out, that he hadn't gone soft, that he didn't have his head in the clouds with some wacko new idea. They wanted to be assured that atop this great pyramid was a man with a brain big enough to tackle whatever might be thrown his way in the coming year. It didn't matter so much what he said as long as he came across sharp in saying it. If Lloyd could just get himself to *shine* for a couple of hours, it would obliterate every gloomy prediction made about Omega in the past year. But Lloyd was dizzy and light-headed. He couldn't hold his water and get rehydrated.

Lloyd made his appearance just as everyone was sitting down to dinner. They were seated around four linen-covered tables, the chandeliers overhead at half strength, the liquor in their glasses at double strength. They wore dark suits; Lloyd wore a San Francisco 49ers jacket, red and gold leather. *Never stay in one place long enough to get too far into an argument that you don't have a snappy response,* he told himself.

He made the rounds, bouncing from table to table, calling everyone by their first names, thanking them for their purchase orders, offering tidbits of inside information.

"Gunter, my man, hell of a first quarter you did for us. . . . Don't think I didn't notice, huh? Hey, I heard Knaur's going to double their warranty, you might want to beat them to it.

"Paulo, always a pleasure . . . The lamb doesn't look appetizing to you, huh? Oh, okay. You know what my wife says? She says 'I am not a vegetarian because I love animals; I am a vegetarian because I hate plants.' " Lloyd hoped nobody recognized his jokes from last year.

Someone asked Lloyd if he was afraid that software in the future would just be downloaded over the internet, cutting them out of the pipeline. Without thinking, Lloyd returned, "Have you ever imagined a world with no hypothetical situations?" He let that sink in, then added, "I know we have to be ready for the future, but don't be so open-minded that your brains fall out. People *want* to come into your stores. Internet distribution won't cut into your market, it will just add on top of your market."

Then, "Do I think Dole has a chance against Clinton? . . . You know that joke, 'What has four legs and an arm? A happy pit bull!' Clinton will let Dole have an arm, but that's all the senator will get. . . .

"No, I don't care about fiscal policy so much as I care about antitrust policy. Under Reagan the Justice Department hired kids out of school, indoctrinated them into a nonlitigious mind-set, only went after criminal violations. . . . Hell, yes, I'm talking about Microsoft, who else? . . ."

Someone asked him about what Papa Lewis was up to. Papa was the chairman of the board of Omega, the one person who had the authority to fire him, and so asking about Papa was not idle chitchat. Lloyd wanted to give the impression that Papa was totally at ease. "Papa went boar hunting last week—came back with a set of tusks and a hundred pounds of jerky. . . . He wanted to send some jerky to our largest customers. You know what boar jerky tastes like? About like a shoelace . . .

"You like this jacket? Lookie here—" Lloyd unzipped the placket and pulled back the breast flap, showing the designer's label. It had been autographed by the 49ers' star receiver, Jerry Rice. "I would give this jacket to you—but if I gave one to *you*, I would have to give one to everybody, wouldn't I?" He scratched his chin and pursed his lips, mocking the process of coming to a decision. "Aww, what the heck," he said, shrugging the jacket off his shoulders and pulling his arms from the sleeves. "Here you go. No, seriously, take it. Come on, take it." The guy wouldn't accept it. Lloyd bent his head toward the man and whispered, "If you *don't* take it, I don't have an excuse to give one to everybody." So the guy accepted the jacket, and on cue someone from Omega's marketing department wheeled in a few cardboard boxes on a pallet truck. Lloyd went over and ripped open the boxes. "Oh, what do we have *here*?" He began throwing leather jackets toward the guests, then let one of the marketing guys take over as Santa Claus. Styrofoam peanuts spilled out onto the carpet.

Lloyd turned to talk to Omega's partner in the Scandinavian countries. Omega's computers were repackaged under a Danish brand name. "You know what I would like to know? When they ship Styrofoam, what do they pack it in? . . . How are you, Peter?"

Peter said, "I've been reading the articles about the six eighty-six in the *Mercury News*. I can't tell if the chip really has the features we need."

Lloyd knew what Peter was referring to. It was the topic on everyone's minds. Computer prices had been dropping steadily for two years. Unit sales were increasing, but margins were disappearing. The sales channel desperately needed a new chip to justify raising prices. Everybody here at the dinner was desperate for the chip to restore their margins. Lloyd knew that at best, Francis's

686 design was five months from completion, and it would be another half year to perfect manufacturing.

Lloyd said, "Let's say we had the new chip today. What would you use it for, Peter?"

"I could raise prices on the average model a thousand dollars."

"But would consumers buy it? Would they really flock to stores just for a faster chip? Don't they need better software, too?"

"Software has upgraded three times since the Falcon."

"And what has that software brought us? Take the most popular application in the world, the word processor. What have the most recent upgrades brought us? Two years ago, you could underline, double underline, or underline with red. Today, you have six color choices for underlining, and you have the squiggle underline to boot. Are consumers really rushing out to stores—are consumers really going to pay an extra *thousand dollars* just to get the squiggle underline?"

"I suppose not."

"Be patient, Peter. Omega's six eighty-six will be available at the same time as truly new software is available, I assure you. We've got a Falcon with a hundred and fifty megahertz clock speed available next month. That'll get your margins up."

"For three months, maybe."

"Patience, Peter. Patience." This conversation was dragging on too long.

Very quietly, Peter said, "Intel's Pentium Pro is available next month."

Lloyd put his hand on Peter's shoulder. "You're not switching to Intel, Peter, and we both know it. Your margins can't afford the premium for Intel. AMD, maybe. Motorola, maybe. But they don't have the chip to offer you any more than I do."

Peter bit his lip. "I can wait for the six eighty-six as long as I know it will be on my shelves in a year. If you don't have it in manufacturing six months from now, I'll have to consider my options."

"I hear you, Peter. We'll keep you informed."

To get rid of him, Lloyd grabbed another man passing by. He was an Eastern European distributor. "Misha, meet Peter Jenssen.

Peter, you've just got to hear some of the crazy stories Misha has about Poland. Misha, tell him that one about the third copper wire in all the phone jacks. . . ." Lloyd slipped away as the story began.

A moment later, at another table: "This company is about profit. . . . I'm not trying to use my position to go down in history as the next Alexander Graham Bell."

And again: "Name one prominent merger that's paid off . . . name one, just one. . . . No, their stock was going up anyway— you can't attribute anything to the merger. . . . No way, they bought a brand name only—the product won't port to the internet . . . Ego driven, solely ego driven—he just wanted to get in the headlines, and a merger was the only way. . . ."

After dinner, they congregated in the bar, and Lloyd's throat didn't get a rest. Someone behind him was smoking a cigar; the acrid smoke was too much for Lloyd. In the middle of a sentence his voice broke, and he began coughing uncontrollably. His eyes watered. He took this chance to excuse himself. He bolted for the nearest exit, took the stairs two at a time. He had left the bath water in the tub and the hot water dribbling from the tap, just to keep the water heated. He threw off his clothes and slipped in.

His pulse was racing. There was no way he would sleep for hours. His body was too wired on adrenaline. He picked up the bathroom telephone and dialed his voice mail to check for messages. His secretary urged him to call Hank about some emergency.

. . .

The next morning, feeling an empty ache in his stomach, Hank heard the phone ring in his kitchen.

"Lloyd?"

There was some static on the line. His voice came from a long way off. "What's the emergency, Hank?"

"Oh, thank god you called, Lloyd."

"I've only got a minute."

"Okay, okay. It's about the sponsorship funds, Lloyd. For the six eighty-six."

"What about them?"

"They haven't been wired in yet."

There was a pause on the line. Hank wasn't sure if Lloyd had heard him, so he repeated his last sentence.

Lloyd said, "Well that's a mistake, I'm sure it'll be corrected soon."

"Is there somebody in Santa Clara I should call?"

"No, I'll send e-mail to our finance department. Perhaps the switch-up confused them."

"The switch-up? What switch-up, Lloyd?"

"I sent three communications. The first one told them to wire the money, the second one told them to hold the money, and the third one told them to wire just this month's money."

"What do you mean, this month's money?"

"One month at a time, I figure."

"But we usually do a whole year at a time. Technically, that's what the sponsorship contract says."

"Technically," Lloyd echoed dully. "I've been trying to tell you, I don't like that three-hundred-dollar computer, I want to take things one month at a time. It's a loaded gun. Why don't you just fire those guys?"

"We can't fire them—we've got a journalist here who would sniff it out. Nobody's ever been fired at La Honda, Lloyd. Nobody *ever*. We don't just fire people."

"Okay, fine. Then one month at a time."

Hank said, "Are you guys having cash flow problems or something? I just don't get this one month at a time thing—"

Lloyd cut him short. "I need you to do me a favor, Hank. About that journalist."

"What about her?"

"Can you get her to write a story about how the six eighty-six compares to Intel's chip?"

"It's probably too technical for her."

"Well, give it a try, will you?"

"All right. Hey, Lloyd?"

"What?"

"If I get her to write that story, will you change your tune on the money?"

"It's late here, Hank. Let's talk about it when I get back."

"Fine, okay, fine. When do you get back?"

"Next Wednesday. I'm spending a few days in Orlando on the way home."

Hank put the handset back in its cradle. He was at a loss. Hank got a mug from the cabinet and filled it with milk. He put it in the microwave and stood watching it while the timer counted down.

5

The Hypnotizer

In early October, Tiny Curtis Reese received e-mail from his friend who had helped him find the motherboards. At last contact he was leaving Florida for the Bay Area to look for a job. He said he was now in Seattle, where some friends had formed a new company that was going to let video game players compete against one another over an internet connection. Tiny's friend had been hired, and though the money was peanuts, they had just taken out a lease on this three-thousand-square-foot warehouse at the base of Queen Anne Hill, on the west side. From the roof they could see Alki Point at the tip of West Seattle and the banana ships being towed by tugboats into Elliott Bay. The warehouse was spacious enough that for the next six months they were going to let the employees live in the loft. He painted a romantic image that put a pang in Tiny's heart, but Tiny had seen a hundred garage start-ups die in the second month without investment capital. All it took was one key person to get a real job offer, and he'd start thinking about his future or his health insurance ("What if a car hit me crossing the street today?"), and just like that the whole house of cards comes down. But Tiny's friend had that angle covered. They already had an exclusive contract with a local multimedia publisher to convert the publisher's multiplayer games to an internet platform, and the contract paid them fifteen grand a month from the get-go. They used the contract to secure the lease on the warehouse.

From Tiny's point of view, this seemed nothing less than a feat of pure magic. Tiny could code in eight languages, but he couldn't balance his own checkbook. Money scared him. It went without saying that start-ups burned money like butane, and if you didn't have a big war chest from day one, then don't even think of dreaming about your own company. That his old friend had formed a new company without any investment capital, without any down payment—well, Tiny felt as if the laws of nature had been suspended.

The e-mail came to Tiny after a particularly hard few days. He'd been trying to imitate the VWPC's motherboard, with all of its nine chips, on his big Falcon computer on his desk. If he built a software model of the VWPC's chips, sort of a computer within a computer, then he could test the logic of his work before they ever had to spend a penny printing circuit boards. Tiny liked to describe it as hypnotizing his Falcon into thinking it was a VWPC, just the way an adult can be hypnotized to think he's a kid again. In order to hypnotize the Falcon—in order to tell it how to think—he had to know what operating system the VWPC would run. But he couldn't decide upon the best operating system without testing each operating system first. And to test it, he needed a fully hypnotized Falcon. It was an infinite loop, and Tiny couldn't see his way out of it. To make things worse, he was pretty sure he couldn't use an existing operating system off the shelf, since their RAM requirements would be too great. He'd have to modify something. This possibility just put too many codependent variables into the equation, and Tiny felt paralyzed by the likelihood of starting on the wrong variable. He was like one of Francis's underlings staring at his first grid, not sure which square to solve first. When he got the e-mail from his friend in Seattle, Tiny hadn't done anything but stare at his screen for three days.

Tiny forwarded his friend's e-mail to Salman and Darrell, with a note attached saying, "Here's what someone else is doing with the internet," but when Salman and Darrell read about the monthly contract, they knew darn well what had captured Tiny's interest.

The multiplayer games weren't the point. The internet wasn't the point.

Every self-respecting young man in Silicon Valley had considered the fantasy at one time or another. You could be pulling down a six-figure salary at Apple or Oracle . . . you could have two patents registered under your own name . . . you could have a division of programmers under your command . . . and it didn't count for *nothing* unless you had taken a crack at the big spin. You had to know: "Could I do it?" It was easy for an older guy like Francis Benoit to ridicule the romance of a start-up, but if you were thirty, like Tiny, or twenty-nine, like Salman, you suspected that you'd never really lived if you hadn't done it at least once. They were always looking for the chance. And what constituted a chance? A decent idea and a team big enough to do the work fast but small enough to survive on credit cards. How many chances would they get like this? Darrell, meanwhile, had tried and failed once before, and he was just gaining enough distance on the experience to see the mistakes he had made. And so he was wondering, *What if I don't repeat those mistakes?*

Nobody talked about it openly, but the idea was never very far from their minds: what if? What if they just collectively resigned from La Honda? Where would they go when they woke up in the morning?

About that time, Salman was riding with his father down El Camino Real one Saturday night, on the way to dinner at a poolside smorgasbord buffet that was their favorite, when his father suddenly turned into a parking lot in Mountain View. He left the engine running, got out of the car, and went over to a patch of grass in front of a two-story ugly gray rectangular building. A FOR LEASE sign had blown off the side of the building and landed in the grass. Salman's father owned a few gas stations and laundromats, and apparently he owned this building, too. The first floor was leased by the School for Contemporary Business, which was really a training school for secretaries. The second floor had been vacant for a year, Salman's father explained when he got back in the car. He'd been trying to sell the building, and he thought he might have a better chance of selling it if no tenants held long-term leases that prevented rent increases. So he hadn't rented it—hadn't even returned the phone calls of potential renters. Salman asked why he bothered with the FOR LEASE sign. In order to write off the lost income on his taxes, his father had to pretend it was available.

"So . . . nobody's up there?" Salman asked.

"Mmmm," his father agreed.

"And it has commercial electrical wiring?"

His father said that it did.

"Like . . . how many amps can it deliver?"

"Dunno . . . got separate fuse boxes for each suite. Five hundred maybe? Does that sound right?"

The next day, Salman came into the trailer with a big grin on his face. *Secretary school!* That was an even more appealing fantasy than a view of the water.

"What are you so giddy about?" Darrell asked, when he caught Salman daydreaming.

"It's . . . nothing. Never mind."

"All right, that does it. Out with it. Come on."

"Naw . . . you wouldn't appreciate it *fully*. You have to be in a certain wistful frame of mind."

"Wistful? I'm wistful right now. I'm wistful that you'll avoid getting socked in the teeth and let me in on your secret."

"Aww . . . your expectations are already too high. I can't tell you now."

"Tell Tiny, then, and he can tell me."

So Salman went to Tiny and told him how in Mountain View there is this secretary school. Not only that, but above the secretary school is a vacant office space, twenty-four hundred square feet. Then Tiny went to Darrell and repeated it to him, word for word, without any expression.

"So what?" Darrell screamed at Salman. "That's it? A vacant office. You got me all lathered up and all you have to report is a *vacant office!* You know I can't work when I get all excited. You *know* that. . . . I've got a little news for you, pal. There's probably a *thousand* vacant offices between here and San Francisco."

Salman leaned back in his seat and shook his head. "Not . . . owned by my father."

"It's owned by your father? Really?"

"Mmmm . . . there's more."

"What *more*? Give me *more*."

"Are you sure?"

"Yes, I'm sure."

Salman clucked his tongue skeptically. "If I tell you, you won't be able to work all day."

"That's *okay*."

"Maybe I should tell you at the end of the day."

"No! Tell me now."

"Okay. It's free."

"What's free? The office? The office is free? Free for us to use? We can use the office for free?"

"Mmmm . . ."

"What kind of wiring does it have?" Darrell's heartbeat was racing. He could tell he wasn't going to get any work done all day. *Secretary school!* It was too delicious to not spend a few moments fantasizing, and then the fantasy took a grip on their brains, so that every time they tried to stare at their last line of code it was like one of those secretaries-to-be was right at their ear, cooing, "Help me, help me, my printer's jammed."

After about two days, Andy picked up on the fact that almost no code had been written. "What's the matter with you guys? Don't you realize our budget is spent in four more weeks? We've got to— if we don't have some results by then, I don't know *what*. This is no time to procrastinate."

"There's no time to procrastinate like the present," Darrell said.

"What's that supposed to mean?" Andy shot back.

"That was a joke."

"It's not funny." Andy sighed. He had barely slept or ate in days, and he hadn't been able to work much as a consequence.

"We might as well tell him," Darrell said, looking at the others. Salman gave his customary mumble of agreement.

"Tell me what?" Andy said.

So they told him.

"Why not?" Darrell asked. "For the next few months, we don't need much money. All we're doing is writing code."

"You think I haven't considered breaking away from here?" Andy responded.

"So let's do it," Darrell said. "What's stopping us?"

Andy moaned. "Our work here—it's not owned by us. The design of the VWPC, the code, the chips and monitors—it's all owned by La Honda. It's their intellectual property. If we took the project with us, they'd sue us for stealing."

"But *we* invented it. It's not stealing to take what *we* invented."

Andy shook his head. "It is too. Forget about it. Let's not have this conversation." As the team leader, Andy had been briefed on the legal issues by La Honda's counsel at the start of the project.

Darrell said, "Then we have to just stay here and wait for the money to dry up? Just like that? We have no other options? We're doomed. I'd rather quit and take my chances of being sued. Just go underground. They can't track us. What do you think? Huh?"

"Mmmm . . ." Salman said.

"You think?" Darrell urged.

"Me? Uh, *no*."

"*No?*"

Salman said, "Be *sued*? You gotta be kidding. I'd rather use peanut butter for deodorant."

Andy interrupted them. "We haven't exhausted our options yet."

. . .

Hank Menzinger was staring at a list of his monthly payables when he got a knock on his door. Hank yelled out that his door was open. Nell Kirkham walked in. She took a seat like she owned it. She brought a rose garden into the room with her. New perfume. He hadn't seen too much of her lately—she'd been coming over to La Honda for an hour or two a couple days a week—but her columns had been adequate and had served Hank's purposes. The ironmen on the 686 regularly pored over her printed text, trying to find their own names.

He said, "I hope they're treating you well enough on the six eighty-six."

She ignored his implied question. "What can you tell me about Andy Caspar?"

Oh, *shit*. Hank stalled. "Caspar? Let me think. Caspar. Hmm. Oh, yes. Caspar. Right. Like what?"

Nell pinched a fleck of lint from her nylons. "You know. His background, that stuff. Some good anecdotes, maybe."

Hank tried not to show alarm. *How much did she know?* "Jeez, hard to recall anything, kid's kinda quiet. You've been talking to him directly?"

"He cornered me, actually. Yesterday. Gave me a rundown on what he calls the 'VWPC.' I think he's hoping I'll write about the fact he's looking for a sponsor. You know, score some free publicity. It's okay. I'm used to being manipulated."

"Hmmm. I want to apologize for Caspar, Nell. Your presence here, it's not for anyone's *personal* publicity campaign. I'm sorry he tried to take advantage of you. I'm sure you'll resist his efforts." Hank gave her a one-hundred-watt smile until his cheeks hurt.

"Ordinarily, I would. But I was intrigued. He seemed—what should I say? *Desperate,* maybe. I haven't met many desperate kids around here. Maybe there's a story there after all."

Hank paused, hoping for an angle to appear. Maybe one already had. "You mentioned that he's looking for a sponsor."

"Uh-huh. That seemed funny to me."

"Funny?" he asked.

"Well, I thought the engineers here . . . were supposed to dedicate themselves entirely to *engineering.*"

"They're supposed to," Hank said.

Nell tilted to her right and crossed her legs. She stared at her notepad, as if she didn't want to be here but her notepad was forcing her to push the point. "So you can understand my surprise to hear that an ironman was devoting his time to chasing down sponsors. If I'm correct, Hank, and I think I am, finding sponsors is your job, isn't it?"

"Well, of course it is. Nell. Ms. Kirkham. If I may help you understand . . . every year, there are a few projects around here that don't succeed, for whatever reason. I have been here twenty years and I have seen some patterns. It is not unusual to find an individual who is a better rabble-rouser than programmer. He's usually about thirty years old, and after programming for ten years has grown weary of mere code. He wants to make deals, be a manager, *find sponsors* to support projects doomed by his own involvement in them."

"You mean he no longer has the right stuff?" Nell said.

Hank nodded gravely, as if a coder who'd lost his stuff was equal to one with a terminal illness. "So if you write about him, you will merely reinforce his bad habits. He will be under the illusion he is actually accomplishing something merely by chatting up a reporter." *Poor delusional chap.*

Nell cleared her throat. "Have you attempted to find sponsors for them?"

"Not exactly, Nell. With a new approach like theirs, I have to have something to demo. And so far . . . I'm not surprised by all this, frankly. Most ironmen can't accept that every once in a while their work just isn't worthy. Not worthy of sponsorship, not worthy of my time, and not worthy of yours."

Nell shook her hair and took a deep breath. "Well, maybe I should open this up. Let's not just talk about Andy Caspar. Do you allow the ironmen to bring in their own sponsors?"

"Always looking for a story, aren't you? Why don't you write about how the six eighty-six compares to Intel's chip? Now *that's* a story the industry wants to read."

She considered this. "I'll put that in my idea file. But there's nothing timely about it."

"Intel's chip will be available next month."

"They've been saying 'next month' for four months. My guess is January. Meanwhile, Andy Caspar is happening today. Now, about those sponsors—"

"Of course, every contract is approved by our board, but we try to allow the teams as much leeway as they need. We don't have a *principle* against it, Nell. But you said it as well as I: an ironman who's devoting his time to chasing down sponsors—he's not a true ironman, is he?"

"So that's the official position, is it?"

"Official position? No, that's just my opinion. Official position? . . . You're not still thinking of wasting a column on Caspar, I hope."

"He might provide a good contrast to the other men. Show them in high relief—brothers in the bond, that sort of thing. I was thinking, if he had a different background, came from a different culture. You know. Black sheep."

"Not that I know of, Nell. He came from Stanford EE, like about a third of the guys here. About as plain vanilla as an ironman gets."

She seemed skeptical. "Hmmm. O-*kay*."

He still couldn't tell if she was going to write about Caspar. "So . . . ?"

"I'd like to talk to my editor about it," she said.

"Of course, yes. You know, I'd hate to see you diverge from writing about the six eighty-six, Nell."

She sighed. "The six eighty-six is so *complicated*. I'm worried I'm losing my audience week to week without some drama."

"What better drama could you want than Omega versus Intel, David versus Goliath?"

"The differences are too technical for my readership."

"Oh, I don't think so. When I travel, people only want to talk about the six eighty-six design. They read about it. They want details. You're a good writer, Nell—you can handle that material."

"You think? Really? You think?" She didn't know how to take a compliment. He let it hang there for a while. Eventually, she got up and left.

Hank ran out of his office to look for Francis. He wasn't in his office. At his lab, someone told him to check the parking lot—they had just seen Francis with his car keys in the hallway. They all knew that Francis liked to think through problems while driving, often at high speeds, on the snaking roads that connected Skyline Road atop the peninsula to the sleepy towns below. Something about the level of stimulation, the way driving fast partially occupied Francis's brain, allowed the unoccupied portion to work without self-conscious second-guessing.

Hank hustled out to the parking lot. Francis was just pulling out in his powder-blue convertible Fiat X19, a car shaped like a wedge of cheese. Hank ran in front of the car.

"I've got work to do," Francis said, looking up at Hank.

Hank never quite believed that Francis actually got work done while driving. Hank didn't deny the importance of Francis's ritual, not that. Hank just figured the driving loosened Francis's mind, at best. At worst, it was a form of hooky. "I need to talk," Hank said.

"Get in then."

"Can't we go to my office?"

"I told you, I have work to do."

Hank walked around the car and slipped into the passenger seat. He moved aside a clipboard with a blank piece of paper on it and put it on the floor.

"Hold that in your lap," Francis instructed him.

"It's okay down here."

"Give it to me, then."

Hank passed him the clipboard. Francis set it in his lap, then shifted gears and pushed down the accelerator. Hank shot back against his seat. The engine was right behind them. There was no backseat to speak of. Francis turned right at Old La Honda and maneuvered the familiar downhill hairpin turns without any effort. The Fiat felt like a go-cart with a rocket on the back. If they hit something, the whole thing would detonate. In a minute Francis had come to the bottom of the hill and let the motor idle.

Hank took this as a chance to speak. "Caspar went to Nell Kirkham. I don't know how much he told her, I can't tell. I think he's trying to get his own sponsor, thought she would give him the needed publicity."

Francis hit the accelerator again. "Is she going to write about it?"

Hank straightened his legs, bracing with fear. "I think I bought us a little time. But the issue's not dead." He explained how she was going to talk with her editor. "This is exactly what Lloyd predicted could happen. What do you think?" Hank was afraid to take his eyes off the road. They had started to climb Skyline again, this time on Highway 84 out of Woodside. Larch trees cast shadows on the road; in places, mudslides had left the roots protruding over the road. The speed limit was twenty-five. Francis wasn't doing more than fifty. Finally, on a hundred-yard straightaway, Hank glanced over at Francis. Hank suddenly felt the urge to urinate.

Francis had his head down to write something on his clipboard.

"Jesus H. Christ, Francis!"

"Huh?" Francis looked up and spun them into a turn. "I know these roads."

"Will you slow down a moment?"

"I'm trying to work."

"Did you even hear what I said?"

"Yup. Caspar got to Kirkham, and if Kirkham gives him ink, Lloyd's going to freak."

"What are we going to do?"

"You don't really think Lloyd would pull the plug, do you? He *needs* the six eighty-six, doesn't he?"

"I don't know! I can't gamble on it."

"How much longer will their budget last?"

"Three weeks, but we can't risk it. Besides, they don't spend any money anyway. It's taken a little creative surcharging to use up their budget this fast."

Francis drove, using every gear, the big engine sending vibrations right through their seats. He steered with his left hand crossed to the right side of the wheel to give his hand leverage. Anise and coriander grew beside the road. Francis passed several cars without even pausing to see if the opposite lane was clear. Hank closed his eyes. When he opened them, Francis was writing again on his clipboard.

At Skyline, Francis turned north on 35, and then four twisted miles later, turned back down the hill on old Kings Mountain Road, which was relatively unknown and usually free of traffic. Francis held nothing back. Francis had a goal to someday race on these roads while doing a grid at the same time. What an adrenaline rush that would be! But he'd never been able to get anybody to race against him. Not even Ronny had the balls.

Francis said, "You're not thinking very well, Hank. You seem tense."

"Of course I'm tense—you're driving like a madman!"

Francis smiled. "The answer is really quite obvious."

"Not to me!"

"That's because you're tense."

"Well, you're driving too fast."

"Driving relaxes me."

"What are we going to do?" Hank screamed into the wind.

Francis downshifted into a turn. "What did Ronny Banks tell you?"

"Ronny? Uh." How did he know Ronny had been to see him?

There was no point in lying to Francis. "He said you forced Caspar into the VWPC just to spite me and Lloyd."

Francis nodded. "Did you believe him?"

"It seemed like a thing you would do."

"So you believed him?"

"Yeah . . . Is it true?"

Francis wrote something on his clipboard again. When he looked up, it was as if he had just woken from a trance and the conversation had been forgotten. "How much did you lose in that botched IPO?"

"About half a million."

"That shouldn't kill us."

"If the board finds out, it'll be the end. If they try to sit on it, there will be a leak, leading to a public disgrace of all of them. They'll realize that—realize they can't sit on it. So they'll fire me to make themselves look responsible. But without me, La Honda is not La Honda, it's just another research lab bobbing for dollars. Don't you see? A chain reaction here, a sequence of events . . . it could be the beginning of the end."

"Fuck."

"Yeah, exactly."

"Fuck!!"

"*Exactly.*" Finally, Hank thought Francis was understanding the severity of the crisis.

"No, I'm not swearing about you. My pen's out of ink." Abruptly, Francis stopped the car in the middle of the road. The car didn't swerve or skid. Francis leaned across Hank and popped the glove compartment, digging through its contents for another pen.

"What are we going to do, Francis? You said the solution is obvious."

"All good solutions are obvious. That's the nature of solutions. If it isn't obvious, then it probably isn't a solution."

"So you *don't* have a solution?"

"No, I do."

"What is it?"

"You give Andy Caspar, et al., a waiver on the intellectual property. They'll vanish into the Bermuda Triangle of bungled start-ups. No story for Nell Kirkham, Lloyd Acheson is happy, you get your Omega money, Quentin Black gets his money, and so on."

"That's brilliant!"

"It's not brilliant. It's obvious."

"But—but do you think they will go? If we give them the waiver? Will that work?"

Francis said, "I know you've got a pen."

Hank finally gave him one he kept in his shirt pocket. It was made of gold. Francis took it without comment. He regunned the car and left rubber on the road.

"Did you hear what I said?" Hank asked.

"Of course I did."

"Well?"

"We'll give them a little more incentive to go."

. . .

Andy Caspar woke up the next morning feeling like he had a hangover.

Why wake up at all? Andy wondered.

Don't even open your eyes.

Why leave the imagination?

Then the thought popped into his mind that today, this day, was Wednesday. *Wednesday!* Nell's biweekly column would run today in the *Mercury News*. The VWPC might be mentioned. The phone might ring, a sponsor on the other end of the line. . . . Andy popped out of bed, skipped his ritual push-ups, and drove to the Sharon Heights shopping center to trade two quarters for the morning paper. He sat down on the picnic bench outside the Safeway and spread the paper on the shellacked (not stained) table surface. This was a ritzy enclave; classical music was piped outdoors, even into the parking lot, where the shrubs were trimmed to the mold of cake tins. Rubbermaid garbage cans and recycling bins had been placed every few paces, to ensure that litter would never touch the ground. Every other car was a minivan. Hood ornaments, Andy noted, were back in style. As a kid he had been arrested for stealing them.

Even as he flipped through the news pages, he felt glad he hadn't told Nell anything about the file cabinet, the night on the sleeping porch, or anything damning about La Honda. It was enough of a violation of the unspoken code to approach her seeking publicity. Though the other ironmen secretly hoped to find their name in her column, they never went out of their way to chat with her. On Wednesday, the *Mercury News* broke out a special technology section, to which some of the business writers such as Nell contributed.

Her column was devoted to the arithmetic-logic unit of the 686. It didn't mention the VWPC.

Andy stared at a small black swallow that was hunting for crumbs off the table. It wouldn't find any.

He was out of ideas. Momentarily, he fantasized driving over Skyline out to San Gregorio Beach to stare at the ocean. He'd had a lot of peace-and-quiet fantasies lately. But he would go back to work just like any other day. Their project, it had become just like life: sometimes it was hopeless and pointless, but there weren't any reliable alternatives.

He didn't think he was the first to arrive at the trailer that morning, since the door was unlocked. Then he saw that stacks of articles and spec sheets, which had been on their desks the night before, had been scattered onto the floor. Perhaps Darrell had blown his fuse during the night and thrown a tantrum. On Andy's desk was a present, wrapped in newspaper and ribboned with a phone cord. It was about the size of a shoe. Andy didn't touch it at first. A suspicious fear overtook him. He checked the monitors on everyone's computers to see if they were turned on—if maybe they had arrived and gone out for coffee. Tiny's screen saver was running across his monitor—a ticker tape of classical poetry. All of the other computers were off.

Andy went back to the present. The wrapper, the newspaper, was familiar. It was that morning's edition of the San Jose *Mercury News*. Specifically, it was Nell Kirkham's article, her cartoonized portrait looking up at him, the look on her face simultaneously friendly and tough. He picked up the parcel. Lightweight, but there was something inside the roll of paper. Andy unwound the phone cord. He looked toward the door. Holding the package with both hands, he unwrapped the newsprint. The contents slipped through the roll and fell onto his desk.

A large gray dead rat.

Eyes half closed, mouth slightly open, little hands frozen in a clutching position.

Who knew he'd talked to her? A shiver ran up Andy's spine. The shiver didn't quite exhaust itself, and it triggered another. His teeth clenched uncontrollably. He covered the rat in the paper, then threw the combination in his trash can. He removed the plastic liner from the trash can and knotted the top. He carried it out the door and down the hill toward the garbage Dumpster. His eyes combed the trees and the upstairs windows of the south building for anyone watching him. He wondered whether to tell his team. He decided not to, which proved to be a mistake, because when Darrell came to work eventually, he opened the drawer to his desk and found a similar present awaiting him.

"Oh, shit!" he screamed. He stood up, his fists clenched at his sides. "What the hell's going on?"

Andy said, "Somebody knows I talked to Nell Kirkham."

"So? Does that deserve *this?*"

"Somebody thinks it does."

Darrell said, "Somebody who thinks we're the Marines. I hate this place, you know? Everything that was once cool about it now makes me claustrophobic."

Darrell tried to burn his rat with a Bic lighter. It wouldn't catch on fire, but the stink of singeing hair made their stomachs turn. So Darrell strung a phone cord around his rat's neck and hung it from the wall.

"You can't . . ." Salman tried to say. "It's going to *decay*. The stench."

"We won't be here long enough for it to decay," Darrell shot back.

Tiny hadn't come in yet. Andy checked Tiny's desk for surprises but couldn't find anything. Andy called Tiny's apartment. There was no answer.

"Have you heard from Tiny? His computer's on but he's not here," he asked Salman.

"Who? Me? Uh, no, not Tiny."

Andy drummed his fingers on Salman's desk. "Did your dad rent that place yet?"

"Nuh-unh. Like I said . . . he doesn't want to lease it."

"What would you do, if you didn't have this?"

"This? Hmm. Go back to school, I guess."

"It's funny," Andy said after a moment. "Six months ago I was afraid to leave school. Now for the life of me, I can't imagine going back. It would be like retracing my steps."

"Mmmm . . ."

In the afternoon, Andy got a call from Hank Menzinger. "He wants us in his office," Andy said, after taking the call.

"All of us?" Salman asked.

"Somebody leave a note in case Tiny shows up."

The three team members took seats in Hank's office. Andy apologized for Tiny's unexplained absence. Hank passed each of them a two-page stapled document. It was a legal contract of some sort, with numbered paragraphs and boilerplate language denying the relevance of the headings to the contract. Andy's hands trembled.

Hank was chewing on some sunflower seeds. The charm had gone from his face. "Do you know what that is?"

"It's a waiver to the rights," Andy said.

Hank nodded. "A *nonexclusive* waiver. You know what that means?"

They didn't. Hank asked them if they wanted to wait for a lawyer to show up. Nobody did, though the mention of lawyers made the paper in their hands seem ominous. "Nonexclusive," Hank explained. "It means you can use your ideas, but it also means *we* can use your ideas—the work you've done so far. We can sell it, license it, sponsor it, publish it, put it in the public domain, anything we want. I can wipe my ass with it if I so choose. But so can you."

"You're giving us this?" Andy couldn't believe it. He *didn't* believe it. Where was the catch?

Hank directed them to the bottom of page two. "You see that line there under my name? No signature on it yet. That paper in your hands is just wood chips and glue without my Hancock. We've got a ways to go here."

Andy asked what he meant.

"Well, we've got to get together exhibit A."

"Exhibit A?"

"Paragraph—let's see, paragraph . . . four. Top of page two. I need originals of everything you've done so far. Put it in a box. You can make copies. I want hard disks, floppy disks, Post-it notes—you name it. If you've got two motherboards, give me one. If you've only got one, it's mine. Memos, e-mail, *everything*. I'm not kidding you. Failure to comply one hundred percent will be a violation of the waiver on your part, and we will prosecute you under criminal law. Do you know what *criminal law* means, Salman?"

"Me? Criminal laws . . . uh . . ."

"It means *jail time*. We don't kid around. This is not some civil disagreement where we sue your ass into bankruptcy, though there's nothing to stop us from doing that if we so choose. But sometimes kids don't have any money to lose, so they get to thinking there's no downside. *Hey, if I withhold this here program, what can happen—they take my mountain bike?* Ha ha. *Right.* Jail time, boys. Don't fuck with it, that's my advice. Get it?"

"Yeah," Andy said.

"Sure," Darrell added.

"We have an understanding then?"

Andy said that they did. "But we have to tell Tiny."

"Well, you all have to sign the paper together. Where's Tiny?"

"We don't know."

"Find him fast. I want a team of security guards up there ASAP to watch you clean house. In the meantime, I suggest you read these two pages carefully. For instance, paragraph five says you can't make any discrediting public remarks about La Honda or it will violate the terms of the waiver. When you walk out these doors for the last time, it's as if you never were here. Can I give you three a little advice?"

"What?"

"Don't ask for job recommendations."

. . .

When they got back to their lab, Darrell said, "Let's get drunk."

"You know what I feel like?" Andy said. "I feel like I'm wearing a flubber suit."

"What's *flubber*?" Salman asked.

"It was from a Disney movie when we were kids. Flubber was a kind of mysterious rubber that was lighter than air, some school science teacher's magical accident. Kurt Russell wore flubber and competed in all these decathlon events."

"No, you're thinking of some other movie," Darrell said. "Kurt Russell was mopping up the science lab when he knocked over some beakers and spilled the combination onto himself. It made him invisible."

"Then what was flubber?"

"That was Fred MacMurray—you know, the guy from *My Three Sons*—in *The Absent-Minded Professor*. He coached a basketball team, put it in their shoes. Phi Slamma Jamma."

"I remember Kurt Russell," Andy said.

"No you don't."

"I do too."

Darrell shook his head adamantly. "He wasn't in it."

"Maybe he wasn't. But in my *memory*, he was."

"What is that, *in your memory*? Either he was in it or he wasn't. None of this *in your memory* stuff."

"I have a picture in my mind."

"The picture is of some guy. You can't remember his name, so for convenience you're labeling him Kurt Russell. But it *wasn't* Kurt Russell."

"Maybe you're right."

"I *am* right. Not *maybe*."

The door to the lab opened. Tiny walked in. He looked like he had slept maybe fifteen minutes in the last twenty-four hours. His face was pale and his beard was covered with flakes of glazed sugar from doughnuts he had no doubt been eating all night to keep himself awake. He was wearing his bicycle helmet again.

"Hey, Tiny," Darrell said eagerly, "was Kurt Russell in *The Absent-Minded Professor*?"

Tiny bowed his head to think. His eyebrows came together.

Andy's mouth fell open. He turned to Darrell. "After all that's going on, you're asking him about *Kurt Russell*?"

"Why not? Let's settle this."

"Because!"

Tiny looked up. Matter-of-factly, he said, "I think Kurt Russell was in *Son of Flubber,* the sequel."

"Christ!" Andy exhaled deeply.

"What's going on?" Tiny asked.

It took about fifteen minutes to explain everything, particularly with both Salman and Darrell wanting to put their own two cents in. They explained about the rats and then the visit to Hank's office and the jail time and the part about having to turn over everything they'd invented so far.

"Everything?" Tiny asked, when they were finished.

"Yes, *everything,*" Andy repeated. "Why?"

Tiny stood up slowly and went over to Andy's Falcon on his desktop. He pulled a floppy disk out of his shirt pocket and fed it into Andy's floppy drive. After quickly copying a file from the floppy to the Falcon's hard disk, he booted the file. The screen went blank for a second, then a new pale yellow screen came up, eight and one-half inches diagonal.

"What's that?" Andy asked.

"The Hypnotizer."

"The computer-within-a-computer that you've been procrastinating on?"

"Yes. Right now, the Falcon thinks it's a VWPC. I've hypnotized it."

"You finished it?"

"I burst through the free variables last night. Finished it about an hour ago."

"And you've got it on just a floppy?"

Tiny said that he did. The Hypnotizer was a pretty small program, it turned out. It acted like a translator, adapting commands intended for the VWPC instruction set into a DOS instruction set. Instruction sets were one of the root languages printed directly into a computer's circuit boards. They were the magical link where hardware (the circuit board) and software met as one. Tiny likened

the link to the "mind-body connection," which was why his Hypnotizer name was so apt.

Tiny said, "Last night, around eight o'clock, I had a seizure. A
big one. I don't know how long it lasted, maybe a minute. When I
came to, I tried reconstructing my thought pattern right before the
seizure. What led to it? What was I doing when I froze up? I wrote
everything I remembered down. And then it came to me. I had it."

Andy said, "You figured out what causes your seizures?"

"No. I figured out how to do the Hypnotizer. It wasn't just a
new operating system. I created a new language, a language that
translates across the mind-body connection of the computer. Now
we can write software in that language and it will run perfectly."

"Wow," Andy said.

"Yeah," Salman said. "Wow is right."

The team had not realized the Hypnotizer would be so small a
program—a mere ten thousand lines of code. Tiny had designed it
with the intention of testing the VWPC, and testing boards or testing programs were common in designing new chips like the 686.
But testing programs were always slow and monstrous, since it
took hundreds of thousand of lines of code to make a Falcon pretend it was a 686; the hard disk acted like the processor, and the
hard disk was slow. That was an *upstream* model, and it's what
everyone had assumed Tiny would run into here. But Tiny was
actually going *downstream*. Since the Falcon had so many more
transistors than a VWPC, it was relatively easy to hypnotize it. And
the program, as a result, was *fast*.

Tiny sat there and waited for what he had invented to sink in. It
took a while, but slowly the faces of his teammates took on smiles
and dropped jaws and scratched chins. "Okay, now if . . ." one
would say, and then answer his own question. "If that's true,
then . . ." Same thing.

If they could use one Hypnotizer to convince any DOS machine
that it was a VWPC, then they could write a similar Hypnotizer to
convince any UNIX machine it was a VWPC, and a third Hypnotizer to convince any Macintosh that *it* too was a VWPC. . . .

And these Hypnotizers were small enough that they could
download over the internet in about ten seconds. . . .

Then any program written for the VWPC could also download and run on any other machine, as long as the proper Hypnotizer had been downloaded first.

One of the biggest stumbling blocks to the explosion of the internet—the kind of explosion that would trigger the "jolt" or lure the "other 50 percent" online—was that programs could never play on different operating systems. All digital bits on computers were either *data* or *programs*. The internet allowed *data* to flow freely, but programs were a different animal entirely. For example, one person can send a digital photograph across the internet, no problem. But video—which is just a stack of rapidly shuffling photographs—can't play across the internet. The stack of photographs transfers fine, but the program that shuffles them at thirty frames a second will only work on some computers—those with the same operating system as the sender. A program meant for Unix is just gobbledygook to a Windows operating system. The easiest solution would be for everyone to stick to just one operating system, but nobody wanted one company to hold that much power. So a half dozen operating systems coexist, creating havoc.

Tiny had come up with an elegant little solution to this huge stumbling block!

His Hypnotizer program would download before the photographs and the shuffler . . . and just like that, the video could play!

When this realization swept the team, they all had to sit down. What Tiny had done, well, it was perhaps far more important—more consequential—than the VWPC itself. As they remembered, the knock on the VWPC was that *anybody* could have built it if they wanted to. The team had set out not just to build it, but to build it "good good good." Tiny's Hypnotizer, though, was an answer to a riddle that had stumped thousands of engineers for several years. And it was elegant. In a way, it was *obvious*. *Of course!* The trick had been in going *downstream;* the computer-within-a-computer creates a simpler standard, but a standard that can work on *any* computer. It was more of a brilliant idea than a brilliant piece of code. Like all great inventions in science, once you knew what you were looking for, it wasn't hard to code. Tiny had stumbled across what they were looking for. Nobody had taken this approach before.

"Well, I was in the front row," Salman said finally. "I was *here*."

This altered their situation at La Honda fundamentally. The whole team knew right away that if they wanted the past five months to be wiped clean, all they had to do was march into Francis Benoit's office and show him the Hypnotizer. They could have a sponsor tomorrow, have as many people on the team as they wanted tomorrow afternoon, be drowning in champagne tomorrow night.

"We'd be heroes," Andy said. His fingers were tingling. He couldn't keep from smiling. He felt like he had taken drugs. "All of this, it would change everything. We'd be right and they'd be wrong. We could make them kiss our ass." *It was so simple! A mere ten thousand lines of code!*

. . .

At the end of the day they went out to dinner to talk about it. They drove down the hill to old Rosotti's Tavern on Alpine Road, a favorite Stanford hangout after football games. Tucked between two foothills and buried under oak trees, Rosotti's had big picnic tables in a dusty corral where you could eat outdoors. It was an old rat's nest of a place, and they loved it for that. The burgers weren't the size of Texas and the hot sauce wasn't fresh off the vine and no matter how hard you looked at the menu on the wall, you couldn't read what kind of oil the french fries were cooked in. There wasn't a buxom waitress wearing a "Vixen" name tag and hip-length shorts who brought out your meal. You had to order inside and pick it up yourself. The beer came in waxed-paper cups and pitchers. A rattlesnake skin, six feet long, was tacked to a pine board and hung on one wall. The NO SMOKING sign was riddled with shotgun-pellet dents. A stuffed deer head kept watch over the tap. Baseball caps hung from each of the antlers' ten points. The crowd here was a mix of contractors, Stanford alumni remembering the good ole days, and exceptionally beautiful women with their hair in braids, wearing down coats and riding tights (leather patches sewn on the insides of their knees). The picnic benches were carved with initials and graduation dates going back sixty years. A small creek flowed along one side of the corral. The roof of the bar needed patching; tar paper showed in places. A ventilation fan rattled like it needed a nut tightened.

The night was warm, and the team drank two pitchers of beer before they started counting, without saying much, just letting it slosh around in their stomachs while they watched the bats dive for mosquitoes across the dark blue sky. The burgers were served on sourdough buns. The condiments were kept on a counter inside. They loaded their buns with sauerkraut and relish and spicy mustard.

Tiny swallowed his in a few bites. He went back to order another. A couple of old bird dogs that were nosing around followed him to the door and wagged their tails when he came out again with a third pitcher. Maybe the dogs drank beer. Tiny sat down and let out a big grunt. He didn't say anything, but occasionally he laughed a little—always when his mouth was full. Relish would squirt from his mouth and ooze down his cheek.

Getting away from La Honda was a good move. Drinking a little beer was a good move. Sitting there in that dusty corral, some of the burning anger from the past few months receded, and it didn't matter to them so much anymore. They melted into the benches. The feeling that came out of that dinner was that turning over the Hypnotizer to La Honda would be like what Andy had said earlier—it would be retracing their steps, going backward.

"But . . ." Salman said.

"But what?" Darrell asked.

"If we leave . . ."

"What about it?"

"We have to *tell* . . . the Hypnotizer would be exhibit A, no?"

He was right and they all knew it. Tiny had realized this when Andy first explained the rules of the waiver.

"I don't know . . ." Salman said. *"Jail time."*

"Fuck jail time," Darrell said.

"That's easy to say *now*. You're *drunk*, now."

"Fuck you, I'm not drunk."

Andy said, "You want to quit and withhold the Hypnotizer from them?"

"Well we can't darn well give them Tiny's idea, can we? They'll run with it. We don't have to give them Tiny's code. Tiny, is the code on your Falcon in the lab?"

Tiny said, "Yes. Although I was at home all day, I was dialed in to work via remote."

Darrell said, "So all we have to do is go back tonight and delete it from your machine and Andy's. They won't know shit."

They left it at that for a while. Andy went inside and brought back another pitcher of beer. Nobody refused a refill. If they weren't drunk yet they were well on their way, and they felt like they needed to be. This was not an easy decision to make.

Andy reached into his coat pocket and pulled out four small plastic salt shakers, white, with grooves down their sides. "Here's the deal," he said. "We take a blind vote. You take a salt shaker, put both hands below the table, bring one hand up. We all do this at once. You open your hand. If your palm is empty, you vote to turn over the Hypnotizer to La Honda, stay at La Honda, get a new sponsor, enjoy the high life, probably get famous, be admired by engineers everywhere. But if there's a salt shaker in your hand, you vote to withhold the code, go at it by ourselves, show up at secretary school tomorrow morning, and potentially spend a year fighting a lawsuit. Everybody understand? Salman?"

Salman nodded. "Salt shaker, quit; no shaker, stay."

"Right. Everybody take one."

Their hands reached for a shaker. Their arms moved underneath the table.

"Wait a minute," Tiny said. "What if there's a tie?"

"Okay, you get two votes," Andy said. He got up and walked back indoors and came out a moment later with a fifth salt shaker. "It's your invention, anyway."

"Not *really*," Tiny said. "It was a by-product of our approach."

"Okay, but it's *your* by-product, so *you* get two votes."

Tiny nodded. Everyone put their arms under the table again.

"Bring 'em up," Andy said.

Five arms came up and stretched into the middle of the picnic table, palms down, hiding their vote.

"Darrell?"

Darrell turned his hand over and unclenched his fingers. A salt shaker lay in his palm.

"Salman?"

A salt shaker was in his hand as well.

Andy turned his hand over and opened it. Salt.

"Tiny?"

Two salts.

. . .

"Jesus, Ronny, don't you think giving them rats for presents was a little melodramatic?" Francis said.

Ronny leaned forward with uncontainable excitement. "Aww, I thought it was brilliant. The kind of thing only you would have thought of. Rats, see? Rat to a journalist, get a rat for breakfast, see? Beautiful."

"I just wanted a little vandalism."

"But it was a *lesson,* see? Something they'll never forget."

Francis took a sip of his drink, whiskey on ice. "A prank like that points to me. Some spray paint on the walls would have pointed elsewhere." They were sitting on opposing twin couches in Francis's living room. His house was a luxury log cabin on ten acres of land; over the years, Francis Benoit had been dealt in on so many friends' lists for IPOs that he'd stopped counting his money. His salary at La Honda was inconsequential. The walls of his house were decorated with his collection of metal-framed antiwar posters, ranging from the Persian Gulf War of 1991 all the way back to the Spanish-American War of 1898. Francis had failed to convince several publishers to print a coffee-table book with the images. Every couple years he gave it another try.

Francis asked Ronny where he got the rats.

"I got a friend at the hospital, she studies amputations. She cuts their arms off, then sews 'em back on. When they're healed, she makes 'em do treadmill tests to failure."

Francis winced. "Sounds like your kind of gal. She probably didn't even ask you why you wanted a couple of rats."

Ronny giggled. "You're right, she didn't. Huh."

Francis topped off his drink. He didn't pour any more for Ronny, even though he could see Ronny was down to his last fingerful. Ronny was driving, and he wasn't the kind to turn down any form of elixir.

"So how did the rest go?" Francis asked.

"Oh, just great. Just like you said. I'm certain they're thinking they got hit by vandals last night. They don't have any idea I copied their hard drives."

"Good, good."

"Except one guy's. I think he was accessing his remotely while I was there, so I had to wait around."

"But you got it?"

"Just like you said. That software is pretty nifty, copy a whole disk that fast."

Ronny went out to his car and brought back four portable hard disks in a cardboard box. Tomorrow, with a lawyer and a security guard present, the VWPC team would make official copies of all of their documents and their hard disks. Of course, Francis had anticipated the team would hit the delete key a few times before making the copies, and he didn't expect anything valuable to get handed over. Instead, they'd hand over so much junk that it would be intimidating to search through it. But now, Francis had only to compare last night's copy to tomorrow's copy, and he could be assured that whatever was missing tomorrow would be the important code.

"So, Francis?" Ronny still stood in Francis's doorway.

Francis had been daydreaming. La Honda wasn't what it used to be. "What?"

"About Hank, about that waiver."

"Oh, right."

"You think he'll give me that waiver now?"

"I don't know, Ronny. What do you think?"

"I figure I've helped you guys out quite a bit here."

"Really? I figure we're even again, after you told Hank about what I was up to."

Ronny chuckled nervously. "Come on, that would have got out sooner or later." Ronny looked down at his shoes, then looked up. A smile came over his face. "How about half of what I earn? Twenty-five grand to you, at least."

"No, I'm not looking for any more money. I've got all the money I'll ever need. Why don't you just get a job? It's inevitable. I mean, I can't sell out Omega, Hank can't sell out Omega. If you need

money, I'll give you money. I'd rather give you money for a while
than have you sell out Omega."

"You? *You'd* give me money?"

"Sure, why not? It's only money. But you're going to have to get
a job, Ronny."

"How much would you give me?"

"Look, enough for a couple months, how about that? Here, I'll
write you a check right now." Francis went over to a walnut secretary and fished a checkbook from the top drawer. He wrote out a
check for five thousand dollars and carelessly ripped it from his
checkbook. "Here. Hey—you gotta get a life, man."

Ronny took the check. "Sure, okay."

Francis stood on his doorstep and watched Ronny walk back to
his car. When he got into the driver's seat, he turned the rearview
mirror to his face and pulled out a comb and ran it through his
hair.

Francis didn't know why he considered Ronny one of his best
friends, but there it was. Of all the changes at La Honda over the
years—the evaporating sponsorship of the military industry, the
marketing bent of the commercial sponsors, the waste of the Falcon—the one Francis missed most was the *humor*. The fun was
gone. Ronny was gone. Francis looked a few years down the road
and couldn't imagine La Honda would survive in its current incar-
nation. If Hank's misplaced investments didn't bring them down,
something else would. It was nothing to be sad about. Ten years
was a lifetime in this valley. They'd had a good run.

6

Too Small for Radar

Darrell Lincoln had been in a start-up four years ago, and in the meantime most of the experience had boiled away, leaving behind only bitter memories. He and some friends had come up with a relatively simple idea: they foresaw this huge boom in compact disk multimedia, and they decided to make a reference disk, storing hundreds of "clip sounds." On the CD would be a little sound-editing system, so that people could copy sounds off the CD and paste them into their multimedia games. In a couple months, they recorded everything they could think of, from the noise of a ceramic plate breaking on a tile floor, to a young boy screaming in horror. While the CD was still in development, they demonstrated their idea to a CD distributor, who was so impressed that they not only offered to distribute it, they offered two hundred thousand dollars to own the project. Convinced they were onto something hot, Darrell and his friends turned down the buyout, figuring there was more profit in selling it themselves. Then, the very week that they were about to manufacture a first run of twenty thousand copies of their disk, Darrell was in an Egghead Software store and saw a "clip sound" disc with five hundred sounds. It was the identical concept to their project. They canceled the manufacturing order and decided to work around the clock to record a three-disc set with two thousand sounds. That took another two months. When their product finally reached the market, it was one of six similar CD packages. Four of the six were from big brand-name software companies, who cut deals that quickly squeezed Darrell's company's package off the shelves. Darrell never saw a penny for his efforts.

Darrell knew that whether the product is a new hardware gizmo such as a pocket scheduler or a software application such as a 3-D illustrator, you're always in competition with other unknown entrepreneurs. The relevant question never goes away: do I ship now, entering the market before my competitors, thereby gaining early market share, or do I wait, improve my program until it's the best on the market, and steal market share with a superior product? To teach this important principle, years ago some manager somewhere had invented a game called "Ten Women."

In Ten Women, each guy has to choose from the next ten women he sees which woman he would like to spend a week with on a deserted tropical island. Every woman counts toward the ten, even if it's an old grandmother feeding pigeons at the bus stop. And sometimes the criterion wasn't a week on a desert island—sometimes it was the woman a guy had to marry or sleep with for one night or have as a sister. The game had one catch: a guy had to pick his woman as soon as he saw her, not after watching all ten. It was like shipping software; if you chose not to ship, you couldn't ever get the opportunity back. So there was no comparing women—it was a constant gamble. If a guy hadn't picked by the ninth woman, then he automatically got stuck with the tenth. Whoever picked the best woman (with the benefit of hindsight) got to razz the loser. Just about every coder in Silicon Valley knew the game and had his own version. Some played it while watching television, to make the commercials interesting. Some played it on the freeways, to keep their mind off the traffic jam. They played it in movie theaters, while waiting for the lights to dim and the previews to run, and they played it while waiting in line for lattes or burritos. And on the first morning of their new life as entrepreneurs, as Darrell and Salman sat in the car outside the secretary school, waiting for Andy and Tiny to show up (they wanted to inaugurate the space together), the two men were playing a game of Ten Women.

THE FIRST $20 MILLION IS ALWAYS THE HARDEST 153

Six women had entered the building that morning, and both agreed that the second woman had been the best so far; but, at the time, they both expected better, so neither had chosen her. Darrell had just picked the sixth woman, who wore a nice white outfit and had shiny thick blond hair.

"But she was fat," Salman said, sipping from a paper cup of coffee.

"She was *full-figured,*" Darrell countered. "Her proportions were fine."

"Nope."

"How the hell could you tell? She was wearing a dress and a sport coat."

Salman coughed as some coffee dripped down the wrong pipe. "Did you see her feet? Her calves?"

"So?"

"A woman doesn't need calves like that unless she's hauling a load."

"That's ridiculous. I know plenty of slender women who have thick legs. It just means they work out."

"Nope."

"Hey, I'd rather have number six than get stuck with what you're going to get stuck with."

"I'm not going to get stuck . . . If number two comes back out of the building, does she count as number seven?"

"Forget it. You're going to get a pigeon lady. I can feel it. Chirp chirp."

"What is that? 'Chirp chirp.' What is that?"

"Pigeons, mister pigeon man."

Salman shook his head with mock disgust. "That's not what pigeons make. Pigeons are like this, kloo-oo, kloo-oo. Sort of purring like a cat."

Darrell said, "You're going to need to know, not me."

Two older women pushing two-wheeled wire shopping carts strolled down the sidewalk.

Darrell said, "Only two chances left, mister pigeon man."

"Okay, the woman on the billboard." On the side of the building next door, overlooking the parking lot, was a Virginia Slims cigarette ad, twenty feet long by ten feet high.

"You can't pick a woman off a *billboard*. She's got to be real."

"Look at that woman in that car over there." Salman was point-ing across the street at the exit driveway to a Burger King. A woman in a car was preparing to enter traffic. She had sunglasses on and the glare of her windshield made it difficult to see any other details.

"She doesn't count," Darrell said. "You can't just pick some woman who drives by. We have to be able to see her."

"I picked her."

"You *can't*."

"She had great legs."

"You couldn't see her *legs!*"

"Dainty little calves, feet soft as slippers."

"If you don't shut up I'm going to make you get out of the car."

Salman got out of the car anyway. He stood in the sun, basking, his eyes closed. Andy and Tiny showed up a minute later, in Andy's Lincoln. In the backseat was an old-model Exercycle, with a heavy iron rear wheel. Andy helped Tiny carry it upstairs. Salman un-locked the front door, and then at the top of the stairs a second door opening into the space. It was one big room, with tinted aluminum storm windows looking out onto El Camino. Covering the opposite wall, four pairs of sliding double doors opened into narrow closets. The walls were gray, and in the middle of the floor was a nest of twelve-foot-long tubes of copper pipe.

"My Dad said we can throw those out," Salman explained. "He was going to put a bathroom up here, then decided against it."

"There's no bathroom?" Darrell said. "Christ. What does he expect us to do?"

"Burger King. It's open twenty-four hours."

Andy went over to the pile of copper pipe, picked up a tube, and studied it. He tried to bend it over his knee, checking its strength.

"What are you thinking?" Darrell asked.

"You know what they used to say at Omega? It's about when life gives you lemons."

"I've heard that," Darrell said. "You make lemonade."

Andy shook his head. "Nope. At Omega, that's what they figure everyone else is already doing. So you've got to do one better: you squeeze the lemon juice into bottles and sell it as organic hair lightener for twenty bucks a bottle."

Andy sent them home to work for the rest of the day, and told them to come in tomorrow with their home computers. The team would rather have hung out and repainted the walls, but Andy was firm that their work had to keep its momentum. Besides, the phone lines wouldn't be installed until the next day anyway.

That afternoon, Andy rented a propane blowtorch at the hardware store, along with a pipe cutter and a level. He went back to the office and removed four of the sliding closet doors from their hanging rails. They were wider than conventional doors, thirty-six inches across. Andy began to work on the pipe with the cutter, blowtorch, and some heavy solder. He began to fashion a box frame. On top of the frame he set one sliding door to make a desk. His work wasn't perfect, but the pipe was a beautiful mottled color and the closet door smooth and varnished. Once he had it balanced and level, he began soldering on support pipes wherever it seemed necessary. The first desk took him six hours, the second half that, and by the time he finished the last two it was past midnight and the pile of pipe was down to a few blunt sprigs he could throw in the secretary school's Dumpster.

"Cool!" Tiny said, when he came in the next morning. Tiny went over to his Exercycle, tilted it up on its back wheel, and rolled it over to a desk he chose as his. He removed a bolt from the handlebar stem, allowing the handlebars to come off. Tiny slid the front of the Exercycle under his desk; he sat down on the triangular seat and put his feet on the pedals.

"You going to try to lose some weight?" Andy asked.

"No, my back," Tiny said. "With my feet on the pedals, my back never stays in one position long enough to go numb. Don't you ever lose the feeling in your legs?"

"Sure—pins and needles?"

Tiny nodded his head. "Kinda. But like my whole body."

"And it happens when you sit still?"

"Uh-huh. Really still. Concentrating."

"I've seen you . . ." Andy said. "What are they like? Blackouts?"

"No . . . I don't pass out. I'm awake, replaying the previous few seconds over and over."

Andy thought about that. "Like in an infinite loop?"

"I never thought about it that way, but . . . yeah."

Suddenly Andy thought of something. "Hey, Tiny, do you have health insurance?"

Tiny said that he didn't. Andy asked him what he would do if he got hit by a car that afternoon.

"Probably die of a punctured lung," Tiny said.

Darrell came in carrying a boom box and a tower case of compact disks. He announced that if he wasn't going to get paid to work anymore, then nobody could order him not to play loud music while he was coding. He plugged it in and hit the "play" button. A heavy metal guitar began to strum.

Andy asked him if he had headphones.

"Nope. Headphones give me a psoriasis of the ear for some reason."

"You can't play that music—"

Darrell interrupted him. "It's okay, I've got it figured out. I'm moving into the closet." Darrell went out to his car and came back with an armful of sheets of plastic bubble wrap and a staple gun. He slid back one door to a closet and began tacking down the bubble wrap. He put the CD player on the floor and slid an extension cord under the door. As he built up several layers of wrap, the sound began to be muffled. He tacked the wrap to the floor and the ceiling and built a flap over the door opening, until he had built himself a womb of bubbles. Darrell's computer, which he'd brought from home, was just a notebook, which he set down on his lap. He put his chair right over the CD player, so the heavy bass came up through his spine. When the door to the closet was closed, the only sound that escaped was a staticky buzz, and when Salman walked past the closet he couldn't help but imagine that Darrell was being swarmed by killer bees.

They quickly fell in love with their office. It was *theirs,* and that was the most important thing. It didn't matter that it had no elevator, no shipping entrance, and no security system; they had no complaints. It was unpretentious: no zoning laws had to be bent to get this place constructed. The flower beds hadn't been overturned to install a sprinkler system. And it was all for the better that there was no gymnasium nearby, or no fitness course down the block—those would only provide distractions. The view of car dealerships and fast-food joints provided a constant note of hustle and bustle. The team was going to get a lot of work done here, they could just tell.

Three days later, Salman began to develop headaches from the flicker of the fluorescent tube lighting. He wore a bandanna tied at an angle around his head to cover one eye. Every couple hours he untied the bandanna and retied it to cover the other eye. Finally he went up to Andy.

"Well, aren't you going to ask me about it?"

"About what?"

"About why I'm wearing a bandanna over one eye."

Andy thought about this for a moment. "Naw, nope, I don't want to pry. If you want to tell me, you can tell me."

"Yeah, but . . ."

"But what?"

"You're like our *manager* now. When a manager sees a model employee such as myself walking around in clear agony with a bandanna over an eye, the manager . . . he's supposed to ask about it, he's supposed to offer to help."

"I didn't want to intrude. Maybe your girlfriend popped you in the eye again. I figured it's personal."

"Would I be switching it eye to eye every other hour if I had a black eye?"

"I didn't notice you were switching it."

"But you're *supposed* to notice those things. That's what a manager does."

"Okay, okay." Andy paused and gathered himself. "Salman, I noticed you're wearing a bandanna over your eye and switching it every few hours. Is there anything I can do to help?"

Salman smiled, then looked away. "No, there's nothing you can do to help."

"What the hell do you mean, there's nothing I can do to help? Why did you have me ask you to help if I couldn't do anything in the first place?"

"Because I wanted you to ask, that's why. It's nice to be asked.

Next time, I shouldn't have to ask to be asked. You should just ask on your own."

"Well, Christ, Salman. What the hell do you have a bandanna over your eye for in the first place?"

"I get headaches from the fluorescent lights."

"I've never heard of such a thing," Andy said.

"I get it from anything that flickers. Monitors sometimes."

Andy looked up. "I don't see any flicker."

"Believe me, it's *flickering*."

Andy said, "We don't have the money for an incandescent lighting system."

"I know. There's nothing you can do. I already said that."

Then Tiny, who had heard this whole exchange, said, "Change the color of the tubes. These are blue."

Andy looked up. "These aren't blue. They're white."

"Blue-white. Try rose-white."

So Andy and Salman drove off to the hardware store and Andy put a case of rose-white bulbs on his credit card. It wasn't cheap. "This better work," he said. When they returned, Andy jacked Tiny's Exercycle seat to its highest setting and stood on it to change the bulbs. Andy expected the light to have a deep rose tint.

"Christ, it looks exactly the same!" Andy said, after inserting the first bank of three bulbs. "I just wasted a hundred bucks."

Salman looked up. "No, that's much better. Tiny was right."

"But there isn't any difference at all!"

"Oh, yes . . . there is. Those blue ones gave me headaches, while these rose ones don't."

"Okay, whatever, as long as you get to work."

"Mmmm . . ." Salman agreed, finally. "But . . . money— what about the money?"

Andy groaned. He was trying to avoid this. He took out his wallet. "How much do you need?"

"Hard to say, maybe fifty."

"Fifty bucks! I don't have fifty bucks!"

Salman looked down. "Not fifty bucks. Fifty thousand bucks."

"What do you mean, fifty thousand bucks? Eventually, sure, but not all at once. You're kidding, right?"

But Salman wasn't kidding. To build the backbone of the VWPC network, he needed a server, the mother computer that all the VWPCs would dial into. Servers are specially designed to quickly handle and fulfill requests for data (such as "gimme that word processor") from many outlying terminals. His home computer, which he had configured to play games, wouldn't cut it by half. Back at La Honda, Salman had been able to work on one of the center's many servers. In addition, he would very quickly need to assemble the other pieces of their internet site: a firewall computer devoted to security; a router computer to direct traffic; a tower of modems to handle all the incoming calls; a high-volume internet link from the phone company. All of these computers, including the server, would run a version of the UNIX operating system, and so Salman had been programming the network to run under UNIX. Salman's home computer couldn't run UNIX. *Nobody's* home computer could run UNIX.

"Can you sneak on one at Stanford?" Andy suggested, searching for anything.

Salman said that he might, but the computers there were already in high demand. One might only be available a few hours a night— like from two to five in the morning.

"Well, what's the bare minimum amount of equipment you need to get started? How much would it cost?"

"Just something that ran UNIX? Maybe three grand."

"Well, that's more like it. You scared me there."

Salman said, "We're going to need more soon."

"You think I don't know that? No point reminding me."

"Sorry."

So they put another three grand on Andy's credit card, while Andy went about begging for fifty thousand dollars. In a valley of so many millionaires, you would think fifty thousand dollars was just bus fare to so many whiz kids who'd be happy to help out fellow start-ups, but in this case their background worked against them: at La Honda they had been so removed from the commercial factors (and one of the commercial factors was the whopping salary) that these four guys just didn't know a soul in town who had fifty grand sitting around earning interest. If they had spent their undergraduate years at Stanford, they might have some old friends who were now bank vice presidents and software sales directors, but as graduate students they had known only other graduate students trying to raise a family on a scholarship and a stipend. So it wasn't a few hours before Andy turned to a source where so many entrepreneurs had turned before him: venture capital.

Andy didn't know enough to realize he should prepare a business plan and send it in advance before making a series of unsolicited, unreturned phone calls; he figured *hey, venture capital?* and got out the yellow pages to look under the *V*'s. Other entrepreneurs sent themselves to business school just to learn how to make a good pitch to a venture capitalist, but Andy just picked up the phone and gave a few of these firms a ring. Lo and behold, he was customarily transferred to some junior partner who had just graduated from business school (where he had been taught a hundred and one ways to turn down an entrepreneur). Not knowing where to start and afraid of wasting their time, Andy started out asking a few of the most obvious categorical questions, such as whether the venture firm was currently making investments, and if they were, then might they be interested in computer hardware, and if they were, then by chance were they open to consumer products, which is just the kind of cascade of questions a young man asking for money should ask, since it allows you to hold a conversation without actually saying anything about your own project that might let the person on the other end of the line start one of his speeches: "Well, your idea sounds like a good one for somebody, but we're just not doing multimedia this year." And after a few minutes Andy had these venture capitalists just wondering who the hell were they talking to, anyway. And right about then Andy would let it slip out that he and his buddies had just left this old research lab up on the hill, *La Honda*—had they heard of it? Most of the venture capital firms in Silicon Valley were located along one main thoroughfare, Sand Hill Road, which actually intersected the winding road that La Honda was located along, and so Andy didn't find one venture capitalist who didn't perk right up at word that a La Honda alumnus was looking for money. Right about then the junior associate partner would put Andy on hold, and some senior executive full partner would come on strong with a prom night's worth of polite manners.

All this time, Andy still hadn't given word one about the three-

hundred-dollar computer his buddies intended to nail on the head. .
Then, taking a cue from Salman, Andy suddenly became evasive,
suggesting his project was nothing, surely not worth their time, and
sorry to have bothered, which only pumped more tension into the
situation. By that point, it didn't really matter what Andy said,
since the password had been spoken. The password was "La
Honda," and without it Andy didn't have a chance in hell of getting a meeting. Their project had enough knocks against it—
knocks that those venture capitalists managed to surface in just a
few polite inquiries—that even with the La Honda connection,
when it was all said and done, Andy only managed to schedule one
face-to-face meeting, for which they had two weeks to prepare.

Two weeks!

"But nothing's working yet!" Darrell complained. They didn't
have any hardware, and all of their software was still, in effect,
unassembled. Even Tiny's Hypnotizer merely displayed a white
rectangle on the screen.

"Well, we're going to have to fake it."

To Darrell, this brought up burning memories of their trip down
the freeway to ModNet, where Andy's old friend had told them
that from a marketing point of view, their box wasn't a computer.
"I'm not going to waste two weeks of work just to embarrass
myself again."

Andy had analyzed that meeting at ModNet a hundred times,
and he had come to conclude how stupid it was to have used an old
Macintosh for the demonstration, because by 1995 Apple was considered a weak company and its Macintosh a failure in the market-
place. To have even implicitly compared their VWPC to a failed
product was a real strategic boner, akin to a presidential candidate's invoking Mike Dukakis in his stump speech.

Instead, Andy wanted to demonstrate the concept through Tiny's
Hypnotizer, running on a DOS computer. The Hypnotizer was the
most revolutionary piece to the puzzle, and it was the most likely to
knock the socks off their audience, since it was a solution thousands of engineers had been unable to find. Andy wanted it to be
the center of attention. It wasn't hard to make the Hypnotizer
display a stack of screen images rather than just a white rectangle.
The Hypnotizer would flip through a *picture* of a simple word

processor, and a *picture* of a simple database, and a *picture* of a few favorite web sites. Off to the side, Andy wanted to exhibit a model of what they figured the VWPC would look like—perhaps molded from plaster. The overall impression he wanted to convey was that the VWPC wasn't a 1986 computer with new tires—they had an entirely new thing in the VWPC. Not just a whole new product, but a whole product category: new hardware, new software, new operating systems, new computer languages. Maybe the VWPC computer would drive demand for the software, but it could also be the other way around: the Hypnotizer might drive demand for the VWPC.

"And that's another thing," Andy said. "We can't call it a 'VWPC' anymore. We're going to need a name."

One might have thought that these hard-core engineers, with their focus on the technology, might have looked down their noses at the prospect of wasting even a few hours on questions like what their box should be called, what the screens should look like, or how the box should be styled. But in fact the opposite was the case—the team took these decisions personally. They were devoting fourteen hours of every day to technical fine print, facing problems written in an obscure logic language. As a result, they *craved* meaning, they *craved* interpretation: what does all my logic add up to? The harder they worked, the more they craved meaning, so the more they cared about labels, logos, and designs.

The next day Andy came in with a fifteen-foot-long stretch of butcher paper and four colored markers. He taped the butcher paper to one wall and gave each team member his own color. This was to be a low-pressure brainstorming session. He instructed them to write up ideas for names spontaneously, over the course of the day. He didn't want them just to write potential names, though; they were to write up any inspirations, root words, logos— anything that would foster creative thought. At the end of the day they would make a choice by consensus, and whoever came up with the chosen name won dinner for two at a restaurant of his own choosing.

"It's not brain*storming*," Andy said. "It's sort of brain*breezing*."

By the middle of the day, a certain pattern had emerged in the four colors. Scribbled in red and green, the colors of Andy and Salman, were terms like:

console	Discman
player	boombox
navigator	Walkman
dashboard	station
viewer	web
window	browser
personal	lunch box
mobile	internet
wired	outpost
network	system

Meanwhile, etched in the little blue block letters of Tiny and the more aggressive, bold-stroked orange capitals of Darrell were terms like:

nanocomputer	internet
notebook	laptop
power	ATM
VCR	XT, AT, DX4
network	webware
online	wired
personal computer	PC
computer	CPU
engine	machine

Andy's and Salman's inspirations were more metaphorical, more playful, while Tiny's and Darrell's were more conventionally descriptive. In the afternoon, every time one or the other of them went up to the butcher paper, all the others watched with growing interest—and sometimes anger. Nobody said a word, though. It was like a game of tennis, all the hatred expressed in gestures and ground strokes. Salman walked up and wrote "NetMan," and on his way back to his desk he got a smile from Andy and a frown from Darrell, who marched up to the wall and scrawled "massively

parallel processing supercomputer." So Salman came right back
with "Pandora," a reference to the Greek myth. As soon as he sat
down, Darrell picked up his pen again to write "32-bit, 3.3 Volt,
Reduced-Instruction-Set-Chip Computer." He underlined the last
word three times.

"Come on you guys," Andy said at the end of the day. "You've
got to have some sense of *marketing.*"

Darrell blew his top. "Marketing? Marketing? Fuck marketing.
All day, and not once do you write down the word 'computer.' Not
once. People are . . . we have a weakness to overcome . . . *computer,* see? Everybody's going to say it's not a computer, it's not
good for business, and on and on like that."

"We can't take them on," Salman offered. "You've seen it . . .
the *ridicule* . . . calling it a computer just provokes the attack."

"He's right," Andy said. "If we go around marketing this as a
full-fledged alternative to the desktop computer, we're going to get
the full weight of a three-hundred-billion-dollar industry squashing
us. Didn't you learn anything from the past six months at La
Honda? If the ironmen hate us, think of companies who really have
something to lose."

"Fuck you wimps, fuck it, pansies. . . . This *is* a full-fledged
alternative to the desktop computer . . . it *is.* . . . If it's not,
then what's the point? Every detail, everything about it, they have
to say—no, *shout*—'computer, computer, computer.' It's about
power, right, Tiny?"

Tiny nodded. "Powerful, powerful. Computer, computer, computer."

Darrell feared that not much separated Andy's vision from "Mister Internet." But Andy believed their unit should be introduced as
a *complement* to the PC, and after a few years people would realize
they didn't need the PC anymore. The sides to this debate were
reproduced when they began to discuss what the box should look
like. Darrell and Tiny wanted something that looked just like a
computer—a big metal box without ornamentation. A no-nonsense
machine. Andy and Salman wanted something that was cooler,
hipper, more stylish than a computer. Pointing out again that the
most important audience for the VWPC was students, Andy
wanted a box inspired by the sleek designs of video game consoles.

Students should take one look at the VWPC and think it was going to be fun. Andy anticipated this argument would have hit a nerve with Darrell. When it didn't, Andy figured Darrell was just being stubborn, that his ego was still bruised from the unfair criticism leveled at the VWPC by Donny Williamson, and that he would come around eventually.

For two days, no work got done. Everyone was too mad to concentrate. Andy felt he'd made a mistake in taking a side on the dilemma—as the manager, he should have played the role of arbiter. But he couldn't take his words back. Maybe he could bring someone else in, someone independent, to help them reach a consensus.

. . .

Darrell and Salman were staring out the window, playing another round of Ten Women. It was the lunch hour, when the secretaries exited the school in bunches and walked up the street to a Sizzler, which had a killer salad bar. An orange Volkswagen Bug turned off El Camino and parked in the lot below their window. When its driver door opened, a slender brunette with shoulder-length hair stepped out. She wore cutoffs and sandals and a coppery leather vest over a black T-shirt. She was a far cry from the secretaries who had been trained to tone themselves down. She didn't control her hips, she didn't cover her arms, she hadn't cut her hair to chin length. She didn't wear a sport coat with padded shoulders. She probably didn't even own a pair of nylons.

"Mine," said Darrell.

"I called her first," said Salman.

"No you didn't! You didn't say anything!"

"Yes I did. Right before you, right as you were speaking. You didn't hear me because you were so busy listening to yourself." Salman giggled.

"You— Shut up, you cheater, she's mine."

Salman looked down at her again. She was gazing around, a bit lost, with her hand up to her forehead, shielding the sun from her eyes. Some strands of her hair were pulled away from her face with bobby pins. Salman looked again at the VW Bug. It had sheepskin seat covers. "Hey," he said, "that car . . . I know that car. . . ."

"This is Alisa Jennings," Andy said a moment later, introducing her to the team. "She's a professional industrial designer. I've asked her here to help us. It's not costing us anything, but it's costing her *time*, so let's not fuck around."

Andy rolled out the butcher paper onto his desk.

Alisa made a big deal out of checking her watch. "Okay, I only have forty minutes, so let's go through this. Please, for me—only one person speak at a time."

The team began to run through their arguments again, but this time, with Alisa present, nobody swore or spoke out of turn or called each other a retard, which is what Andy had been counting upon. The boys were on their best behavior. Frequently, Alisa restated in simpler language what one of them had just said. If one of them began to grow animated, all she had to do was give the guy a smile and he melted. After forty minutes, nothing had been decided, but for once it didn't feel like a dogfight.

"Okay," Alisa said, looking at her watch again. She began to roll up the butcher paper. "I'll get back to you in a couple days with some ideas." She turned to Darrell. "Do you work on Sundays?"

He said that he worked every day.

"Then I'll see you on Sunday, say, two o'clock?"

Andy walked her to her car. "I know it seems like we couldn't agree on anything, but that was really . . . really a lot better than it's been."

Alisa cracked a smile. "I don't think you have any idea how perfectly normal that was. You know Pacific Bell spent half a million dollars to come up with the name *AirTouch* for their cellular spin-off? I don't have any clients who know what they want."

"You don't?"

"If they knew what they wanted, they wouldn't need *me*—they would need a draftsman." She popped him on the arm with the butcher paper and leaned into her car. "Relax, this isn't permanent. You just need a concept to get you through your meeting."

Alisa went straight home from their office; the impression she had given—that she had to be back somewhere in forty minutes—was just mumbo jumbo to make her seem more professional. Since graduating in June, she had discovered there weren't as many jobs for industrial designers as some of her professors had conveyed. In the meantime, she tried to get freelance jobs while she built her portfolio. She'd never seen herself in some other line of work, but sometimes the vision of herself was foggy. She had been debating whether to move to San Francisco, where most of the design work was assigned, but her university department hadn't changed the door lock to the industrial design studio, so she could still go into the lab at night and use all of the equipment, from computers to pottery wheels to sewing machines. None of the other students seemed to realize she wasn't still attending classes.

Alisa spread out the butcher paper on her bedroom floor. As far as she could tell, her goal could be defined by the following oxymoronic parameters, which she wrote down in a notebook:

1. Look enough like a powerful computer to defray critics, yet—
2. Not look so much like a computer that a $300 billion industry feels threatened, and—
3. Be made of one piece (to save cost), yet—
4. *Don't* look like the old one-piece Macintoshes (a failed product)

Well that shouldn't be too hard, she said to herself facetiously. Instinctively, she agreed with Darrell that it would be a dangerously slippery slope to *not* emphasize their device was a computer with a lot of power. But Alisa never thought that computers were designed very well in the first place. One of her pet peeves was the spaghetti wiring and cabling hooking parts together that always plugged into the back of computers and the bottoms of printers— places that were usually hard to reach. The alternative wasn't much better, to have cables popping out the front, where they could easily be accidentally unplugged. Besides, wires were considered ugly, though this didn't have to be the case—there was no reason Alisa couldn't do something that made the wires cool. She remembered that she had been into the basement of the engineering school once, where there were about fifty computers on steel racks, and each computer had about five cables sticking out. Some engineer had taken the time to braid the cables into a big net; it wasn't quite *pretty,* but it was a creative approach. So she realized that there was no reason this computer had to have *four* separate wires—the four (one for power, one for the phone line, one to the printer, and one to the monitor) could be braided together. Or something. Alisa was just getting started. She pledged to herself that by the time she was done, she would have solved the wires question.

She turned the page of her notebook to focus on the name. She would need two names—one for the *category* of computer, the other for their specific model. Alisa had smothered the walls of her bedroom with pictures from catalogs and magazines of all sorts of gadgetry. Furniture, cookware, book covers, machine tools, car parts. All she had to do for inspiration was stare at her walls, but sometimes it also helped to have a little wine.

Andy had become attached to the name Salman conceived, *Pandora*. Alisa thought the myth of Pandora's box was too loaded with feminist interpretation and reinterpretation to work for a computer. But she knew Andy and Salman would never be happy unless the name conveyed some metaphorical meaning. On the other hand, Darrell would have been perfectly pleased to call the thing the GX50550—just some meaningless string of numerals. To Darrell, numerals made it seem serious, scientific, and powerful. So Alisa figured the solution was in a long word that, when pronounced, was also a set of meaningful numbers. For a while, she played with variations of 686, since the next generation of computer was supposed to be the 80686. She knew this computer wouldn't be one tenth as powerful as the inevitable Intel 686 Pentium Pro, but so what? It was just a name. Her notebook filled up.

    C3PO = Seethreepio
    R2D2 = Artoo Detoo
    12345 = won, too, three, phore, phyve
    678910 = sicks, syx, sephin, ate, aty, nyne, teyn
    686 = sicksatysicks, 6ATY6, SYXATY6
    syxatysyx, SYXATYSYX, SyxatySix
    512 256 128 64 32 16 8 4 2 1
    1   0   1 0 1 01   110
    686 = 1010101110

She liked the idea, but none of the results. She went to put on some rice, and when she came back she started thinking about a phrase

Andy had used to explain the virtues of their product: "Ninety percent of the features, for twenty percent of the cost."

> Ninety-four, twenty = 94-20
> Ninety, four-twenty = 90420
> Pandora, Pandorum, Pandorii, Pandoro
> G8 = gate
> The Power of One $= X^1$
> U^{INTERNET} = The Power of the Internet to You
> PC^{INTERNET} = The Power of the Internet to the PC
> 904202U = Ninety for Twenty, to You

Then she started looking at a diagram of a network that Salman had sketched for her. It included things called *servers, routers, modems,* and *firewalls.* That last word, *firewall,* reminded Alisa of a comment she'd read so many times in so many places, how the internet would be such a massive flow of unverified information that trying to use it for research would be like trying to take a sip of water from a fire hydrant. Though it was meant as a criticism, Alisa liked the image of the internet as a fire hose of data. It conveyed power and speed, the rush of it all. She wrote down, "Fireplug." Then below it she wrote, "90420 Fireplug, a Web Computer."

That got her thinking about those wires again. What if the Fireplug was designed with a big fat cable as big as a garden hose coming into it? That would give the impression that the computer hookup was faster than a skinny little phone line. She could use the one fat cable to actually hide several cables inside—the power cord, the phone line, and the printer cable. The fat cable would run to the wall outlet, where there would be a little box. The phone line and the printer would plug into the box at the outlet, so there wouldn't have to be three wires coming up to the computer. The more she thought about it, the more she liked it. Consumers would take one look at that fat cable and say to themselves, "yeah, the whole internet's coming through there." She wasn't so sure about the word *Fireplug,* but she had grown attached already to the 90420 and the fire-hose cable.

. . .

On Saturday evening, while sitting in his bedroom folding his laundry, Andy started to panic about what would happen to their project if they didn't find money. Pretty soon he was fretting about his own financial situation. He'd been eating rice for dinner since they left La Honda. Rice "smothered with a thick layer of steam," as Alisa had taught him to call it. He wasn't hungry but he wasn't satiated, either. Washing and drying his clothes had taken on the aura of self-indulgent luxury. Although he'd entered graduate school with about ten thousand dollars locked up in short-term CDs, as a student he didn't want to possess money—he wanted to feel like he could live off his talents at any time, the way animals can live off the land. At the time, he believed that holding his nest egg was undermining that desire. So he spent his savings. It took him eighteen month's to deplete it all. Now he didn't even have enough in his checking account to avoid the ten-dollar monthly fee. And a big credit card payment was looming.

He'd never prepared for the possibility that he might someday have a passion that needed nurturing.

Looking at his laundry, he realized that most of it had been mail-ordered from L.L. Bean (he hated shopping). He fingered the labels and then he remembered that L.L. Bean had a lifetime money-back guarantee on anything ever purchased from them. Lifetime! This provoked his curiosity. So he dug around in his bookshelf and found an old catalog, and sure enough, it promised a money-back guarantee, "no questions asked." He really didn't think he would go through with it, but he was just curious as heck to find out how much his wardrobe was worth. Andy scrambled around his bedroom, piling up clothing on the bed. Wool sweaters, several pairs of boots, two overcoats, a pair of gloves, some scarves, every pair of pants he owned. Then he opened a storage closet in the hallway (he hadn't looked inside in months) and found three sport coats, eight ties, and five dress shirts—his old clothes from his Omega days. The mountain on his bed was three feet high. Even the flannel sheets were mail-order. The charm of L.L. Bean is that the style never changes, so just about every item was listed in the catalog.

He was surprised at how much some of it had cost him—several of the sweaters were over eighty dollars, and the sport coats were over two hundred each. He totaled it all up, and it came to almost twelve hundred dollars. That was three months' rent! Or two months' rent plus food! He still couldn't believe this was going to work, so he called the toll-free number and asked for the return procedures, trying to stifle a laugh. *No way could this work.* But the lady on the line didn't ask him any accusing questions at all. She was just as motherly as could be. She looked him up in her records, and she verified that he had made all these purchases over the years, and then she gave him a return authorization number, and that was it! He would receive a check about a week after they reacquired the clothes. That was what she called it, *reacquired,* as if they were valuable artifacts that had been sold by mistake.

While he was boxing it all up, his phone rang. It was Alisa.

"Where are you?" he asked.

"I'm down here at the design studio. What are you up to?"

He told her the story about his clothes, and she laughed.

"I'm going to have to check my closet," she added.

Her asked her how the concept was coming.

"That's why I called— You want to come down, take a look?"

She gave him directions to the building, hidden behind the student union. He didn't waste any time walking down there. The air had grown cold in the past week, and he was wearing shorts since he had boxed up all his pants. The old brick building was covered in ivy; as a student, he'd walked past it a hundred times without knowing what was inside. The entrance door was the size of a barn door. She was waiting for him, her body in the crack of the door.

"My, what a big set of doors you have," he said.

She laughed, then said, "Oh, what a small-sized monitor you have." She smiled at her own joke. Then Alisa explained the door's purpose—so that large design projects could be wheeled in and out on skids.

She escorted him into the studio. The huge warehouse-style space was partially divided by head-high temporary walls into sections for pottery, metalworking, and painting. In a separate room were a dozen workstations for computer-aided design.

"I worked up the preliminary model design on the screen," Alisa said, "but then I switched to clay. Working with my hands . . . I don't know. It stimulates my creativity, I guess."

She had a wet towel thrown over something that sat on a slab of plywood. Alisa said, "I was fiddling around, and every design I came up with seemed to call attention to the fact your screen is so small—which it is, I checked. Then—then it was hard not to look like a Macintosh, with just one piece. I tried it circular rather than boxy, but it looked like a trash can. Also, oh yeah, I was afraid if it was too small, then people would think it was a gadget, not a real computer."

"Well, can I just see it?"

"All right, just a second. Close your eyes."

He did. She told him to open them. The wet cloth was removed. The design was sort of a head, neck, and shoulders design—the monitor sat at a slightly backward cant on a fluted neck, three inches wide at the top and five at the bottom, which curved gently into a much wider square base, about fourteen inches to a side and an inch and a half tall. Andy walked around it. Below the base, rather than stunted peg legs, quarter-inch beveled rails ran front to back. Coming out the left side of the base and dropping off the table was a dark green garden hose that had been plugged into the clay. The neck was about seven inches tall. The monitor was tilted back ten degrees, and tapered slightly toward its back. Alisa was right. In this design, the screen didn't *feel* small; something about the size and shape of the neck made the monitor seem as big as the neck and shoulders could support—as if a bigger monitor would be unwieldy and unstable. Andy loved it. He loved the whole thing. Secretly, he'd been trying to draw possible variations the last few days, and all of his sketches ran into the problems she had solved— if it didn't look like a Macintosh, it looked like a toilet bowl.

Alisa said, "The design is very computerish, so for the color, I'm thinking something not very computerish. *Black,* with just a touch of gray mixed in, like stereo components. Not glossy, though— matte. To the touch, it would feel like super-duper fine sandpaper."

"You know, Alisa, this is so—so *good.* Tiny said it had to be good, good, good, and it is. It is. *Wow.* It doesn't look like a three-hundred-dollar machine. It looks like a three-*thousand*-dollar machine. Do you have a name?"

"Yeah, but, okay, you ready?"

He said that he was. She handed him a piece of paper. On it was printed:

Universe's *PowerStation 90420* Web Computer

He liked the way it sounded. "Who's 'Universe'?"

"You guys are. That's your company name."

"Cool. Wow." Then Andy repeated the numbers, except he said it like a Southern California zip code—"Nine-oh-four-two-oh."

"No, no . . . not like that. Ninety-four-twenty."

"PowerStation Ninety-four-twenty. Ninety for twenty. Ninety *for twenty*. Hey! Cool! Cool!!"

"I was at Radio Shack this morning, that's where I learned about your monitor. And, well, they were calling anything with a CD-ROM inside a 'multimedia computer.' So I thought: we call yours a 'web computer.' That's what the cable is for." She explained her fire-hose idea. Then she talked about how she would create a mold over the clay, and then paint a form of liquid plastic into the mold. When this dried, she would sand down accidental ridges and fill pits with a hard wax, until she had a prototype that she could paint.

Andy loved all of it. It not only pleased him, but she had solved all of the problems that the team—heck, not the *team* anymore!—the *staff,* the *Universe* staff. Her concept solved all their problems. Her concept was more "like a computer" than Andy had *thought* he wanted. But now that he saw her design, he realized he'd been wrong about what he wanted. *This* was what he wanted. A *computer*. Not just a computer. A *PowerStation!*

Andy told Alisa about how he had offered the guys a free dinner for two to whoever chose the name. "I'd like to take you to dinner, if you'd go."

"It's ten-thirty."

"Okay, well, another night then maybe."

"No—I mean I'd love to go, but what's open at ten-thirty?"

They drove into town and found a Hunan dive, all silver-flecked

Formica and fluorescence. *Blue* fluorescence. Andy had been here a
couple times before; they didn't use MSG and they didn't serve
vegetables that were out of season and they didn't build a dish
around baby shrimp when the menu promised prawns. Andy
wanted to do something nice for Alisa, so he ordered the most
expensive dish on the menu, the Chef's Special Taiwanese Fish,
which set him back all of nine dollars. They drank hot tea and sake
over ice. Andy was at a loss for words. He struggled to finds topics
of conversation. He looked across the table at this woman; if he
knew her at all, it was by deduction from her habits. She didn't
take long showers, except on Sunday. She didn't play music loud.
She didn't bring men over, but she didn't stay home on Saturday
nights either. She didn't sleep with makeup on. She wasn't frail.
She wasn't frilly. She didn't seem confused. She didn't wear nice
shoes when it rained, and she didn't own five pairs of comfy
sweatpants—she had maybe one pair, worn down to the thickness
of a T-shirt. The world had not taken much out of her. She didn't
own a TV and she wasn't on the phone three hours a night, and
Andy adored her. He knew she wouldn't have solved his problems
if she didn't like him a little bit too.

When the fish came, Andy started rambling, telling jokes. All of
a sudden, they were flowing off his tongue. The fish was a flat
bottom fish, probably a flounder, baked and smothered in a light
brown teriyaki glaze with slivers of scallions. Andy just started
rambling: "You know what I'd like to know? I don't see any eyelids on this fish. What does a flounder do when it gets a little speck
of sand in its eye? It can't reach up there with a fin and flick it out,
can it?" He made a struggling motion, holding his splayed finger
down at his side and trying to put his head to his finger. "What
does it do? . . . I mean, frogs have eyelids, right? Look at this—
no eyelids." Alisa giggled and watched him. "Actually, here's what
I really wonder: does a flounder swim like this, horizontal, like a
manta? Or when it wants to go somewhere, does it twist ninety
degrees upright, like a normal fish, and wiggle side to side? Maybe
it does both, sort of first gear–second gear. The James Bond flounder . . . being chased by a dogfish, and just when it's about to be
eaten, it tips up on its side and speeds away." Andy didn't have any
idea where these jokes were coming from. He cut Alisa some fish

and spooned some sauce over her portion. "A flounder is sort of built like a sail, or a wing—thicker on one side than the other. I wonder if a fish can use the current the way a sailboat tacks into the wind. Doesn't even have to flap its fins. Just turns forty-five degrees to the current, shoots forward, tacks back to the left, shoots forward again. Maybe the fish have sailing races, no fins allowed. Though it would be hard to tell if your opponent was cheating." He held up two paper napkins like puppets. He shook one. "I saw you pumping water through your gills!" He shook the other. "No I didn't. I was just breathing!" "Cheater." "Crybaby."

By the time his roll petered out, Alisa was bent over, half under the table, trying to get her breath.

"Sorry," Andy said, for some reason.

"Please, no, I loved it."

As they were coming out of the restaurant, they joined a crowd from a theater down the block that had just let out. They tried to mix in.

"So what did you think of the movie?" Andy said.

Alisa said, "Not enough big explosions. I need my fix. If I don't get some trains and planes exploding every hour, I'm just unsatisfied."

Andy looked ahead, and a few feet in front of him were two brunettes with beads in their hair. Not just any two brunettes. It was Salman's girlfriend and her sister—he'd had dinner at Salman's one night. Andy tapped her on the shoulder.

"Hey, I know you," he said.

They swirled around. They were wearing big coats, the top buttons clasped. Both of them had big dimples in their cheeks. Both wore lipstick that looked like it had been reapplied in the women's room on the way out of the movie. Andy introduced Salman's girlfriend as the chef of the most delicious lemon lamb pie he'd ever tasted. Andy introduced Alisa as the designer of the computer Salman's girlfriend had of course been hearing so much about.

She said, "No, I'm not really up on that stuff anymore."

Andy sensed something like bitterness. "You should see the design Alisa did . . . talk about *wow*."

His girlfriend said, "Well, I'm glad it's going well for him."

Andy was no fool. This was not the language of a girlfriend.

"Umm, you know, I'm not . . . Salman, he holds things inside. . . . I remember this time he had this great idea, took him two days to get it out. He holds things . . . in here." Andy put a fist to his chest.

"Tell me about it."

Andy felt Alisa clench his arm. Andy took a stab. "He hasn't told us anything."

"That's just like him."

"I'm not trying to pry . . . but when did this happen?"

She looked to her sister, as if her sister was the one counting weeks. Her sister said, "In August."

"August? But that was— That was . . . two months ago. He hasn't said . . . not a word, nothing."

"Well . . ." Salman's girlfriend, who wasn't his girlfriend at all, began to drift away.

Andy said, "But his phone number . . . I've called him at home. *Many* times."

She said, "I let him take the number with him."

"Well, where's he living?"

"With his father." She put her hand up, not quite a good-bye wave. Her sister took her under the arm and escorted her away.

Andy turned to Alisa. "Nothing! He said nothing! What do I do? Do I say something now? Do I? What do you think?"

She had one arm on his, the other arm around his back. "I don't really know Salman," she said. She pushed him to walk toward his car.

"I can't believe . . . nothing. You don't understand. It's not that he just hasn't mentioned it. He continues to talk about her. Just yesterday morning, he came in and said she'd cooked this fudge cake for him the night before. . . . He was talking about this whipped cream she'd made, a taste of Kahlúa liqueur in the cream. . . ."

"Maybe he meant his mother."

"No, you don't know Salman, he *brags*. . . . We have to go see him."

"You think he wants you to show up at his dad's house late on a Saturday night?"

"Absolutely he does. Salman *wants* me to notice his pain—he's always trying to tell me how to be a considerate manager, how to be a friend. It's his way of asking for attention."

Andy had Salman's father's phone number and address in his wallet, in case of building emergencies. It wasn't far away. They were there in five minutes.

"You want me to stay in the car?" Alisa said.

"No, come in." Andy got out and walked up to the front door and rang the doorbell. Most of the lights were on in the house. They heard a television being turned down. Footsteps approached the other side of the door, then went past the door. Window curtains moved aside, and Salman's face appeared behind the glass.

"What are you doing here?" Salman said, opening the door.

"Can we come in?"

Salman stepped aside. Andy took Alisa's hand. They took a seat on the living room couch. The coffee table was marble topped.

"So what's up?" Salman said. "You guys want a beer or something?"

Andy said, "We were out to dinner, and after dinner we ran into your girlfriend coming out of the movie theater. Except she said she's not your girlfriend anymore, and hasn't been since August. We came to see if you're okay."

Salman showed no expression, just a sad blankness. But then his eyes kind of softened as a thought occurred to him. "You came right away, then?"

"Well, yeah, of course."

This brought a full smile to Salman's face. "You saw her, and you came right here, right away?"

"Yeah."

This seemed to embarrass him. He put a hand over his forehead, his fingers splayed over his eyes. "Well, I'm all right," he said. "I'm just fine, actually. But I really, really appreciate you coming." He patted his thighs and stood up, as if he expected them to now go.

Andy said, "Salman, *why*— What happened between you two?"

Salman looked to Alisa, then back to Andy. Looking at Andy, he jerked his head in the direction of the hallway.

Andy stood up. His touched Alisa's shoulder. "We'll be right back," he said.

Andy followed Salman down the hall and into a bedroom. On

the wall were pennants from every team of the National Football
League. The wallpaper pattern was of one-legged pirates and
schooners. Framed and hung over the bed was a certificate from
the United Nations.

"You grew up here?" Andy said.

"Mmmm . . ." Salman sat on the bed. "So . . . you and Alisa
. . . you were out on a date, weren't you?"

"I dunno. But I won't lie to you. I like her. I feel something."

"Well, watch out."

"What do you mean?"

Salman twisted his finger into the bedspread. "Well, why do you
think my girlfriend and I broke up?"

"I don't know."

"Well, what do you *think*?"

Andy didn't want to make the wrong assumption and offend
him. "Why don't you just tell me?"

"*Come on— Because I was working too hard,* of course. She
wanted a boyfriend, not the *idea* of one. She looked into our future
and she saw that it would always be this way, that she would
always come in second to my work."

Andy bowed his head. "You gave up your girlfriend to work on
the project."

"Of *course* I did! Yes!"

"It matters that much to you?"

"No! Of course not! I don't know. Maybe. I didn't make the
choice consciously. . . . She just said she was leaving me unless I
quit, and I didn't quit, and then one night I came home here. You
can't do it, Andy—don't fool yourself. Go *slow* with Alisa. Don't
think you can have a good relationship. A relationship . . . I
know this sounds corny, but I would rather say it badly than not
say it at all: it's a living thing. It needs to be nurtured just as much
as a plant needs water and sun and air. Every day. If it doesn't get
it, it will die."

Andy felt a hole open up inside. He took a deep breath. Salman
was right, dead right. If he denied his feelings and pulled away
from Alisa, it would only hurt. But if he fell in love with her, he
would probably end up hurting her worse.

Andy said, "Why did you lie about it, Salman?"

"I don't know. It was easier than to tell the truth."

"You used to lie about her, all that stuff about her being some sex kitten."

"Mmmm . . ."

"When did it start?"

Salman's eyes squinted, and his mouth pursed tight, and he brought his knees up to his chest. Andy moved and sat down beside him. Salman pinched the bridge of his nose with his fingertips, hard, to push back imminent tears.

Salman said, "Okay, I will tell you something, but don't tell anybody, okay?"

"I won't."

"After a while, like after a year, when we would have sex . . ."

"Go ahead."

"I would close my eyes, and in my mind, it wasn't *her* anymore. It was usually someone else. I think I stopped loving her. I felt so guilty. I was lying to her, then soon lying to everyone else."

Andy sighed with relief. "But Salman! That's *normal*."

Salman sniffed and brushed his nose. "How can that possibly be normal?"

"Have you ever asked anyone about this but me?"

"No . . ."

"It happens to everybody."

"To people who *really* love each other?"

Andy was going to say yes, but then he realized he had only his own experience to go on. And who could say that he had *really* loved? "I don't know."

They sat there for a while.

"You'd better go take care of Alisa," Salman finally said.

Andy stood up.

Salman added, "Can you let yourself out?" He rolled over and stretched out on the bed. Andy left the room. Alisa was leafing through a magazine.

"All right," he said, pulling his car keys from his pocket.

On the way home, he told her how Salman had been forced to choose between his work and his girlfriend. It was an uncomfortable story to tell, but he didn't want to hide it from Alisa. Afterward, they rode in silence, and the story sat in their minds like a wet fog. When he pulled up to their house, he got out of the car slowly and walked ten feet behind her.

When he got to the top of the stairs, she was watching him, half in and half out of her door, like back at the design studio. They said good night to each other, and when he had passed her and was almost to his door she called out.

"Andy?"

He turned around. "Uh-huh . . . ?"

"You can take me out to dinner again sometime."

"Really? . . . Good . . . I'd like that." He paused a moment, looking at her in the dark night. She came over toward him and as quick as a bird gave him one kiss on the cheek and another on the neck. He kissed her hair. It was as if he'd never touched hair before, never seen it before, never had anything so precious in his hands. She slipped away from him and went back to her door and closed it behind her. His heart was pounding so hard it hurt in his chest. He took several deep breaths.

. . .

Early in the morning on the day of the meeting, Andy was at the office with the rest of the team, double-checking the stack of screen images they intended to show the venture firm. In the previous week, Tiny had written a third Hypnotizer, one that translated to Macintosh. In order to fully demonstrate the power of the Hypnotizer, Andy intended to "hypnotize" a DOS computer and a Mac side by side; both computers would display the screen images simultaneously. Their meeting was scheduled for 9:30 A.M., about an hour away. Alisa showed up around 8:45 carrying the prototype, which she had gussied up with a paint job, a PowerStation label, and a plate-glass screen. Behind the screen was a swatch of gold lamé fabric, which gave the screen an eerie luminescent quality, as if it were already pumped with electricity. The rest of the team had seen Alisa's clay model on Sunday, and this was even cooler than that one.

"Okay, you guys only have forty-five minutes to get dressed," Alisa said.

Get dressed? Andy had been so focused on the appearance of the prototype that he had totally forgotten to consider his own appearance. He hadn't shaved in four days, and he was standing there in some of the few clothes he hadn't sent back to L.L. Bean—a pair of maroon athletic shorts and a T-shirt with a surfing logo. There was time to drive by his apartment, but Andy realized he didn't own a pair of pants! Here he was, a half hour from one of the most important meetings in his life, and he didn't own a single pair of pants!

Then Andy looked around the room, and he realized that everybody on his team was wearing shorts of one kind or another. They might have time to drop by Darrell's house on the way, but Darrell surely didn't own a pair of pants that fit Tiny's forty-six-inch waist. Furthermore, at nine o'clock on a Wednesday morning, there wasn't a clothing store open in town. With anguish, he explained all this aloud.

Alisa glanced through the phone book but came up with no ideas.

"It's fate," Darrell said.

"It's not *fate*," Salman said. "It was subconscious self-determination. We don't want to sell our baby."

"How can you have *subconscious* self-determination? That's an oxymoron. Self-determination is when you *choose* your life and make it so."

Salman shook his head methodically. "It doesn't have to be. Take *destiny*, for instance. Destiny is self-actualization, but you don't *choose* your destiny. You just *are* your destiny. You're born with it."

Darrell sighed with exasperation. "Destiny and fate are the same thing."

"Nope."

"Come on, guys," Andy said. "Not at a time like this. We have to go."

"I'm not going," Darrell said.

Andy groaned. He turned to Salman. "Salman, admit that destiny and fate are the same thing so that Darrell will get in the car with us?"

"But they're not the same thing," Salman said casually.

"I'm not going anyway," Darrell said. "I'll fuck it up. I'll only get mad and say the wrong thing."

"No you won't. We *need* you. Christ, your legs aren't *that* ugly."

"It's not my legs. I'm not going."

Andy didn't have time to argue. They carried the boxes of materials down to his car and got in. The venture capital firm was located in an office park on Sand Hill Road, five miles away. At about the fourth mile, they passed between the front nine and back nine of Stanford's golf course. Andy had an inspiration and pulled off, then turned around and drove up to the clubhouse. He parked beside the practice green. They all jumped out and ran into the sport shop, which was having a clearance on some plaid pants made from stretchable fabric. Kelly green was the dominant color, crisscrossed with blues and reds. They even had a size forty-four, which stretched to a forty-six without much trouble.

"Do you have this in a blue?" Salman asked the counter clerk. "Maybe a Campbell or a Royal Stewart?"

"Not now!" Andy screamed. He put it on his credit card. Alisa drove the rest of the way while the three men changed into their new pants.

The venture firm was in a sort of eco-office-complex, with one-way asphalt roads winding amid the cedar-roofed buildings. The architect couldn't decide whether to imitate a ski lodge or a dude ranch, so he had done both. Every building was partly obscured and cast in shade by a taller Pacific oak. Pumice walls lined the roads. There was no dirt; every inch of ground was covered with wood chips or gravel. In the sense that no detail had been left to chance, there was nothing natural about it at all. Andy got the feeling that if one of the big eucalypti shed a long strip of bark, a little Mexican man would run out of some unseen basement door and catch the bark before it hit the ground. Alisa tried to find a parking place among the Mercedeses, Volvos, and Jaguars. Speed bumps slowed her every twenty yards. All of the parking places were marked "Reserved," with the initials of the occupant. They found a satellite lot and were able to walk back on a railed path.

In their tartan pants, they felt terribly out of place. When they strolled through the frosted-glass front doors and into the posh reception area of Marquee Venture Partners, the three men looked like a Scottish rock band.

. . .

Each of Marquee Ventures's eight full partners and four associate partners had his specialty. Andy's main contact, Travis Grissom, was a hardware man: he could quote the labor costs in Singapore, the memory refresh times of RAM, and the cost per square inch of flat-panel displays. And though he had his own opinion on the various legal questions raised in the hardware industry, when it came to Marquee business, Travis Grissom had to defer to the opinion of their legal man, Lenny Smythe. For the past three days, Travis Grissom had been trying to get Lenny Smythe to read the La Honda intellectual property waiver that Andy Caspar had faxed over. The problem was, Lenny Smythe was on vacation in Cabo San Lucas, at the tip of Baja California, and for the past three days had been on a yacht, fishing for adventure. This yacht was a fully rigged communications vessel, equipped with a cellular fax machine that would make office managers everywhere drool with envy, but there was one little unforeseen problem. Four executive men and their four executive wives had commissioned the yacht, and on the first day so many faxes had been received from various parts of the world that the damn thing had run out of fax paper. Not to be beaten that easily, Lenny Smythe had spent several hours of each day trying to connect his cellular phone to his laptop computer—which had a fax/modem inside. Travis kept suggesting that he just *read* the contract to Lenny over the phone, but Lenny prided himself on always being in "full digital contact," and wouldn't give in. Finally, on this morning, while Andy Caspar was setting up his demonstration in the room outside Travis Grissom's office, and while Lenny Smythe's wife had hooked a black sea bass off the stern, Travis was reading the contract to Lenny one sentence at a time.

"Christ, Travis, can't this wait till I get home?"

But Travis didn't want to risk the wait. Marquee Ventures hadn't found a single internet business to throw some money at. It was obvious that the internet was the big growth area for the future, and if Marquee wasn't invested, then in another five years there would be no Marquee. They had to get on this juggernaut. It was just so damn hard to find a *company*. . . . Individual people were making money on the internet, marketing consultants and web programmers and the like—but there in the fall of 1995, *companies* were still just giving away software for free. Nobody had booked much revenue, let alone a profit. So when Travis Grissom picked up the phone one day and Andy Caspar was offering a chance to invest in a *hardware* product, Travis wasn't going to make the mistake of being slow to pull the trigger. Nobody gave away hardware for free, and though the margins for a low-price computer weren't very enticing, they were a hell of a lot better than on free software. Eighteen months ago, a start-up that designed internet routers had come to Marquee looking for a million bucks, and Marquee had done the usual venture capital games—stalled, checked around for competition, tried to negotiate more shares for their money. In the meantime, the internet router market boomed, and the company funded its own growth through profits. They stopped returning Travis's phone calls. Now it was about to go public. If Marquee hadn't diddled around and just given them the money, that million would soon be worth twenty. Travis Grissom wouldn't make the same mistake twice.

But three months prior, Lenny Smythe had bowed to pressure to "go with gut instinct" and prematurely authorized a five-hundred-thousand-dollar investment in two aerospace engineers who had left Northrop Grumman, the defense contractor. They had designed an air-pressure system that prevented leaks in underground storage tanks of hazardous materials. Northrop Grumman had since sued, claiming partial property rights to the technology. What a mess! Most of the five hundred thousand dollars was going to be spent defending the lawsuit. So Lenny Smythe also was not going to make the same mistake twice.

He said, "I'm just not comfortable unless I see it on paper."

Travis moaned. "Didn't you write it down as I read it to you?"

"But it's in my own handwriting. I can't be critically minded of my own work."

"You're being paranoid. This is a *waiver*. Do you see anything here that's suspicious?"

"The whole exhibit list . . . how do I know that what they will present is what's on this list?"

"Let's assume that it is, for a moment. Is everything else okay?"

"I'd really like to see their presentation myself."

"Lenny, be reasonable."

"All right. If—and I mean *if*—the technology on the list is the technology they present, then the rest is okay."

Travis ran out of his office and into the conference room, where three kids in goofy plaid leisure pants were standing around, staring out the window at the parking lot. One was tall, one was fat, and one was neither. Travis fought off the urge to judge them on their appearance. For all he knew, plaid leisure pants were all the rage among coders these days. Travis made a mental note to look for a pair for himself, next time he was at the shopping center.

Travis introduced himself. Seven other partners filed in for the demonstration. "No need for a dog and pony show," Travis said. "Just a little show-and-tell. We'll ask plenty of questions."

Andy spoke sitting down. He talked about how in the early eighties the price point for a computer dropped from ten thousand dollars to a couple thousand. But it had stayed around two grand for twelve years. Granted that far more power was being bought for the same amount of money; still, another revolution in pricing, on the scale of what happened in the early eighties, seemed inevitable. As he spoke, Alisa's PowerStation prototype sat in the middle of the table. Andy noticed as many eyes were on the prototype as on him. Several of the partners reached out to touch the screen.

They weren't asking questions, though. Andy switched subjects over to the Hypnotizer. He turned on the two computers, and then he talked about the riddle that had stumped so many engineers and was a stumbling block to the boom of the internet—how to make one program run on different operating systems. Then he booted up Tiny's Hypnotizer on both computers, and up came the screen images Alisa had designed. Andy asked them to notice how *quickly* the Hypnotizer loaded—a couple seconds. He reiterated how it was small enough to download rapidly over the internet, and would travel just in front of programs, which could then be booted. Using two hands and two mice, Andy clicked through identical screens on both computers. The venture capitalists began a flurry of questions, from how far along the team was in their software development to what their exit strategy was for recouping any investment in their company. When they started talking about exit strategy, Andy knew he'd made an impact. He admitted that his team didn't have any business acumen and hoped to sell or license the technology to a company who could manufacture it or market it. They asked him how much money he was looking to raise and he admitted he didn't have any idea, it just wasn't his field of expertise, and if they invested he hoped they would bring in a person who could cover those bases.

"We like to come in with a two-stage investment," one of the partners explained. "We give you some money up front, get you through premanufacturing. If it goes well, we have an option and right of first refusal to fund your next stage."

Andy wasn't stupid. When they started explaining the process by which they gave money, that money wasn't very far off.

Then an older guy in back cleared his throat. The room got quiet. He had a slightly distressed look on his face, as if he were in the middle of pushing out a large turd. "I don't get it," he said. "Why isn't this project being sponsored at La Honda? It's too *juicy*. The internet's hot."

Andy referred him to the legal waiver, which he had mailed to Travis Grissom the previous week for assurances. "Most of the good stuff you see here was invented in the past month."

The guy grunted. "The past month?" He looked skeptical.

Travis Grissom interrupted. "Lenny gave his nod."

The old guy asked, "Did he call La Honda?"

"He didn't see a need. The waiver language is standard."

"What about just to check their references? You know, what's the harm in *asking*?"

There was a long pause. Andy looked out the window. In the parking lot was a basketball hoop with glass backboard.

Finally, the guy said, "We ought to give a call up there." He turned to Andy. "Nothing personal, but we just met you. We like to know who we're dealing with."

"I'll call up there this afternoon," Travis Grissom said quickly, trying to get past this uncomfortable moment. "I'm sure this will get cleared up quickly. Francis Benoit's an old friend of mine." He turned to Andy. "You guys know Francis, right?"

Andy nodded. "Sure . . . not well, actually. Just professionally."

"The hardware man of hardware men. I'm sure he'll vouch for you guys."

. . .

"We're fucked," Andy said, when they got back to the car.

"What happened?" Alisa asked. She had been waiting in the reception area during the meeting. Andy explained it to her.

"We're fucked," Andy said again.

"Fucked, fucked, fucked, fucked," Tiny clarified.

"*Maybe* we're fucked," Salman said.

"It was going so well . . ." Andy mourned.

"Is it really that bad?" Alisa asked.

Andy spelled it out for her. "At best—at *best*—Francis will tell them we're pea-brained schmoes who rank just below ex-cons in terms of trustworthiness. It's also possible he hears about the Hypnotizer and takes some interest, and suddenly a detective knocks on the door to our office with a warrant for our arrest. At worst—I don't know what at worst would be."

"Can't you just go to another venture capital firm?" Alisa suggested.

Andy slung himself into the driver's seat of his car. He slammed the door. "Every firm in the valley is going to ask the logical question, 'Who the fuck are these guys?' Nobody's gonna invest without checking references, and that means a call to Hank Menzinger or Francis Benoit."

"Are you sure?" Salman said quietly.

"How could I have been so *stupid*," Andy said. He slapped the dashboard with his palm. "I shouldn't have showed them the Hypnotizer. It was too risky."

Tiny said, "But we didn't have a chance of getting money without the Hypnotizer."

"I know. Just like we never would have got a meeting without La Honda on our résumés, but because La Honda is the only reference on our résumés, we'll never get any money." It was another infinite loop, and there seemed no way out. He drove in silence.

Salman said, "You remember the end of *Butch Cassidy and the Sundance Kid?*"

Nobody answered. Finally, Alisa said that she remembered. "They're at a restaurant in this little town in Bolivia, surrounded by the Bolivian army, except they don't know it. They think they're just shooting against ten guys."

"Right. And the very end?"

Alisa thought hard. "They load up their guns and run into the plaza toward their horses."

"And?"

"I don't remember."

"The camera freezes. Credits roll over the image. We never see them get shot."

Andy interrupted. "What's your point?"

"I didn't have a point. I was just thinking about it, that's all."

"You were just *thinking* about it."

"Yeah," Salman said. "Like, you think that's where they got the term 'going out shooting'?"

Andy raised his eyebrows. "From the *movie?*"

"Yeah."

"The movie was made in *1969,* for crying out loud. That term was around for a century before the movie came out."

"How do you know?"

"What do you mean, 'How do I know'? Of course it was. You're saying it wasn't?"

Salman shook his head stubbornly. "I'm not arguing one way or the other. I'm just saying you don't *know* whether the term was around. What were you, maybe three years old when the movie came out? You have some distinct memory, from the age of two, lying there in your crib, hearing the phrase 'going out shooting'?"

"I can't believe we're talking about this."

"My point is, you don't *know.* Not for sure."

Andy waited a moment. He tried to stop arguing and understand what Salman was after. "So you're not afraid of what might happen?"

Salman said, "Just don't freak out too soon. Grissom's gonna make a phone call. Big deal. Hank was glad to get rid of us—what does he care what we're up to? He's got plenty to keep him busy already. We're too small to appear on his radar. We're just four nobodies. I doubt he even remembers all our names."

"You believe that?" Tiny said.

"I'll tell you what I believe," Salman said. "I believe in our project. It will attract money, one way or another."

7

Selfish Generousness

They didn't have to wait long to hear from Travis Grissom. Salman answered the phone that afternoon, and Grissom was on the other end of the line. Salman put him on hold, notified Andy, and then went outside to sit down on the curb of the parking lot. He didn't want to overhear. Nor did Darrell, who disappeared into his closet. Andy picked up his handset and thanked Grissom for calling so soon.

"Let me say right off, Andy, that it's our policy not to give any advice or make any comments when we turn down entrepreneurs for funding. We don't like to open ourselves up to criticism, and sometimes our reasons for turning people down have to do with internal complications going on here at Marquee, despite the worthiness of an entrepreneur's technology."

"Uhmm . . . I kinda missed that. . . . Did you just tell me that you're not interested?"

"Well, yes, but like I said, it may not be in any way a *criticism* of your business idea. We have certain criteria, certain risk profiles, and many good ideas are still very *good* ideas, even if they don't meet *our* criteria, which can often be quite narrow."

"All right. Well, thanks." Andy waited for him to hang up. He didn't.

"What I'm trying to say, Andy, is that your project is . . . Look, we invest in *businesses,* run by *business*people—that's our thing, see? But what I'd like to do, if it's okay by you, I have an individual in mind who might be interested in investing in your company. A friend of a friend. I think it might meet his profile, he's invested in several other start-ups. I'd like to tell him about it, if you'd let me."

Andy had a hard time following him. "You know a guy who wants to invest?"

"No, I don't *know* he'll want to invest. I haven't told him about it. Mind you, I've signed a nondisclosure agreement with you, I can't talk about your work with anybody unless you clear me."

"Well please, by all means, talk with him, you're cleared, whatever I need to do."

"Fine. I'll call him now. If he would like to meet with you, then I will call you back."

"Okay. Good. That's great. Thank you."

. . .

A few days later, team plaid drove ten miles south to the office of a semiretired accountant named Conrad Goss. The building had a motel look to it; its exterior walls were covered with white gravel, its doors pastel. On the building directory, there were a lot of DDSs and MFCCs after the tenants' names. The air in the hallways was slightly noxious, a medical smell. Faint jingle music wafted through the doors. Conrad Goss's receptionist was entirely forgettable. She showed them into his office. He was in his middle fifties, had a downward-turned nose, droopy eyelids, and his skin was slightly waxy. His hair had separated into two islands. The big island began on both sides and met in a thin bridge on the top. The small island was over his forehead. This extra clump was thicker, wilder. It hadn't receded so much as seceded. Goss wore an accountant's suit but a golfer's polo shirt, well worn and open at the collar. He didn't wear a watch. His office walls were covered with gilt-framed degrees and credentials from various boards and agencies. There were lots of Japanese trinkets around the room—samurai toy soldiers marching across the coffee table, fans on the walls, bonsai trees to book-end the couch they sat down upon. Two long swords crossed on the wall behind his desk. On the front corner of his desk, in a place nobody could miss, there was an autographed photograph of him standing with President Clinton, probably at some fund-raiser.

Conrad Goss broke the ice by talking about the bonsais, which apparently weren't bonsai trees at all—they were baby cypress pines injected with chemicals to petrify their growth. In Japan, bonsais take forever to grow and therefore are extremely expensive. These runt cypresses had a 23 percent share of the imitation bonsai market. "The cubic zirconium of bonsai trees," Conrad said, and laughed. He had invested in the company's petrification technology. Tiny promptly reached down to feel the plant and accidentally broke off a snippet of leaf. Bright green dye oozed out. Tiny looked up, flustered, afraid he had made a terrific blunder.

Conrad Goss whipped out a white napkin and held it out to Tiny. But instead of chastising him, Conrad said, "Sorry about that. Happens all the time. We're working on the problem."

He apologized! *For having his plant broken!* Well, that put the team at ease. Conrad Goss seemed like the most at-ease guy they had met in a long time. They set up their demonstration on the coffee table and ran through their routine.

Conrad Goss watched with rapt attention, leaning forward out of his seat and asking almost no questions. Occasionally he whistled with appreciation; other times, he nodded his head, trying to stay with them. His eyes squinted when Andy's terminology veered too technical. Andy finally asked him if he had any questions.

Conrad Goss chuckled and leaned back. "Don't look at *me*. I don't know tech from tock." He chuckled at that a little. "Tech from tock . . . not bad. But I take Travis's advice on the technology, and what he says is you guys got something on fire here. Red hot. Sure I read magazines, tool around online, try to stay up to speed. But you guys, you're on the *inside*. Wow, I would love to be twenty-five again, I'd do it differently. I got no kids, see? What am I going to do with my money? I got eight million bucks—it's bought me nothing. I wasted my life auditing public utilities, nuclear power, hydro power, all *x*'s and *o*'s. Spreadsheets—debits and credits. Thirty years. Was that a life? I got a house in Bolinas above a beach where the women walk around topless, and I never go there. What's wrong with me? Why do I wake up every morning? There was a time in my life, I thought that I would never tire of seeing bare bosoms. But is that enough? What lasts, if not that? They say sex and money, those impulses will never fail. I say: 'love.' And what is love but illusion? So what am I saying? *Illusion,* that's what lasts. My fantasy, it never goes away. My money means nothing to me. My fantasy, though—without it, *nada.* My money buys me my fantasy. My dream is: *drama.* There it is. Simple. A stranger on the beach with coconuts dangling from her chest is not drama. She is a stranger forever. Spreadsheets, audits, adjusting entries—that was not drama. I want to risk my money. I want it to be at stake. I want to be along for the ride."

Andy said, "So you're interested?"

"Like I said, I'm taking Travis's advice on you guys. How much money are you looking to raise, total?"

Andy said that they needed about sixty thousand for the next couple months.

"Couple months?" Conrad Goss laughed. "No, I'm talking about how much money do you need to get to a point where we can sell the technology? If you spend sixty grand and then stop, that's sixty grand wasted. I need to know what gets us from *today* to the point where we either win or lose."

Andy explained that he didn't have that analyzed yet.

"Of course you do! I know entrepreneurs, and I know they can't sleep at night before scribbling the latest budget on some napkin. What's the figure that you can be sure will get you through a year? A hundred thousand? Two hundred thousand?"

Salman and Tiny looked to Andy. They too were curious what the figure might be.

Andy said, "With what kind of salary?"

"Salary? Oh, right, you guys are broke. How about a thousand a month per person, living expenses. C'mon, what's the figure?"

"Maybe a hundred thousand to proof-of-concept, two hundred thousand to alpha."

"Two hundred thousand?"

"Right. About that."

"Okay, here's how I work. This is the only way I'll do it. Since I don't know you guys personally, I have to get fifty-one percent of the company, and I have to put each of you under an employment contract so you guys don't walk. It's to protect myself. Now don't get me wrong, I'm not a control freak, I don't want to run your company, I don't even understand half of what you said in your demo. Hah! As far as I'm concerned, as long as you three—or four, I'm sorry, four—as long as you four spend the capital on legitimate business, we don't even have to talk to each other. I'm a silent partner, fine. But in case it gets strange on me, I need to be able to take over and liquidate, without a hassle. That's where the fifty-one percent comes in. I'm willing to pay for it. You want two hundred thousand, I'll write you a check tomorrow. Wait, are you guys even incorporated and all that mumbo jumbo?"

Andy admitted that they weren't.

"We'll have to take care of that. Where's a good accountant when you need one? Hah! I can take care of the paperwork, actually. Can do it in my sleep. Hey, not bad—one less trauma for you guys to worry about. I'll get you a bank account, a checkbook. Hey, I'm sorry. I don't want to jump the gun on you guys. I can see I've got you a little shellshocked. You probably thought getting two hundred grand was a lot harder than this, huh? Hah! You guys have probably never seen two hundred grand in your life."

On the way home, they stopped for Popsicles. They kept saying how incredible their luck was—but not one of them actually believed that luck was a significant factor. *Travis Grissom said we were red hot!* If anyone deserved credit, they had to look no farther than down to the ends of their noses. By the time they had those Popsicles sucked down to the sticks, the three men had themselves convinced that with such a red-hot product, stumbling across a guy like Conrad Goss was no accident. Hell, there were hundreds of guys like Conrad Goss in the valley, middle-aged men looking to relive their lives through their money. And all it took to find one was to show your stuff to someone who had the connections; a few phone calls later Mr. Moneybags would be drooling on your shoes!

You want two hundred thousand, I'll write you a check tomorrow!

"Let me get this straight," Darrell said, when they tried to explain it to him. "You walk into this office, and this guy who doesn't know a thing about us, who says he doesn't know a thing about what we're doing . . . he offers you a fifth of a *million dollars,* for a majority of a company we haven't even yet incorporated . . . and he wants to give us the check tomorrow?"

"That's right," Salman said, so giddy he wanted to pinch himself.

"Just like that," Andy said. "Maybe he's a fool, but he's *our* fool." Andy was in the middle of the room taking baseball swings with an imaginary bat.

Darrell shook his head. "And you really believe for a second that he truly *doesn't* understand the technology? Nobody gives you that kind of money without knowing his stuff."

"He just did," Salman said.

"That guy was an accountant," Andy explained. "I don't think the money matters to him as much as the thrill."

"So you believed him?"

"What's to believe?" Andy said. "He had a picture of himself with the president. He's not some shady underworld character, like you're probably thinking. You had to be there. If you'd met him, you'd understand."

But it just didn't sit well with Darrell. "Maybe it's good I didn't meet him. Maybe it's good I don't. I don't want . . . Look, we have to have some *composure,* we have to keep some *distance.*"

"What are you talking about?"

"Why does he want to give us the check tomorrow? Why so fast? Why this shotgun marriage? What's he after that it can't wait?"

"For god's sake, Darrell!" Andy said. "*We* need the money fast. He's not forcing it on us, he's helping us out. He's going to do the paperwork, take care of everything."

"What do you mean, he's doing the paperwork? We should have a lawyer do the paperwork! We don't know shit about contracts. I don't know, I don't know, you guys have . . . you guys. I just don't like the *feeling* I get on this. Why do we have to sell him fifty-one percent of the company? Why can't he just buy twenty-five percent for a hundred thousand?"

Salman sighed with disgust. "He doesn't do it that way. He doesn't know us, he doesn't have any reason to trust us. The fifty-one percent, see? . . . I don't blame him. . . . It's not like *you've* got a picture of yourself with the president on your desk. I mean, it's not like you have venture capitalists for friends."

"Wait a minute, wait a minute. . . . Let's slow down here. . . . Nobody, and I mean *nobody,* sells a majority of their company to outsiders—it's unprecedented. . . . That's not how it works. It's, like, you're supposed to sell as *little* as possible. If you're confident you're on to something big, something red hot, then you want to *hang on* to the shares. And if you don't hang on to them, then, why—that's just like putting up a sign that says 'no confidence.' Listen to me. *Listen to me.* I've been in a start-up before, I've even waited too long to sell, so I should be eager to sell now. But fifty-one percent. I mean, did you think for a minute that the reason he wants so much is not because he wants to control the company, but because he knows the more he buys, the more profit he's going to make? Maybe two hundred thousand isn't enough, maybe that's what I'm saying. Maybe our idea, maybe what we've got here, maybe it's worth a *million* bucks, and he's getting an eighty percent discount, maybe that's what I'm saying."

Andy listened and tried to jot down some notes on what Darrell said, tried his best to treat him with respect, an opinion that he was on the verge of losing. "Two months ago, Darrell, two months ago we were sitting in a tin can on a hill making thirty-five grand a year and dreaming that one day we might be able to give away our VWPC design for free, just put it in the public domain and let anybody get rich building it. It wasn't about money, and it wasn't about getting credit for the design, and it wasn't about protecting our turf. We wanted to see it get built, we wanted to see a VWPC on the desk of every kid in a high school. Now you're—now you've got this in your head, this, this *paranoia,* and this *greed.* So maybe the PowerStation technology is worth a million bucks, maybe it's worth ten million, so what? So somebody else gets rich and we don't, so what? I want to see it get built. I want to see one on every desk. That's all it's ever been about. Just because we left La Honda doesn't change that."

Darrell pursed his lips. The tip of his tongue stuck through the side of his mouth. "No, I'm not . . . This isn't about *greed,* it's about *self-respect.* Giving away software, giving away the computer to school kids, that's not the same as giving the design to some rich accountant who's already got his eight million. I don't care about the money. I *don't*. Stop that, Salman—I *don't*. We can't be these innocent babes in the woods here—we can't trust every guy with money who comes along."

"He's not just some guy," Andy repeated. "If you had been there—"

"You're too trusting! Our La Honda principles didn't serve us very well at La Honda, and they will serve us even less out here. We've got to *think*. We've got to stay on our toes, and never give someone a reason to doubt us."

"But nobody is doubting us!"

It was never so clear to Darrell. All of a sudden, he couldn't believe he had joined a start-up company with three programmers, not one of whom had been in a start-up before or had one ounce of business savvy. His own decision, in retrospect, seemed utterly foolish. He'd taken his eye off the ball. How could he have deluded himself into thinking they could pull it off? It was one thing to stand in the front acreage of La Honda looking down on Silicon Valley, and from a distance think *I'm going to show them*. Because when you got down here, when you were just one of a hundred other start-ups this month, it was hard to remember who you were trying to prove yourself to. "We're going to get eaten alive out here," he said. "We don't know anybody, we can't trust anybody, we say yes to the first guy who offers, and what's more we sign away the company."

In the next few days, while Salman went shopping for servers, Darrell tried to find some precedent for entrepreneurs selling a majority of their company in the first round of financing. He called old friends, he posted queries to online bulletin boards, and he cold-called some multimedia companies. People were reluctant to provide confidential information, but those who would talk to him took his side—selling 51 percent was nonstandard. If anybody else had sold that much, they weren't talking. During this time, Conrad Goss kept sending over couriers with contracts for the team to sign. The signatory pages were flagged with little yellow tabs, and Darrell couldn't help but notice how *easy* Conrad had made it to sign the contracts without reading them. His cover page assured them that he would make copies of the fully signed contracts, which meant it would be several days before they got their own copies of everything they had signed away.

"You're paranoid, man," Andy said, watching Darrell stare blankly at a copy of the shareholder agreement. "Let's go meet the guy, have lunch with him. C'mon. You'll feel a hell of a lot better."

But Darrell wouldn't sign the agreement, and he wouldn't go to lunch with Conrad.

"He's frozen up," Salman said, when Andy asked him for advice.

"Should I tell Conrad? I don't want him to think we've got cold feet. The last thing we want to do is appear indecisive."

"Mmmm . . ."

"So you think I should tell him?"

"Do I?"

"Yeah. Should we?"

"Umm. No, we can't really, can we?"

"I don't think so."

Salman had been thinking about how Conrad Goss was *supposedly* putting in two hundred thousand dollars. Perhaps Salman was a little confused, but when they formed the company, it would have two hundred thousand in assets. And if they liquidated the company, then the shareholders would divide the assets proportionally—and Conrad Goss would get back 51 percent, or $102,000. So, under this logic, Conrad Goss hadn't really given them 200 grand. He'd given them 98 grand, and the other 102 was just given to himself. Salman tried to explain this to Andy. "Ninety-eight grand. He's really only paying us ninety-eight grand, right?"

"No, there's something wrong with your logic."

"I mean, ninety-eight grand is a whole lot less than two hundred grand." Salman had convinced himself once that they had just earned two hundred grand, and now he'd convinced himself that their two hundred grand had shrunk by slightly more than half, and he was feeling the sadness of taking such a heavy hit. "I mean, is our PowerStation really only worth ninety-eight grand? That's not very much."

Now Salman had Andy all confused. "No, no, see, it's the *inverse*. If two hundred grand buys him fifty-one percent of the

PowerStation, then the whole one hundred percent of the Power-Station has a value of three hundred ninety-two thousand."

"That's what I'm *saying*," Salman said. "It's *worth* three hundred ninety-two thousand. But he *buys it* for only *ninety-eight*."

"Now you've got me really confused."

"For a couple of math whizzes, we're pretty lame when it comes to money."

"Money is, like, another *planet*." Andy asked, "Do you think we should be worried?"

"I'm *always* worried."

The next day, Darrell announced that he was going to see Conrad Goss, but by himself, one-on-one. "I don't want any of you there, trying to keep me from confronting him," he said, going back into his bubble-wrap closet for his coat.

"Don't piss him off," Andy said.

"I'll do whatever I have to do to work this out." He marched out the door. He had a kind of stoner's stride—his arms had no swing, and his walking power came from his ankles, causing his whole body to rise and sink with each step.

He came back a couple hours later and, without comment, signed every one of the large stack of contracts that had been held up.

"How'd it go?" Salman asked him.

"I'm signing."

"Did you guys . . . talk?"

Darrell gave Salman a cross-eyed goofy face. "No, we used sign language."

"Well, what did you talk about?"

"Christ, Salman, I'm signing the papers and we're getting his two hundred grand and I don't want to hear anything more about it, all right? Put it to bed, okay?"

A courier arrived and took the papers away.

Andy thought Darrell was just greedy. He was a selfish person anyway, selfish even in his generousness: if he did something nice he made sure everybody knew about it. If he went across the street to Burger King to buy a round of coffee, he made a big show of taking down orders on a notepad, including the number of creamers and sugar packets desired, which he would go out of his way to stir in himself. Then, when he got back from Burger King, he would yell, "All right, the coffee man has arrived!" rather than just walking desk to desk passing it out. He made you come to his desk and get your coffee, and you had to stand there in front of him and taste it, and he'd ask, "Enough creamer?" And he wouldn't let you give him a buck for your cup. It was always on him. On the one hand, Darrell was so nice and generous; on the other hand, it was just *coffee*, for god's sake, not a visit from the queen.

So Andy just figured Darrell was performing one of these self-delusional routines. He was greedy about the shares and what they were worth, but he couldn't admit to himself that he was a greedy guy, so he invented this whole distrust-and-beware act to make it appear as if he were looking out for the team's best interest when he was really just hoping to get a higher value for his shares. He would settle down soon. Money just wasn't an interesting enough topic to hold Darrell's interest for very long.

Everyone went back to work, and Conrad set up a bank account, into which he deposited his promised money. Copies of the paperwork arrived for each of them, in yellow three-ring binders, perfectly organized. Andy wanted to give Darrell his binder, to show him all was well, but Darrell was in his closet.

"Don't go in there," Salman said. "He doesn't like to be interrupted."

Andy stood by the closet door. "I don't hear much buzzing or tapping." But it was hard to tell, with the car traffic from El Camino bouncing around the room.

Andy waited for Darrell to come out. An hour later he said, "Doesn't he have to go to the bathroom or something?"

"Not if he's in a zone," Salman said.

"What if he's passed out? He might need help."

"It's not worth it. He might be in the middle of something very important."

Andy leaned Darrell's three-ring binder up against his closet door.

About six o'clock, Darrell walked in the front door.

"Where've you been?" Andy asked. "I thought you were in your closet."

Darrell sighed and wouldn't look at Andy directly. He went to his closet, opened the door, and reached under his chair for his CD player.

"Were you working at home today?" Andy asked. "You should have called."

"I wasn't working at home," Darrell said. "Look, we've got to talk."

"All right. I'm listening."

"No. All of us. Everyone. A meeting."

The four of them went across the street and sat down in a booth at Burger King. Andy ordered the table a bucket of fries, which they devoured without speaking.

"See, look at this," Darrell said. "We have our meetings at *Burger King,* of all places."

This was somewhat of a heretical statement, since the Burger King had practically become their satellite office. They always talked about how much they loved the place. You didn't have to buy something to use the bathroom. You didn't feel bad for paying for a coffee with a twenty-dollar bill. You never paid too much for your food.

Salman said, "The fries are better than McDonald's."

"*No,* man, see? We're so *small-time* you couldn't find us with a microscope. Meetings at the BK? We're nobodies."

"Hey, not for long," Andy said.

"You're deluding yourself. Look, I'm not saying we can't build this thing, I'm not saying anybody can beat us to the punch. But to make a deal, to license the PowerStation to a multimillion-dollar manufacturer . . . it takes more than what we've got. I've been here. . . . I've seen it. . . . We had a good product, a three-disc set, but we got *killed.*"

"Relax, Darrell," Andy said. Andy noticed that lately he had been stating the first name of the person he was addressing, just like Hank had done. "One step at a time. Finding money was just one step. Break it down, remember? Batches, chunks, fragments, tasks. Tiny, how do you climb a mountain?"

"One step at a time."

"See?" Andy said. "You can't look at the next year, two years, as this mountain."

Darrell just shook his head, looking down at the table. His hands didn't sit still. He kept pressing his fingers down into the bottom of the bucket of fries, picking up salt on his fingertips and licking it off. "I have something to tell you guys, and you're not going to like it, so let me just get it out before you ask questions, okay?"

"Sure," Salman said.

Darrell reached into his pants pocket and brought out a folded piece of paper. He shuffled away from Salman so nobody could read what he had written on the paper. His hands were trembling. Without letting go of the paper, Darrell mopped his brow with his forearm.

"Jesus, what the hell's going on, Darrell?" Andy said.

"Let me just . . . Okay? I'm going to read it, I couldn't—the *words*—I had to write it . . . crap." He folded the paper in half and put it down on the table, covering it with his hands. "All right, I'm just not comfortable with the deal, but you guys so clearly *are*, that's what you have to remember. This is your first start-up and you're going to get a thrill out of it, if nothing else. It's *your* deal, not mine. You're getting what you want, so you can't—you can't let my experience erode yours."

"What the hell are you talking about?" Salman said. "Ours, yours, what is this?"

Darrell wouldn't look up. He turned and looked out the window at the traffic going by. "I worked a deal with Conrad, in order to sign the papers."

"What kind of deal? What?" Salman begged.

Andy said, "What, you don't want ownership? You want to be an employee instead?"

"No, I—it's in the shareholder agreement, it was my right, I sold him my shares."

"You sold him your shares!" Andy said. "But, but—hell, Darrell, you were the one—you were the one who said not three days ago that we were selling too much. Now you sold him the rest?"

"Believe me, it's logical," Darrell said. "You are—you did sell him too much. I don't like it and I don't want to be a part of it and I don't think I'm going to ever get more for my money than I got at the initial valuation."

Salman asked how much Conrad paid him for the shares.

"The same valuation as the first fifty-one percent," Darrell said. "I owned an eighth of the company, he paid me forty-nine five for it."

"Just like that, you get fifty thousand bucks," Andy said in disbelief.

"That's right."

"And Conrad now owns sixty-three percent of the company?"

"That's right."

"The deal is done?"

"Money's in the bank already."

"So you didn't trust this guy, and because you didn't trust him you did a separate deal with him that required you to trust him?"

Darrell paused, thinking that through. "I guess that's right. But my deal is closed. You're still in bed with him, I'm not. I just—I went through a start-up before, I got diddly-squat for the effort. I'm not being stupid twice."

"But this is not some stupid clip-sound CD! This is *important*."

Darrell said, "It's not important yet. The importance is still just a glimmer in your eye."

They all let that sit out there like that for a while. Salman slid out of the booth and went to the counter to buy a soda. When he came back, Andy said, "Okay, then. What's done is done. We're just going to have to move forward. We shouldn't let this concern us."

Darrell said, "I'm not sure you guys understand."

"Understand what?" Andy asked.

"I cashed out. I'm out."

"Out of the owner pool, sure. But so what? The money doesn't really matter anymore, does it?"

"No, you see . . . I'm *out*. I don't like the situation. I took a job at ModNet today."

"But you can't just take a job!" Andy said. "The employment contract, you're locked in for a year, you read that, I know you did."

"That was part of the deal. Conrad let me out of my contract. I'm *gone*."

"You quit?"

"That was the *deal*."

"But ModNet! ModNet was the one who said the ninety four-twenty wasn't a computer! They insulted you! You went back to *them*?" The whole thing was a shock to Andy. They had gained a bookkeeper and two hundred thousand, but in the trade they had lost one of their own. It was just like Darrell to do this. It wasn't the first time he had gone against his stated principles when it suited him: he wanted the VWPC to play video games, but he didn't want the VWPC to look like a game player; he insisted the VWPC couldn't cost more than three hundred dollars, unless it was to add a feature that *he* thought was necessary. Darrell would always look out for his own hide, no doubt about that.

They went back to the office. Nobody was ready to say good-bye to Darrell or wish him well or even to talk to him. He cleaned out his closet in silence. The others just sat in their chairs, trying not to think about what this meant. Salman wished he had a bottle of whiskey in the office.

Darrell came up to him. "I was thinking," Darrell said.

Salman didn't say anything.

"About the difference between self-determination and destiny."

"Mmmm."

"See, this is my self-determination. I make my move. But you, you're more of a true ironman; that place . . . it's *in* you. Loyalty, righteousness, importance—it's in your blood. You are those values, and they control your destiny, not you."

"Mmmm."

"I'm trying to say you were right."

"I know you are. But you're trying to sound smart at the same time. Like I don't already know the difference between fucking self-determination and fucking destiny. I told you already; you didn't listen. You never listened to anybody but yourself, Darrell. That closet, the whole thing—you cut us off from you."

"That's me. That's who I am. I'm not shy about being me."

"Just go, get out of here, will you? Go to your *job*, go to your *salary*, go to your health benefits and your elevators and your name tags and your parking spaces and your coffee breaks and your little cartoons on your cubicle walls and don't ever think about us again, okay?"

Darrell took his box of belongings and went out the front door. Instinctively, the other three walked to the window and looked down to the parking lot, where Darrell was pushing his box into the backseat of his car. When he backed out of the parking lot and pulled into traffic, he cut off two oncoming cars. There was a lot of honking, and Darrell's arm flew out of his window, making obscene gestures at his attackers.

"Well, I'm going home to get a blow job," Salman said, putting on his coat. He left without any more comment. Andy heard it and it gave him the spooks, to hear Salman pretending he still had a girlfriend. Everybody had his secrets. Right then it didn't seem like a team at all. It felt as fragile as glass, as illusory as a dream. What kept it together? What kept it going? Tiny was sitting at his desk, staring at his monitor.

"Hey, Tiny," Andy said. "You didn't say word one all night. You all right?"

Tiny nodded. "What was there to say? He's Darrell."

"Okay, but maybe we should talk about it, you know, just to help us process it."

Tiny shrugged, showing little interest. "All right," he said.

"By saying 'He's Darrell,' you meant he wouldn't listen to us even if we said anything?"

"Yes."

"So why try to convince him, why try to change his mind, or even to get mad at him—why even bother to waste your anger on him, what good will it do?"

"Yes."

"You know, Tiny— Crap, I keep doing that, like Hank did."

"What?"

"Saying your name when I speak to you."

"Like a salesman."

"Right. Sorry, I'll stop. But you know, sometimes it's good to get angry. Sometimes it's good to scream and yell and get it out of your system, so you don't bottle it up inside forever."

"Maybe."

"Like, sometimes I look at you, and I can tell you're thinking something. I can tell there's something in you that wants to come out. I don't know what it is. Maybe it doesn't have anything at all to do with what we're talking about right then and there. But I've been your friend now for nearly six months, every day and night.

Two months into it I thought 'Okay, he'll tell me when he knows me better.' But now it's been six months, and I'm wondering if maybe you don't like me, that's why you don't say what you have to say. It's getting harder to be your friend. It's like, either you say what it is, and we become that much better friends, or you keep it cooped up forever, and you push me away."

"I don't know what you're talking about."

"What do you mean? You have more secrets than a bag of fortune cookies. I'm getting worried. . . . I thought I knew Darrell. I thought we could count on him—he was rock solid, maybe a little hotheaded but that would be an advantage in this environment . . . And Salman—" Andy wanted to tell him but knew it wasn't his right. "Or you. I don't know you at all. I'm wondering, jeez, maybe I can't count on Tiny either."

"You're taking this too hard."

"Don't tell me how to take it and not to take it. I'm telling you how I feel. Don't tell me my feelings aren't legitimate."

"Don't compare me to Darrell."

"I'm not."

"*Andy*, he was just being Darrell. Darrell is Darrell. *He* made this decision. We didn't drive him to it. We didn't do anything wrong. This doesn't have anything to do with our deal with Conrad—fifty-one percent and all that bull. Darrell was pulling away before we even went to see Conrad Goss—he didn't go with us to Marquee and he didn't go to meet Conrad. He thought he wanted back into a start-up, but he realized he was wrong, and he's blaming us rather than blaming himself. That's *Darrell*."

"Maybe you're right."

Tiny added, "We just shouldn't take this as a knock on *us*."

"But we need him, if nothing else then as a programmer."

"You sure?"

Andy asked, "What do you mean?"

"Have you taken a close look at his output?"

"Not really. I try to give you guys loose reins."

"You might want to take inventory of his code. He works a little on this, a little on that . . . nothing's ever done. I don't even mean gold-master done. I mean first-draft done."

Andy said, "Yeah, I know what you mean, but I just figured that was the way he worked. I tried to accommodate his style."

"It wasn't his *style*. Darrell was avoiding your criticism. It was a cover-up. As long as he never finished a program, you couldn't test it or evaluate it. He didn't make the transition from programming in C to the Hypnotizer language very well. He knew he was in above his head. The guy was an act."

"Tiny, are you being straight with me? This isn't some battle between you and Darrell?"

"Nope. He skipped town before you found out."

"That's why you didn't say anything while he was making excuses! You wanted him to leave!"

Tiny smiled. "Andy?"

"What?"

"I think you're two hundred times better than me at managing people, so I won't give you advice more than this once. But . . . well . . . just *stop* giving us so much freedom. I know that last June that's what it took to get us to sign up for this project. But you've got to be the commander in chief now. Nobody's kidding anybody. We need you to stop holding back. We need everything you've got. Don't worry about stepping on toes. It's time to stop pussyfooting around."

"Am I pussyfooting around?"

"I don't know," Tiny said, "but I wrote the goddamn Hypnotizer code, so I know for sure *I'm* not pussyfooting around. I know I'm not holding anything back. The question is, are *you*?"

"Am I?"

Tiny said, "Are you?"

Quietly, "Yeah."

"Why?"

"Because . . . because I think, 'An engineer wouldn't do this.' "

"Fuck that. This is *survival,* Andy. I don't care if you have to rewrite my Hypnotizer code."

"Are you sure about that?" Andy asked.

"Do what it takes. If you believe in what we're doing, you'll do whatever it takes. And if you don't do what it takes, there's only one conclusion I can make."

"What's that?"

"You don't really believe."

"I *do* believe, Tiny."

"All right then." Tiny nodded. He took a deep breath. After a while, he said, "What were you gonna say about Salman?"

"He hasn't had a girlfriend since August." It just slipped out.

"That's not too bad," Tiny said. "I haven't had a girlfriend since 1988."

. . .

Before going for the big home run with licensing or selling the PowerStation to a major manufacturer, Andy wanted to sell a short-run of alpha-phase "kits," just a few hundred units. This was a guerrilla marketing tactic known as "seeding the market." Andy wouldn't spend any money marketing; he would promote the kits over the internet, and would just sell them at the sum cost of all the components, about four hundred dollars. Despite what Donny Williamson had warned about there not being any early adopters for this product, Andy was sure a few hundred innovators would be curious enough to buy one. The company would receive some feedback from early users, and if the run was successful, it would stimulate word of mouth in the industry. This way, when it came time to pitch the big deal, Andy wouldn't be walking in cold—his audience would have heard some gossip and want to see what the fuss was all about.

All of the parts could be purchased except for the case, which had to be manufactured as an original. From his days at Omega, Andy remembered a plastics manufacturer down in Watsonville—a blue-collar city about a hundred miles south—that printed the hard plastic cases for Omega laptops. He called up the company, San Juan Cast & Die, and got a meeting with the president, Jimmy Porter, then drove down there the next day with Alisa's prototype. San Juan Cast & Die was inside a thirty-thousand-square-foot corrugated tin warehouse. Jimmy Porter was a fifty-year-old guy wearing a short-sleeved polyester dress shirt closed at the neck by a short, wide, collegiate-striped tie. His hair was a sort of beige color, as though he was using chemicals to keep the color from leaving. His desk was covered with a tasteless slab of half-inch

clear Lucite, and under the Lucite were newspaper clippings of his
son, who seemed to be some basketball star at a local high school.
Andy saw he didn't have a single thing in common with Jimmy
Porter.

Now, the economics of manufacturing are such that the first
mold, the cast, would cost about thirty thousand dollars to create.
The cost per unit after that would be comparatively minor. Andy
only wanted to order a first run of three hundred cases, and he was
willing to pay up to fifty dollars a case to get them. But that was
less than half of what San Juan Cast & Die would incur in the
process; Andy was, in effect, asking the guy to take a loss of fifteen
thousand dollars on the order. But if the PowerStation took off, or
even if the kits took off, San Juan Cast & Die could spread the cost
of the mold over thousands, tens of thousands, maybe even millions of units. Andy was asking the president to gamble on that
chance. So Andy turned on every bit of charm he had, talking
about how the internet was going to boom and this box was darn
near a sure thing. The president just listened. Taking risks like this
was standard procedure in his line of work, but he had to trust the
companies he was taking orders from. He didn't have any reason
to distrust Andy, but history had taught Jimmy Porter to be cau-
tious.

After Andy gave his pitch, there was an awkward moment for
both of them. Jimmy Porter kind of sighed, and then he just started
chatting to fill up the vacuum. He said something about how half
his line workers had called in sick that morning, but he knew better. It was the first day of king salmon season, and if you took a
skiff out on Monterey Bay and puttered around the kelp beds, you
would see a lot of guys wearing San Juan Cast & Die baseball caps
to shield their eyes from the sun. He said most of his workers were
lower class, who only cared about three things: fishing, hunting,
and fucking. Jimmy Porter said that he got two Laotians in here
once and put them on the line, and boy were they hard workers!
But when it came time to shut the line down for coffee break, they
wouldn't leave their stations. Two weeks like that, never left their
stools. Finally, Porter got a translator to come by the plant, and it
turned out the two Laotians were afraid if they left their stations,
someone would take their place. Porter was so impressed that he

got himself two more Laotians, and suddenly the productivity plummeted.

"What do you think it was?" he asked Andy.

Andy leaned forward. He could smell Porter's aftershave. "Maybe two men and two women?"

That wasn't it. Porter brought the translator back, and it turned out he didn't have four Laotians after all: he had two Cambodians and two Laotians, who apparently are like oil and water, can't work together. His story finished, Porter laughed, then settled down and looked hard at Andy's specification sheet. His eyes looked up.

"You want a Coke?"

Anxious for anything to extend the meeting, Andy said he wouldn't mind one.

Porter spun around and opened a cabinet without leaving his chair. Andy could see a case of soda cans in the cabinet and a liter of hooch.

"You take anything in it?" Porter said.

"I'll have what you're having," he said, playing it safe.

"I can't decide. The day feels shot already."

Andy started talking. He mentioned how his father had owned a telephone-casing refurbishing plant, back in the seventies, when all telephones were rotary dialers made by AT&T. In order to clean the plastic casings for recycling, Andy's father had discovered that the best product was a universal solvent made by Amway. So Andy's father kept buying these fifty-five-gallon drums of solvent from a friend who ran an Amway dealership out of his basement. On the revenues of these regular orders, Andy's father's friend became the Amway king for a couple years, and was flown off to Amway conventions in Las Vegas to deliver speeches.

Andy's story wasn't completely true, but it sounded true, and it had the desired effect. It made the point to the president of San Juan Cast & Die that although Andy was half his age and living in a different era, the two men were cut from the same cloth. The president listened to Andy's story, and a big smile came over his face, he laughed heartily, and then he stood up and stuck his hand out and told Andy to send him the order whenever the beta system was ready.

Andy was so excited that on the way home he decided to stop off at Conrad Goss's office and give him the good news. The beta system might not be ready for two more months, but just knowing that their work was going to see the sun would keep the team encouraged during the long dark hours of programming. Conrad seemed happy to see him. Leaned up against Conrad's desk was a Sam Snead golf putter; three neon-yellow balls and a highball glass were on the carpet. Andy plopped down on the couch and told Conrad about the deal he'd struck.

Conrad started to ask all sorts of nitpicky questions about the kit strategy.

"Who would assemble the kits?"

"I can get a chop house retail store to assemble them after hours for next to nothing."

"But you'll sell them at cost?"

Andy nodded. "I'm buying only three hundred of everything—in those small lots, I can't get good prices."

Conrad walked back and forth behind his desk. "I don't like it," he said.

"Why not?"

"Why do you need to strike a deal with San Juan now? Why don't you wait two months until the beta is ready? Then, with a working computer to plop down on this guy's desk, it won't seem like such a risk to him. You can cut a better deal, maybe twenty bucks a case. Then we have a little profit margin in the kits."

This seemed like splitting hairs to Andy. The goal of the kits wasn't to make money, it was to seed the market. It was purely a marketing strategy. He believed they were lucky not to be selling the kits as loss leaders. He explained this to Conrad.

"No, nope, I don't like it," Conrad said. "No matter what you say, even if it's a marketing strategy, we're going to record sales on our income statements, and it helps to show a positive margin on those sales. I want to show a profit from day one." Conrad said there was no point going out to Toshiba or Apple—when it came time to swing for the home run—and try to persuade them to manufacture the PowerStations unless there was a fat margin in the product. Andy thought this was ridiculous, totally ignorant of the way the computer companies lose money for years in order to gain market share. Andy thought that Conrad's accounting-background outlook was naïve. But Conrad was insistent; he argued if they were making money on the kits, then they would never be desperate to sell licenses for too low a price. Profit on the kits would give them more time to negotiate, and let them drive a harder bargain.

Andy couldn't believe it. He tried not to lose his cool. "Conrad, you said yourself that you didn't want to—that you weren't going to tell us how to run this company."

"I said that, sure. And I meant it. For *technological issues*. This isn't a technological issue. It's a strategical issue. I've been around business a lot longer than you have. This whole kit thing—it's dangerous, you could blow it, striking deals before we're ready."

"Still . . . strategical, technological, you *said* you weren't going to—I mean, I didn't stop by today to get your permission on this decision, I was just notifying you, filling you in."

"Don't be ridiculous. I own a majority of this company. *Of course* all strategical decisions have to be cleared by me. That's final. Now I don't want you to cut any deals, or place any orders, or shake hands on *anything* until you get the alpha system working. You should be spending a hundred and ten percent of your time on the technology, and we'll revisit the kits at the appropriate time."

Andy was so shocked he didn't know what to say. He didn't want to have a terrible outburst in front of Conrad, something he would regret later. He forced himself to keep his mouth closed and walk from the room. He tried to tell himself that this would sort itself out.

• • •

With Darrell gone, the burden of programming the small applications had fallen entirely upon Andy. The team had taken to calling these applications "utilities," to differentiate them from traditional multifeatured applications. By calling them utilities, they hoped users wouldn't expect too much. You wouldn't get a three-dimensional pie chart at the touch of a button, but on the other hand they wouldn't cost sixty-nine dollars each just for an upgrade, and you wouldn't have to plop down another thirty-five dollars to get a book to tell you how to use the new upgrade. As a team, they had decided upon the following priority of utilities, with those highest on the list to get programmed first: e-mail manager, newsgroup browser, spreadsheet, word processor, database system. Some other utilities would just be spin-offs from these originals: an address book was just a variation on the database engine, and a web-page publisher was just a variation on the word processor. Tiny's operating system was, in effect, a web browser, and Salman's network server interface was just another web site. Salman's work on the network was vital, but it ran in the background. Users would judge the 90420 primarily on the basis of Andy's utilities.

Salman was terribly worried whether Andy was up to the job. For the past six months, only a small portion of Andy's time had been spent coding, and even then just to code simple functions that didn't require Salman's or Tiny's skill. Salman couldn't imagine how a guy as good as Andy at selling and strategy could be any good at coding. Salman had utilized Andy the way a mother might use her son to help prepare a meal: "Here, you chop these carrots into sticks while I work on the soufflé."

Particularly crucial to the utility programming was accomplishing each task in as few lines of code as logic allowed, so that the finished utility would download fast over the network. Nobody doubted that Andy could write any old word processor program, since there were a dozen word processors on the market to use as examples. The question was whether he could make it elegant enough—small without sacrificing too many features. Andy would be spending a lot of time choosing what to omit and what to include. Their word processor, for instance, didn't have to be able to display the document in outline mode, page-layout mode, and full-page-view mode—one mode was enough. He would also be eliminating simple redundancies; for instance, toolbar buttons activate the same function as menu commands, so they would drop all toolbars.

Another reason that Salman was worried was that he had begun to suspect Andy was slightly dyslexic or careless, or both. His e-mail was always full of misspellings and empty of punctuation. At first, Salman figured Andy was just substituting "economical" phoneticisms for full spelling, such as the word "brito" instead of "burrito," or "powr" instead of "power." Some of these became confusing, though, and were frustrating: "cod" for "code," "tech" for "teach." Salman feared these patterns might lead to syntax errors in Andy's code. Andy insisted upon giving it a whirl without any help. Salman fretted that Andy wouldn't ask for help when he needed it, and so he would not only fall helplessly behind, but he wouldn't tell anyone.

To make all of this worse, Tiny had been exactly right about Darrell—he *had* fallen woefully behind the pace set by Tiny and Salman. Darrell hadn't completed *any* of the programs on the priority list. Instead, he'd focused on two objectives. First, he had written simple versions of a couple of popular games. Games! Darrell had been in that closet for a month, and the only program that ran was a five-card-stud poker game. Second, the team had decided to create utilities of "modular functionality": clicking on the word processor icon caused the simple word processor to download, but not the function that printed envelopes, the thesaurus, or the word counter. Those required another click and another download; Darrell had been calling these "subutilities." Well, Darrell had programmed a variety of subutilities for several programs, working from the smallest tasks up toward the more complex ones. He'd never gotten around to programming *any* actual full utilities, or even the complex subutilities. So he'd left the most difficult work for Andy.

Andy tended to hum while he concentrated. Not a meditative hum, but melodic humming, like Winnie-the-Pooh. It didn't annoy Salman, but it gave him the impression that Andy was a simpleton. After a week, Salman began to panic. He felt an irrepressible urge to butt in—a real taboo among programmers, who take great pride in rescuing themselves from the brink of despair without help. Most programmers would rather crash and burn than ask for assistance. So Salman handled it this way: he intentionally inserted a few obvious errors in a batch of his own code, and then he went to Andy and said, "This isn't working, I need help." It was a test; if Andy found the errors, Salman would keep quiet, but if Andy couldn't find the errors, then Salman and Tiny would insist on supervising Andy.

The test was in the code for the thesaurus subutility, which crossed both Andy's and Salman's turfs. Rather than the whole thesaurus downloading each time a user wanted to search for a synonym, only the interface would download. When the user typed in a word and clicked "OK," the search criteria traveled upstream to Salman's server, where a little search engine located synonyms and sent them back downstream to the interface. Andy was writing the code for the interface, while Salman was writing code for the search engine. It was here that Salman inserted a few logical flaws and syntax errors.

Not only did Andy find the flaws, but he had taken Salman's request for help so seriously that he found several other minifunctions that could be accomplished more elegantly, in fewer lines. In other words, he found solutions where Salman didn't even realize he had problems. From that point, Salman stopped worrying, and soon came to regret ever questioning Andy. Andy had taken Salman's single request for help as an open invitation to scrutinize Salman's code, and so every few days Salman would come into the office in the morning and find on his desk a printout of his own recent work, scribbled with editing marks and suggestions in Andy's handwriting.

· · ·

Andy was combing over the business pages of the newspaper, a habit he'd taken up to look for news of competitors and to hunt for potential companies that might want to buy or license the Power-Station. Every Thursday there was a column on insider trading; it covered purchases and sales of stock by corporate officers, who had to file their trades with the SEC, a requirement designed to prevent them from manipulating their own company's stock and taking advantage of minor price changes. This week's column reported that Lloyd Acheson, the CEO of Omega Logic, Inc., was slowly selling 25 percent of his holdings in Omega over the next two months. At that day's stock price, that 25 percent stake was worth over twenty million dollars. According to the SEC filing, Lloyd Acheson had given the reason for his selling as "diversity of personal portfolio," which is what they always said, along with "retirement planning." Everybody knew that Omega stock had stayed flat for a year, while the rest of the high-tech market had jumped an average of 40 percent. With Acheson selling shares, investors in Omega would probably be getting even more nervous.

"Now why in the world would Lloyd Acheson be selling stock in Omega?" Andy asked Salman, somewhat rhetorically.

"I guess because he thinks it's going to go down," Salman said. It was an obvious answer, but also undeniable.

Andy thought about it. "Unless he needs the money for something else."

"Aww . . . twenty million? Nope. It's not like he needs the money for his daughter's college education."

"You're probably right," Andy said. "Maybe Francis Benoit is having a hard time delivering the six eighty-six, and Lloyd knows it."

"Francis?" Salman said. "No way. He could design the six eighty-six in his sleep."

. . .

After nearly two months of solid programming, Andy decided it was time to rekindle the kit strategy, and he decided to push ahead without telling Conrad Goss. "What's he gonna do, *fire* me?" Andy said to Salman. Besides, Andy figured this was one of those chicken-and-egg problems: once Conrad saw the positive feedback from selling alpha kits, he would realize he had been wrong in blocking the endeavor.

Before he went back to Watsonville, Andy called Tiny's friend up in Seattle. Their web site, which let gamers compete over the internet, had become really popular. Andy asked if he could add a page to their web site which would allow people to download the Hypnotizer, along with the utilities Andy had written. Since these could run on any operating system, they weren't dependent on the PowerStation. Andy was hoping to get some preliminary user feedback, and possibly entice some programmers to write their own utilities. It was possible the platform would build up steam, and there could be a whole army of entrepreneurial programmers coding for the Hypnotizer.

Tiny's friend in Seattle not only agreed, he went a step further. His company offered to create and maintain the web site in exchange for a free license to the Hypnotizer. In their current game system, Macintosh users could compete only against Macintosh users, and Windows users could compete only against Windows users, et cetera. If they ported their games over to the Hypnotizer standard, then anybody could play against anybody, and the whole distracting question, "What kind of computer do you have?" would go away. This was a perfect example of how the Hypnotizer was revolutionary, regardless of whether or not the three-hundred-dollar PowerStation ever made it to market.

Confident and pumped up from this arrangement, Andy called the president of San Juan Cast & Die again, but the guy just wouldn't return his phone calls. Andy sent a few faxes, which also went unanswered. Finally, after about a week of being spurned, Andy just loaded up his Lincoln and drove down to Watsonville.

Jimmy Porter welcomed Andy back into his office, apologizing repeatedly for avoiding his calls. On Porter's desk were two small black plastic cellular phone casings.

"Let me ask you something," Porter said, pushing the two casings toward Andy. "Do those look alike to you?"

"Sure."

"How about the color?"

"They're black."

"*Exactly!* Black paint is black paint, right? That's what I keep trying to tell them!"

"Tell who?"

"Ohhh, this cellular outfit down in Phoenix. I've been trying to break into cellular casings for years, I figure it's got to be big business, but I'm competing on huge runs against overseas companies. So, finally, by nearly bending over backward, I get a contract from this outfit in Phoenix, stealing the business from their regular supplier in Texas. I'm making no money on the first six months of the deal in the first place. So the guys in Phoenix tell me I have to match their existing casings, and I say 'no problem.' I run eight thousand units pronto. Then they turn around and reject them! For the *color.* They say mine aren't *black* enough. I tell them I'm using a hundred percent black plastic, it can't get any blacker. So they say maybe it's in the finish. Well there *isn't* a finish on these. So they ask me to put a gloss finish on. Gonna cost me another two bits a unit. . . . I've got to rerack them, redry them. Mind you, I'm already making no money on this, and suddenly I'm beginning to understand why that outfit in Texas didn't fight harder for this contract. I should have sold this business three years ago. My father, before he died, told me just as much. 'Good things don't last,' he said, and he was right."

Porter seemed talked out and worn down. He was just on the dark side of the difference between something's being funny and its being depressing. Andy tried to bring him back. "My father, in that phone parts company I told you about, OSHA made him put in these stand-alone shower devices, in case anyone ever got sprayed with paint. You have those?"

"Yup. Never used 'em once."

"Well, neither did my dad. But one day, he notices they're missing. He does some figuring and some asking around and pretty soon he figures it out: one of his line workers sold them for cash, thinking nobody would notice them missing. So Dad brings the guy into his office and accuses him. The guy gets so mad at the 'insult of being accused,' which is a sure sign that he did it, that he stands up and punches the wall by my Dad's desk, putting a hole in the plaster. Dad says that's gonna cost him another fifty bucks. The guy's holding his punching hand like it's hot liquid he doesn't want to spill."

The president of San Juan Cast & Die let out a laugh.

Andy went on. "So Dad fires the guy for stealing. The guy's lucky Dad doesn't call the cops. He's getting off light. But Dad has no *idea* how light he was truly getting it, because three months later, at the quarterly renewal of their worker's comp policy, it turns out that this guy had broken his wrist hitting the wall. And in the meantime, he'd been living off worker's comp, getting eighty percent pay! He'd conned the comp board, told them he broke his wrist on the last day of his job while lifting boxes."

The president chuckled again, then sighed and seemed to make a decision. He rubbed the fingers of one hand in the grip of the other, as if his hands were cold. He stood up from his desk and went to his office door and closed it. He sat back down. "I like you, Andy, and so I'm going to be straight with you, but what we say here doesn't leave this room, okay?"

"Sure."

"I'm sorry I haven't returned your phone calls. About two, three weeks after you were here last time, I got a call from my Omega Logic buyer. Now I didn't tell him—I didn't tell anybody—but he'd heard I was going to do some work for you, and he asked me to pass on it. Back off, turn you down, not take your order. Now, that's an illegal restraint of trade, as far as I know, but business is business, and I'm pretty small-time. Omega is thirty percent of my revenues, so they're the eight-hundred-pound gorilla here. I don't know what's between you, but you want my opinion?"

"Yeah, 'cause I'm not sure what's between us either."

"My orders for Omega are down twenty percent from last year. Their stock is flat as Nebraska. I think they're getting paranoid—they see threats from all sides, even a little guy like you."

Andy thought about this. It just didn't make sense. No way in the world was a small start-up with only two hundred grand in the bank a threat to a six-hundred-million-dollar company. That wouldn't be paranoia, that would be delusion. Something else was going on—somebody at Omega didn't want Andy to do this kit deal . . . or somebody friendly with Omega. It wasn't too hard to figure this went back to La Honda.

But how did Omega find out that Andy had struck a deal with San Juan Cast & Die? Andy's instinct was to believe Porter when he said he hadn't told anyone.

Andy had told only four people: Alisa, Tiny, Salman, and Conrad Goss.

"Hey, you okay?" the president said, snapping his fingers in the air.

Andy focused. "Sorry . . . I'm fine."

"Maybe we can try again in six months."

Andy stood up and drifted toward the door. "Sure, sure," he said, not even hearing himself.

8

Standard, Regular,
Normal, and Legal

His pants would stick to the booth vinyl. His palms would stick to the linoleum tabletops. There was nothing on the menu worth eating. By the end of a meal, a dozen of the flimsy little paper napkins they gave you to wipe your hands with would be wadded up amid the dishes. He'd push them toward the aisle, hoping someone would come along mid-meal and take them away. Conrad Goss hadn't come this far in life to keep eating lunch at a place like the Peninsula Creamery.

But on this day, when he sat down, it didn't seem quite so dingy, quite so . . . in focus. The atmosphere wasn't as glaring, and the table was set with white cloth napkins. It made waiting for Francis not as intolerable. Francis had asked to meet him at 1:00; it was now 1:20, and the waitress was giving Conrad hostile glances for not ordering anything yet. Being Francis's accountant had its share of headaches. But it also had more than its share of benefits—oh yes, it certainly did. Francis Benoit had cut Conrad Goss in on some IPOs the last few years, and Conrad had doubled his assets. It wasn't eight million—how wonderful that had sounded, just to pretend it!—but it was nearing a million, and this latest deal with Francis would put him over. The idea of that, *oh*—his whole life Conrad had wanted to say he was a millionaire. And that he wanted it so much scared him. Even though Francis said this deal was a sure thing, guaranteed, Conrad still had the sense that it was a whole lot riskier than IPOs.

"So what's the latest?" Francis asked, when he finally slid into the booth ten minutes later.

"For crying out loud, you're a half hour late. You're always a half hour late."

Francis smiled and signaled to the waitress. "Then why don't you just show up a half hour late too?"

Conrad didn't want to let it go; he wanted Francis to recognize how much Conrad hated getting the runaround. It had always been this way. Francis never told him where his money came from or where it was headed, the kinds of things an accountant needed to know. "I'm on top of it," Francis always said. Even all those IPOs were a form of torture: Francis would give Conrad a stock symbol, but he would never explain who the company was or what they built. Conrad just had to invest on blind faith. The result was that after six years of being his accountant, Conrad still didn't trust Francis.

"So what's the latest?" Francis asked again.

"I don't know. I haven't heard anything from them in a while."

"Has he come back to you about that kit strategy?"

Conrad shook his head. "Do you think he would go ahead and not tell me?"

"Maybe. That's what I'm afraid of. How about the software— have you seen a recent demo?"

"He hasn't shown me anything for six weeks."

Francis said, "That's too long. Have you asked for updates?"

"He said he would rather give me a tour of the full alpha when they have it, rather than calling me every day with minor advances."

"Dang."

"What do you think he's up to?"

"He's cut you off. He's probably wheeling and dealing behind your back right now. You've got to get back on his good side."

"What do you think I ought to do?"

"Encourage him. Tell him to put on the full-court press. Admit you were wrong about stalling the kits, suggest he try to license right away, and make sure he gives you a daily update. You've gotta know his moves. Without that information, you're in the cold."

"But six weeks ago, you told me to squash any deals. I thought we didn't want him to enter into a licensing contract."

"We don't."

"Then why encourage him?"

"Don't worry. He won't get a deal with anyone. It's too big of an investment. He's a stranger to them. There's no momentum behind his product. Believe me, he'll fail. Deals aren't that easy to strike."

Conrad hated the way Francis talked as if he was just giving advice, as if he didn't have anything at stake in this. "So, Francis?"

"What?"

"Our deal is still on, right?"

"A deal's a deal, isn't it?"

"Well, sure, it's just that, well, you haven't *referred* to it in a while, as if maybe you forgot about it."

"Do I forget things?"

"No, but . . . you talk about this company as if I own the damn thing."

"But you do own it. Sixty-three percent, I believe you said."

"Sure I own it, technically. For now. I just want to make sure our deal is still on, that's all. Whatever I spend, plus twenty-five percent, right?"

"I said so, didn't I?"

A deal's a deal, isn't it? "Yeah, a deal's a deal. But Francis . . . we never said, we never agreed on *when,* at what time, we would execute the deal. This week, this month, this year?"

"Soon enough."

"I'd like to know, I need to plan how long the money will be tied up. . . ."

"Just trust me, all right?"

There it was again. Conrad could tell he wasn't going to get anywhere with this, so he tried another angle. "So, what do you think you're going to do with the company, down the road?"

Francis stared hard at Conrad. "I don't know. What do *you* think I'm going to do with it?"

Conrad chuckled nervously. "Well, sometimes I think you're going to run it into the ground."

"And why do you think that?"

"I don't know. Squashing the deals and all that."

Francis grinned. "That seems an awful waste of money, doesn't it?"

"Sure does." But that was the whole point! Only a person with a lot of money that he didn't care about would drive a company into the ground. Conrad thought Francis fit that bill. "Sometimes I think you're trying to let them get as close as possible to success before squashing them."

"Let me ask you something, Conrad. As long as we have our little deal, as long as you get your twenty-five percent on the top, what business is it to you what I do with the company? Christ, like twenty-five percent isn't enough."

"Well, jeez, I'm just interested, I do *own* the company, like you said. I think an owner has a natural curiosity."

Francis stood up abruptly.

"Aren't you going to eat lunch?" Conrad said.

"Naw," Francis said. He looked around the restaurant. It had been refurbished since his last visit. He could hear Simon and Garfunkel playing out of classic chrome Seeburg teardrop speakers mounted over every booth. The windows were painted with candy stripes. And the lighting—above each table hung a pink glass globe, while track lights along the upper walls had been aimed at the ceiling. In refurbishing the place, the owners had scoured the authenticity right out of it. He didn't want to eat here anymore.

He told Conrad, "My stomach doesn't feel so good lately."

"Just order light."

"Naw. We'll talk again soon, okay?"

. . .

Andy Caspar began his search for a licensor with the few companies that, in the past year, had agreed to license the Apple Macintosh operating system to make Mac clones. Andy knew he couldn't approach the major manufacturers of Intel-based computers running Windows software, since that was exactly the syndicate the web computer would eventually undermine. There was a current shortage of Intel chips, and it didn't take much to suddenly find your chip orders were late being delivered. Nobody was going to risk pissing off Intel or Microsoft.

The next logical choice would have been Apple Computer, but they seemed, from a distance, to be in dire straits. Their chief financial officer had just resigned in a bitter dispute with the CEO, and the biannual rumors of the company's demise were floating around the industry again. On top of that, Apple had spent half their war chest developing the handheld Newton personal digital assistant, which never became the ubiquitous hit the company was hoping for and had cost the previous CEO his job. Andy couldn't imagine that Apple would take another chance on a whole new product category.

So this left the Mac clone manufacturers. They had raised all this money in the past year to build Macintoshes, only to enter the market at a time when the Mac seemed doomed. Andy was gambling that these companies would be desperate to find some other piece of hardware to manufacture.

One of these companies, Star Computer, was based in Taiwan but had a corporate office on Montgomery Street in San Francisco. Andy naturally began with them. He drove up to the city, parked underground, took an elevator thirty floors up, and after waiting half an hour gave a demonstration to three Asian men, each of whose business cards listed their title as "President, Dept. of International Liaison." Andy didn't know what that meant, and he didn't understand how there could be three presidents of one department, but by now Andy had a demo that really worked, and it knocked their socks off. After running through the different features of the PowerStation, Andy walked over to one of Star Computer's Mac clones and inserted a floppy disk with Tiny's Hypnotizer on it, and suddenly this clone was running all the PowerStation utilities. These three men opened their mouths and were struck nearly silent, because the clone Andy had just hypnotized *wasn't even on the market yet*. In fact, one of the reasons Star Computer hadn't released it to the market was they were having trouble making all the older-version Macintosh software run properly. Yet here comes this kid into their conference room, and his software works perfectly, without a glitch! So the men nodded and made kind comments and suggested Andy return in a couple of days to meet with some more important people.

In the meantime, Andy did a little research on the internet on Star Computer. He discovered that they were only a couple of years old, but they had raised half a billion dollars. The money had come from half a dozen chip manufacturers in Taiwan. So Andy looked into those chip manufacturers, and it turned out that they used to make Intel-clone chips, under a license from Intel, but that Intel had sued them for violating unspecified conditions of the license. Andy could read between the lines: under that licensing contract, they probably weren't allowed to export their Intel clones to America, but had done it anyway. As part of the settlement, in which they admitted no wrongdoing, the six chip companies lost their licenses with Intel. So they created Star Computer, and were now manufacturing chips for Star. Well, this didn't bode very well for Andy. Here he was, begging to license the PowerStation to a company that had already violated its license with Intel, and may even be violating its license with Apple. Suddenly Andy realized how far in over his head he was. What if Star took his technology and didn't pay him, what would he do? They were all the way over in Taiwan! It would take a team of lawyers and a lot of clout in Washington and—well, Andy wasn't sure what else, he didn't have any experience in this. But if *Intel* couldn't even stop them, then how the heck was *he* going to enforce a deal?

Andy went back to Star a few more times, meeting with successive layers of management, running through his product. They wanted to send his prototype model to Taiwan for their CEO to look at. Andy refused, and it made him really nervous.

Then he waited. After a few more days, they asked him back and told him that they liked his product, but that it seemed just too risky for them. They didn't want to be the only company in this web computer market. The market needed momentum, it needed hype. In particular, they wanted software companies to be writing utilities for the operating system. Andy explained that the software companies wouldn't write utilities until they knew there would be a manufacturer, but it didn't help. So then Star suggested that Andy work with CompuServe or America Online, or one of the internet providers. If, for instance, America Online had a version of their

interface for the PowerStation, then Star would be a lot more in-
clined to strike a deal.

After this gauntlet of meetings, Andy softened in his attitude
toward Conrad Goss and began to communicate with him again.
Conrad had been nothing but encouraging of late, and advocated a
full-court press on striking deals. He'd even admitted he had been
wrong in stalling the kit strategy, so the more Andy thought about
it, the less it made sense that Conrad had snitched to Omega. The
guy had two hundred and fifty grand in the company—what
greater sign of loyalty did Andy need? Andy eventually came to
believe that the president of San Juan Cast & Die must have called
Omega to check Andy's references, and the story slipped out that
way. It was Andy's own fault—he'd mentioned to the president
that he used to work at Omega. It was logical, wasn't it, that the
president would do his homework?

So Andy spent the next week holed up in a Best Western motel in
Vienna, Virginia, the home of America Online, eating two meals a
day at the Denny's restaurant on the ground floor and spending his
evenings dialed in to Salman's server while MTV played in the
background. Getting away from Silicon Valley for the first time in
so long made him reflect on what he'd been through. He couldn't
believe how much had happened. The stress of it all made him
hyper to the point where he couldn't sleep more than a couple
hours a night. And he missed Alisa, so he called her often.

"I hear more from you when you're across the country than
when you're sleeping in the next room," she said one night. The
tone in her voice was distant, not warm. Not a night to make jokes
about Denny's.

"I've got more downtime here," Andy said, "less for me to do at
night."

"You missed my point entirely," she said.

"I did?"

She didn't say anything, just let him figure it out.

"Oh," he said. "You're wondering why you don't see more of
me when I'm at home."

"Well, that's a little bit overanalytical—let me check with the
judges . . . Yes, they're going to give it to you, Andy, but the
answer we were looking for was just that I want to see you more."

"All right." As soon as he heard his own words he knew they were the wrong thing to say. He should have said, *I want to see you more too.* And he did, but he kept thinking about Salman, and he didn't want to create an expectation he couldn't fulfill.

With cynicism, she said, "Well, that's reassuring, that's it's *all right* with you that I want to see you more."

Andy sighed. "*Alisa* . . ."

"What?"

"I thought—we talked about this, didn't we? I've been honest from the start. . . . My work right now, it would detract from a serious relationship."

"Well, that's very reasonable of you, isn't it?"

"Did I say something wrong?"

"It's not wrong, Andy—it's just very *controlling.* . . . I would love to think a man's feelings for me would overwhelm his intelligent decision making, but I suppose that's improbable when the man in question is the Great Brain."

"I'm not controlling my feelings—"

"You're not?" Doubtful, hurt.

"*No.* I'm just simultaneously feeling what it would be like if we fell in love with each other and then my work kept us apart. I don't want to do that to you . . . that would be *unfair* to you."

"You're not protecting *me,* you're protecting your work. You're avoiding a distraction."

"You're not a *distraction,* Alisa. You're a woman I am starting to care about."

"Well, don't protect me. I can protect myself."

"Okay, but then don't you push this to happen faster than it has the time and space to happen. Okay?"

"Okay . . ."

Andy heard the drift in her voice. "What? What is it?"

"Andy?"

"What?"

"So you think it's going to happen?"

"*Alisa!*"

"Sorry . . . sorry. So, what's it like there, in Virginia?"

Andy drew open the gauzy window curtain and looked out. "Well, it's kinda scary. Because *it's no different at all* from looking out the window on El Camino Real. Car dealerships, minimalls, fast food. I could be anywhere. I don't know what to make of it. We live in Franchiseland."

"How are your meetings going?"

"They're all alike. Same demo, same strategic questions, same wonderings aloud. Only the names and faces change. It's hard to remember everyone. They're all my age, or even younger, and they're as new at this as I am. I take their business cards and when they're not looking I write down memorable details on the back, to help me remember who the card comes from. Here's one: umber hair, cropped; keeps a shoe-phone in his briefcase; showed me pictures of family skiing in Alps."

"The Alps? A guy like that must be pretty high up in the organization. Sounds like you're getting through."

"Or beating them down with persistence."

After two days of meetings, America Online had told Andy that they were reluctant. They didn't want to spend much time and money developing a PowerStation interface unless they knew for certain that someone was going to build the device. If he had a manufacturer guaranteeing units, they might jump on board.

Andy told them, "But Star Computer says *they'll* jump on board if you promise to write an interface." Andy spent the next two days on the phone with both companies, trying to get either one to jump first. That's all it seemed to take—if one jumped, the other would follow. But nobody wanted to jump first. It was an infinite loop again: you can't get hardware unless there's software already written, but software people won't write code unless there's hardware to run it. Andy couldn't crack it. It would take a big hitter to close the deal, somebody with a lot of clout that these companies could trust. Andy was just an outsider.

So he changed gears. He pitched to America Online that they buy his company, Universe, outright. If they bought Universe, then they could sign a deal with Star Computer directly, removing the middleman. Well, this pitch was a whole different angle involving numerous departments, and it led to two more days of meetings, at the end of which the answer was the same: if Andy had a licensing deal with Star Computer, then America Online would be happy to buy Universe, while Star Computer would be happy to license from

America Online if they bought Universe. But nobody would pull the trigger. Andy lay on his king-size bed staring at the ceiling for two more days, waiting for a break.

"Come home," Alisa told him, and so he did.

"Is the deal dead?" Salman asked, when Andy got back to the office.

"It's still afloat, but the wind is out of the sails."

"So there's still a chance?"

Andy sighed. "I get the feeling . . . it's like, all it would take would be some hype, some fear. . . . These guys I'm talking to, they can take it or leave it. The PowerStation isn't *crucial* to them. You know how we get afraid we're going to be left out, going to be left behind?"

"Mmmm."

"We need *them* to feel that way. Like, 'If we don't buy Universe, somebody else will.' I think, I *feel*, like all it would take would be a big article in the newspaper or a speech by some CEO pronouncing the category of web computers as the next big growth area. Something just to start the hubbub. A columnist endorsing the concept."

"Mmmm . . . Hey!"

"What?"

"I got it! Wait—no, naw, wouldn't work."

"What? Tell me anyway."

"Naw, sorry, totally ridiculous. Forget it."

"Just tell me, will you? Maybe your idea is stupid, but maybe it will trigger an idea in me that *isn't* stupid. Just brainstorm, will you?"

"Okay, all right. So . . . I was thinking, 'get a product placement in a movie.' "

"Put the PowerStation in a movie?"

"Mmmm."

"That's ridiculous!"

"I know, but— How about you? It give you any ideas?"

Andy thought for a moment. Nothing came. "We could just take out an ad during next year's Super Bowl."

"Mmmm. Or we could shine a picture of the PowerStation with a big spotlight onto the moon. Then everybody would look up and go 'hey!'."

"Or we could kidnap the president and make 'a PowerStation on every school desk' one of the ransom demands."

"There you go." Salman looked down. "We're way in over our heads, aren't we?"

"Just remember one thing. I'm in those meetings and I start thinking, 'What the hell do I know about a licensing deal?' So I remember: all these people we talk to—all the CEOs and marketing executives who control the jobs of hundreds of workers—these guys are just people like you and me. They went to school, got a job, worked up. They wonder the same things we wonder, they have the same fears. They're just doing their job. They're not geniuses and they don't have it out for us. They're just trying to get by and not fuck up."

. . .

"Talk to me."

"Francis?"

"You dialed my number, didn't you?"

"This is Conrad."

"I know your voice."

"Andy was just here. He's back from Virginia."

Francis didn't say anything.

Conrad went on. "After a couple days, he offered the company to them."

"To buy it?"

"Right."

"What'd they say?"

"Well, they said no. But the way Andy described it, they were right on the cliff. He said it just needs a nudge. I looked it up—America Online has bought about six companies this year already. They pull the trigger pretty fast."

"Did they talk price?"

"Price?"

"Yeah, price per share."

Conrad didn't remember Andy mentioning it. "He didn't say anything about price."

Francis said, "Then they're not as close as he thinks. We've got time."

"You sure? Offering the company, after all . . . we don't want something to happen under our noses."

"I suppose you're right. Thanks. Perhaps I should make my move. I need a few days. Don't go out of town."

"I'm not going anywhere. Hey, Francis, are you really going to run them into the ground?"

"Look, just let me handle this, okay? I got enough balls in the air without you."

"Well, I was thinking . . . maybe I could hang on to a few shares, maybe ten percent, stay in the game, hang around, be part of the excitement. . . . That is, if you're not going to run them into the ground."

"A deal was a deal, no changes."

"Sure, I was just thinking, though . . . I mean, it *is* my company right now."

"Oh, don't start thinking that way. I'm counting on you."

"A little *slice*?"

"*Please*. We've got a deal, Conrad. Let it be."

. . .

Gordon "Papa" Lewis was the chairman of the board of Omega Logic, Inc., and he lived for moments like this one, as he strode out of the boardroom and grabbed the first lackey standing around outside and ordered, "You know who I am, right? Good. Now go in the boardroom and sit down beside Lloyd Acheson and don't let him out of your sight and don't you dare let him touch a telephone. I'll be back in fifteen minutes. Treat him like just another guy who walked in off the street and snuck up here and don't ask me any questions. Got it?"

The lackey nodded with fear and hustled off in the direction Papa Lewis was pointing.

Other board members were filing out of the conference room, standing around Papa Lewis to discuss what had just happened. Lewis waved them off. "Let me handle this," he said. "Stay away from the phones. Don't leave the building. If a reporter sees you leave the building they'll know our meeting is over and we've got some announcement. I don't want them even to suspect it. Not a word gets out until the market closes at one-thirty." It was Friday mid-morning. If they kept this under wraps until the afternoon, they would have all weekend to address the situation before the stock reopened for trading.

Papa Lewis marched down the hall to his office. On the way in, he told his assistant to get the director of media relations and the general counsel of the legal department on the phone right away.

"You want them in conference?"

"One at a time."

He sat down behind his desk and tipped back in his chair with his feet on the edge of the desk.

The director of media relations came on the line, and Lewis told him, "I don't care if you're in the middle of taking a piss, stop what you're doing and get up here in two minutes. Don't talk to anyone on the way."

Meanwhile, the general counsel was on hold. Lewis told him, "I want you to do an exit interview for Lloyd Acheson, right now, today. Do it yourself, don't send one of your grunts—draw up the paperwork within a half hour. Don't give him an inch on the non-competes. Make him sign it."

There was a television recessed into the bookshelf across the room. Papa Lewis pulled a remote control out from a drawer and turned the television on, then hit Play for the VCR. A videotape of highlights from the Detroit Lions superstar running back Barry Sanders came on, juking and dancing and banging through men twice his size. Sweep right, nothing there, reverse direction, spin through the linebacker's hands, leap over a safety, accelerate toward the end zone. Being the chairman was usually a fairly cushy role except for times like these, and Papa Lewis liked to get psyched up. He went over to the window and slid it open to let in some fresh air. The Omega buildings were built like greenhouses, so the air inside required so much cooling that Papa Lewis sometimes felt like he was in an airplane. His sliding glass window had been installed in violation of several fire and safety codes, but it was one of the conditions of his chairmanship and had been written into his contract.

Papa Lewis had the saggy neck, chunky chin, and wide-set eyes of a Brahma bull. He was notorious for never being afraid of a fight, and that reputation usually kept anyone from trying to pick one with him. He was living proof that a guy could be supercompetitive without having to be an asshole. He was getting older, but the trick to getting older was not to eat when you weren't hungry and not to sit down when you weren't tired and not to pay others to do things you could do yourself.

The director of media relations popped into his office.

"I sure love Barry Sanders," Papa Lewis exclaimed. He turned the sound down but let the tape continue to play.

"What's going on?"

"We've got a hot one. Lloyd's out, ASAP."

"Amicable or hostile?"

"Well, we're all in agreement, there's no debate on his severance package, but I'm treating him hostile anyway."

"Why's that?"

"Because I want it to look that way. If we treat him hostile, the press will think we've forced him out. We'll look decisive—the board making a move for the best, give the stock a boost, the whole rigamarole."

"I couldn't agree more. But do you mind me asking if he was really forced out?"

"Hell, no, he wasn't forced out, but he didn't quit on us straight away, either. He called a special meeting of the board, at which he gives us a condition, holds us hostage: he says Omega can't stay up with Intel and that we ought to change strategy. If we don't agree to the change, he'll resign."

"And you didn't agree?"

"Hell, no! He wanted Omega to start making smaller computers, for more specific purposes. Maybe that's not a bad strategy if you were starting out today, but Omega's got 'bigger and faster' in its bones. It'd be like a bear trying to learn to ride a bicycle. We could do it, it's not impossible, but we'd sure look funny and we'd never be very good at it. Omega has to play to its strengths. That's what the board decided, and Lloyd's out and now we gotta prepare a statement. He's all in a tiff, wants to speak his mind to the press. Christ, that would be a disaster! Come on, let's go." Papa Lewis jumped out of his chair and left the room with the director of media relations still staring at his chair.

On the way down the hall, the director of media relations caught up with him. "There's a rumor going around downstairs . . ." he said.

"I imagine there's a hundred rumors going around right now. Don't do anything to inflame them."

"There's this one about the six eighty-six . . . about it being in trouble . . . or it's a disappointment—something like that. I need to know about these things, if something's going on."

Lewis stopped abruptly. He gave the director of media relations a fierce stare. "The six eighty-six is the most technologically superior chip ever invented, and it's right on schedule." There was nothing untrue in his words.

"I'm in the dark here . . . If there's something, you can't hide it from me."

"Will you listen to me, goddamnit! You're not in the dark. There's no story. Forget about the six eighty-six, will you? Now I'm going to go make a phone call. You stand here and don't move until I come back. Right here. Okay?" Papa Lewis didn't wait for an answer. He dove into the nearest office and kicked some vice president out. He pulled out his cellular phone and dialed Hank Menzinger's office. He got Menzinger's answering machine, so he hung up and dialed again, this time to Menzinger's cellular phone. Hank picked up on the second ring.

"Menzinger? This is Gordon Lewis. I've got a situation over here that's confidential right now, but I need to ask you a favor—"

"What kind of situation?"

"No, I can't *tell* you about it. You'll know soon enough. You know how it is. Fiduciary duty and all that crap—"

"What is it, a merger?"

"No, don't ask, no point to it. Listen, one of the side effects of our situation is you're going to get the bright lights for the next few weeks about the six eighty-six project. Your answer is, 'No comment.' I want a blackout until I give the green light."

"You can't—I can't—a *blackout?* Come on, that makes me look weak, makes me look scared. Deal me in, Papa. I can't—"

"I'm used to getting what I expect."

"But I've got a journalist here. She's putting out a weekly column, if we interrupt her it looks bad . . ."

"This would be a good time for her to take a vacation. Blackout, Menzinger. Blackout. Don't give this fire any wood to burn, it'll die down, and I gotta hop."

"Let me at least give her a concrete date to resume her access. Next Friday?"

"No date. Wait for my call."

"She's got to plan, schedule . . . the bitterness this will create . . . two weeks?"

"No, nothing firm."

"You've got some nerve calling me up out of the blue and telling me how to run my organization."

"Aww, put a cork in it."

"I'm gonna call Lloyd—"

"Don't second-guess me, Menzinger. I'm gone."

Papa Lewis closed his cellular phone and slipped it back into his breast pocket. He took a deep breath, then charged out of the office and tapped the director of media relations on the shoulder and marched into the boardroom, where Lloyd Acheson was sitting with a glass of water, looking out onto the marshlands of San Francisco Bay. "All right, Lloyd, you know the drill, before we sign some paperwork and before I take you out for a farewell drink we gotta agree upon a statement, and I don't have to tell you that if you say what you want to say then we get hurt, and that's not gonna happen—so let's not dick around, okay?" Papa Lewis turned to his left and glared at the lackey. "You still here?" he said, and the guy scuttled off.

"You're treating me hostile," Lloyd said.

"No, we're not. We're just covering our asses. You'd do the same in my spot."

Lloyd said, "You want the press to presume you forced me out."

"Look, the press can put two and two together on their own, but we don't have to give them the chalk and the blackboard too. I just want to make a simple statement that you've resigned, on your own initiative—"

"Good."

"Wait, hear me out, *on your own initiative,* nobody's forced you out. But I want you to say you're resigning in the best interests of the company . . . that as a CEO you've had your fill and you took us to this level and we need someone else from here on out. Standard stuff. Boilerplate resignation. Ink's already dry."

"But that's not the *truth*, Papa. I have a vision for this company. You just don't want to hear it. But the press will."

"Look, Lloyd, we take the gloves off, we both get black eyes. Think it through. You say to the press what you told the board this morning, then our stock drops ten percent first thing Monday morning and I come back with a statement about all the dumb decisions you made in the past six years so that you never work in this industry again. Is that what you want? I don't think so, so don't be dumb and let's work this out."

"What do you propose?"

"Give us a week. You make one short terse statement today, nothing critical. Let us appoint a successor, steady the boat. Next Friday, after the market closes, you can speak your mind and we won't come after you."

"Wednesday."

Papa Lewis looked across at the director of media relations. "Can you blanket the media before Wednesday? I want someone to *personally* call every reporter and every columnist and every editor in America, I don't care what it costs, hire some goddamn phone-sex girls if you have to. Everybody hears our side before Wednesday."

The director of media relations nodded in agreement. "But not Wednesday afternoon. Wednesday *night*. *Business Week* closes their editorial at nine o'clock Eastern. I want our side only."

Papa turned to Lloyd. "Okay, six P.M. our time Wednesday, I assume you can live with that?"

Lloyd said that he could. Then he added, "But I want to tell the press *today* that I will have a comment next Wednesday night."

"No go on that. You can say you'll have a comment in 'the future,' but not where and when."

"Okay, how about 'shortly'?"

"You'll have a comment *shortly*?" Papa Lewis turned to the director of media relations. "What do you think?"

He answered, " 'Soon' would be better than 'shortly.' 'Shortly' sounds like 'in a few hours.' He can have a comment 'soon.' "

Papa turned back to Lloyd. "Okay, you can say you will make a statement 'soon.' Are we done here? I don't have to tell you guys this is going to be hot. We've got—" Papa looked down at his watch. "We've got an hour and twenty minutes till the market closes. What do you say we go down the hall to my office and see if there's a basketball game on, and that's an order, not an invitation." Papa Lewis stood up. He looked out onto the marshlands and the hazy bay beyond. A flock of egrets was moving north, flying about twenty feet above the marsh. Papa Lewis briefly considered going hunting this weekend, then the reality of finding a successor to Lloyd sank in.

Papa and Lloyd went back to Papa's office. Papa found a basketball game on ESPN, Alabama versus Missouri, two teams he knew nothing about. They watched for a while. "Let's make this interesting," Papa said. "How about a bet?"

"I still haven't figured out which team is 'Bama."

"The team in red. What do you say, hundred bucks to the winner, if you win by five or less. If the spread is six to ten points, then two hundred. Eleven to fifteen points, four hundred. Sixteen to twenty, eight hundred, et cetera. Take your pick of teams."

"I'll take 'Bama."

"Big mistake. 'Bama's got no rebounding. Mizzou's gonna kick their butt." God, how Papa Lewis loved being in the fray again.

"Watch," Lloyd said. "Mizzou's big men can't shoot free throws. Late in the game it's gonna kill them."

Missouri took a ten-point lead into the half.

Papa said, "So you got any ideas for a successor?"

"I'm not sure we should be talking about this."

"I'm just asking. So, I know you got an offer or something, or else you wouldn't have given us an ultimatum this morning. What's doing?"

"Nothing's doing. It was just suddenly clear to me, that's all."

Papa didn't believe that for a second. Lloyd Acheson had a plan, that was certain. He didn't look very stressed for a CEO who just resigned amid controversy.

In the second half, several Missouri forwards got in foul trouble, and Alabama hit all their foul shots to pull away. With a minute to go and Alabama up by five, Papa said, "Double or nothing—'Bama wins by less than five."

"Done," Lloyd agreed. It came down to a meaningless two foul shots, with Alabama up by four points and three seconds on the clock. If the shooter made one shot, Lloyd won a hundred on the first bet, doubled to two hundred. If he made both foul shots and Alabama won by six, he won two hundred on the first bet, doubled to four hundred. But if he sank neither, Lloyd won nothing. Lloyd stood up. "Come on, Crimson Tide!" It was the most emotion he'd shown all day. But the shooter missed both.

The two men headed downstairs, escorted by several assistants and members of the media team. On the ground floor off the front lobby was a briefing room full of reporters who had been called in during the last half hour. You could hear their buzz from down the hall. The event was also being broadcast on videoconferencing equipment to analysts on Wall Street. When the two men entered, they were besieged by questions and the popping of camera flashes. Papa Lewis felt Lloyd Acheson grab for his arm.

. . .

On Saturday morning, Hank Menzinger pulled into the parking lot at La Honda and saw Nell Kirkham's car in the lot. He hadn't been able to contact her the afternoon before, which had been just fine with him, since at the time he didn't have any idea what Omega's situation was. Now Lloyd's resignation was all over the papers.

Hank didn't bother stopping by his office. He went right to lab A, looking for Nell Kirkham. The lab was quiet. Only David Kim was in there. "Have you seen Nell Kirkham?" Hank asked.

David Kim looked up from the keyboard only briefly. "Uh, I just saw her down in the cafeteria with Link Smith."

Hank found Link Smith in the cafeteria eating a bagel. "I thought Nell Kirkham was with you," he said.

Link Smith looked at Hank for a long time.

"David Kim said she was with you," Hank said.

"Oh . . . she *was* with me, but she went up to Francis's office to talk with the advanced logic unit team."

Hank took the tunnel under the quad to the back staircase of the north building. He walked up the two flights of stairs and down the hall to Francis's office. The door was open. Landy Eng was sitting at Francis's desk, typing into his computer.

"Link Smith just said Nell Kirkham was over here," Hank said. "She just went down to lab A."

"With the ALU team?"

"Uhh . . . right. Right."

Hank ran back downstairs and halfway across the quad, hoping to catch Nell before she interviewed any more of the 686 team, when he suddenly realized he'd been tricked into the infinite loop prank again. Didn't these men have any respect? What a time!

At that moment, Nell Kirkham was where she had been all morning: waiting in Hank Menzinger's anteroom. She'd been talking with her editor on her cellular phone. The *Mercury* was a union paper, and as a member of the union she wasn't supposed to work weekends—the recently renegotiated labor contract was very strict on this—even though she was the logical one to get the La Honda angle on Lloyd's resignation. That morning her editor had assigned another staffer to make her calls, but no way was Nell going to let some other writer get her story. She wouldn't tell her editor where she was. When Hank lumbered in, he nearly tripped over her.

"Why, you're *here*," he said. "Thank *god*."

Nell gave him five seconds to sit down and get settled. "Will Lloyd Acheson resign from La Honda, too?" she charged.

"Look, Nell, hold on, whoa, this is a sensitive time around here. . . . I know you've got your copy to get out, but you're going to have to give us a few days to get our act together—" He looked uncomfortable, shifting his weight in his seat from side to side. He was riding his chair more than sitting in it.

"So I assume you haven't spoken with Lloyd since his resignation?"

"I can't comment. Look, Nell—"

"So I was right, you haven't spoken—"

"Now hold on, I didn't say whether I had spoken with Lloyd or not."

She kept peppering him, hoping he would say something out of frustration. "Is the funding of the six eighty-six in jeopardy? Do you think his resignation could have anything to do with the six eighty-six? Is there any truth to the rumors that the six eighty-six project is in trouble?"

"Stop, hold on . . . a few days, Nell. I can't comment on anything. . . . It's the weekend, you understand—some of our board members are all over the country. . . . I'm afraid what I'm going to have to do, Nell, I'm going to have to revoke your press privileges around here for a few days, until this settles down. I'm sure you understand."

"You can't do that! You can't just *revoke* my access—it's not something you turn on and off. The whole point—the *whole* point of hanging around here for the past eight months was so that I would have the full story when something significant happened—"

"I'm sorry—"

"And the first significant event occurs, and you tell me the deal is off!"

"The deal's not off. A few days, that's all I'm saying. I can talk again on Thursday."

"The deal was start-to-finish access. I've put up with the most mundane drama in the history of the newspaper, for what? For *this*?"

"Don't be naïve. You knew darn well this would happen if we had to protect our sponsors."

Nell saw an angle. "Your *sponsors*? So is this blackout on your orders or on Omega's orders?"

"What does that matter? That's irrelevant. It's common courtesy to respect a sponsor's wishes in this situation."

"Who runs this place, you or Omega?"

"I'm not going to comment on that. *Thursday*. You and I should talk on Thursday."

Nell *had* to get this story. If she didn't get at least a quote to build a story on, her editor would probably run some AP reporter's analysis. This was her chance. She took a stab. "I'm writing a column for tomorrow's edition in which several industry experts speculate that Lloyd Acheson resigned because he must know something about the six eighty-six design being in trouble." She'd just made that up. "Do you want me to print that without any rebuttal? How is Omega going to feel come Monday, when the rumor of six eighty-six's troubles hits the market, and Omega finds out you failed to defend the project?"

She watched Hank stew on that for a moment. It was getting

harder and harder for him to hold his tongue. He was now sitting on his hands. He said, "You've been covering the six eighty-six closer than anyone. Tell me—have you seen any signs of trouble?"

She hadn't, but she didn't say that. "So you insist that the project is still on schedule?"

"Well, you've seen the schedules on the bulletin board in the hallway. What do you mean, 'Is it on schedule?'—of course it's on schedule."

She said, "And as far as you've been notified, the six eighty-six is still central to Omega's plans?"

"I'm not going to touch that, Nell."

"What about Lloyd's speech yesterday? Among other things, he said that 'in today's market, the right direction is to go small and specific.' Doesn't that seem to contradict the direction of the six eighty-six?"

"No comment."

"When are you going to be able to comment? Monday?"

"*Thursday*. Believe me, Nell, on Thursday I will tell you more than you want to know."

"I need this story *today*. All year I've been good to you."

"And we've been good to you. Call me Thursday. You're going to have to go now."

She stood up. She didn't give him the courtesy of a good-bye. She didn't have enough for a story, but she would have to fake it and try to get it past her editor anyway.

. . .

When he read in the Sunday paper that Lloyd Acheson had proclaimed "small and specific" as the next wave of computing, Andy Caspar came into the office at six A.M. Monday to fax an enlarged photocopy of the article to America Online. "I'm telling you," he told his contact person in Virginia, "the dam's gonna burst, and when it does you'll be lucky if you can still get me on the phone." His contact promised to circulate the article and add a discussion of it to the agenda for a strategy meeting to be held that afternoon. "Call me before you go home tonight," Andy made him promise, then hung up and dialed the *San Jose Mercury News*. He asked the operator to be transferred to Nell Kirkham. He reached her voice mail and after a long preamble reminding her why his name might sound familiar asked her to return his call.

"Did you see it?" he asked Salman before his partner could sit down. Salman had spent Sunday with his family.

"Mmmm."

"The very *king* of iron, talking about the end of an era!"

"Mmmm—wait, what are you talking about?"

"The article. I thought you saw it."

"Oh . . . I thought you were talking about something else."

"Are you kidding? What else would I be talking about?" Andy said.

"A movie."

"You think I'm *this* excited, jumping up and down as soon as you walk in, all about a *movie*?"

Salman considered this for a moment. "Well, depends upon the movie, I guess."

"Have you ever seen me this excited about a movie?"

"That's my point. You *never* get excited about movies. So if you finally saw a really good movie, then it might release all those years of pent-up thrill you've suppressed. You'd be overjoyed . . . bubbling, giddy—like you are now."

"I don't have years of pent-up thrill!"

"Sure you do. We all do."

"Ahh, forget it." Andy walked back to his desk and threw himself into his chair.

Salman watched him go. "Hey, what was that article you were referring to?"

Around noon, Conrad Goss walked in the front door carrying a briefcase as wide as two briefcases. The team wasn't expecting his visit, but he dropped by now and then.

"Hey Conrad," Andy said. "You buy that briefcase at Price Club? 'Twice the size for the price of a regular briefcase.' "

Salman took it up. "You ought to put a sticker on the girth side. 'Wide Load. Do not pass.' "

Even Tiny put his ten cents in, though he laughed at what he was going to say before he got the sentence out. "Or put it on the SlimFast plan. 'Okay, briefcase, you only get *two* pens today and *one* slice of paper, but you can have all the paper clips you want.'"

Conrad didn't seem to find it funny. "This? It's a standard regular normal legal briefcase," he said.

Andy said, "I always wondered why lawyers have such buff arms . . . and I thought it was something they ate."

"I could have been a lawyer," Salman said, somewhat wistfully.

"What does that have to do with anything?" Andy said.

Before they went off again, Conrad interrupted them. "We need to have a meeting . . . a board meeting, actually . . . a meeting of the board."

"More papers to sign?" Salman said.

"Let's sit down," Conrad said. "We can go over it."

They brought chairs together and sat around Andy's desk. Conrad opened his briefcase and brought out a stack of documents along with a corporate seal. He passed each person a copy of a thick document. It was the shareholder agreement for their company.

"Well, now . . ." Conrad said. "I brought you these just so we have them right here in front of us, in case there are any disputes."

"Disputes?" Andy said. "What's going on?"

"Hold on, I'm getting there. I have to do this by the book. Now, let the record show that all of the stockholders of Universe Corporation are in attendance and—" When Andy made another move to interject, Conrad caught him merely by stopping and looking in his direction. "As the majority stockholder I have called this meeting to order. First item of business: this morning I received an offer to purchase one hundred percent of the shares of Universe Corp. from a California corporation named Everyware Incorporated, for the amount of five hundred thousand dollars, which, let the record show—"

"Who the hell is Everyware?" Andy said. "I haven't heard anything about this!" He jumped out of his chair and paced as he listened to Conrad.

"Now hold on, let me finish. Let the record show that this amount of half a million dollars is a twenty-five percent increase over the previous valuation, only four months prior, and would represent a substantial return on the stock's value—"

"Now what the hell is going on here?"

"In addition—hang on, I'm almost done—this offer is in cash, for a settlement date of as soon as the law allows, which would be in thirty days, and as the shareholder owning just over sixty-three percent of the company, I vote to approve of this offer—"

"Well, we don't!" Andy said.

Finally Conrad faced him. "You don't have to. I control the shares of this company; your vote is inconsequential, but let the record show that the minority shareholders opposed the transaction."

"We're not selling our shares," Andy said.

Salman added, "How much would that be for each of us—about sixty grand?"

Conrad said, "The offer is for one hundred percent of the shares. Look at your shareholder agreement, its standard terms. Minority shareholders are bound to act with the majority block."

"You can't sell our company!"

"I'm sorry, it's not your company."

"There's got to be something illegal about this!"

"Not only is there nothing the least bit illegal about it, there's nothing the least bit out of the ordinary."

"But we don't know the first thing . . . who the hell is Everyware . . . my god . . . this is unfuckingbelievable. . . . Don't we have to do due diligence or something? What about a fairness hearing, and the attorney general?"

"That's fine, Andy. All of that will be done, and it will all be in order, and there is nothing even remotely unfair about earning a return of twenty-five percent in just four months, which is how the attorney general will see it. Grow up, will you? Just because you don't want the company to be sold doesn't give you the right to block it. This deal happens with or without you—you don't have to *sign* any papers, you don't have to *give* your permission, you just have to cash the check when it arrives. Now, my business is done here, gentlemen, I will draw up the appropriate corporate resolution and sign it myself this afternoon. I consider this to have been a very successful investment and it was good doing business with you. Have a nice day." Conrad stood up, smoothed down the sides of his suit, and walked out, his briefcase at his side.

"You can't just *leave!* . . . Oh god, no, I can't—do you believe this?" Andy turned a circle, staring at his office. Nothing seemed different. This was *his* place, how could it belong to anyone else? That calendar over there, that was *his.* This chair, this desk, they were *his.* He had built them with his own hands. The work on his computer, every line of code, it was *his,* wasn't it? Nobody could buy this from him any more than they could buy the rest of his body—this was not something that could be *sold,* this was not something that could be taken away. Andy knew *logically* what it meant to sell the company, but he couldn't *feel* it. He looked around and tried to feel a sense of possession, but it wasn't *possession*—it was him itself. You don't *possess* your hand or your foot. Andy felt so alone, such a stranger to this world. If a wind came it would just push him along. He couldn't feel anything at all. The fire in him had just been put out, like a match blown out. He didn't hurt, he didn't want to cry, he didn't want to yell aloud, and he wasn't hungry; he didn't want to make a joke and he didn't miss Alisa or his parents, and he didn't want to go anywhere or do anything at all.

"Hey, Andy," Salman said. "Let's find out who the fuck Everyware is and go fuck them over."

"We need a lawyer," Andy said. "Does either of you know a lawyer?"

Neither of them did. Andy asked Salman to search SEC filings on the internet to look for Everyware. Meanwhile, he called the secretary of state's office in Santa Clara. It took him five minutes to get a woman on the line. He asked if they could tell him who the officers of a corporation were and where it was located. He was told they couldn't give that information out over the phone. He had to come to the office and fill out a request and pay five dollars. It took a day to process.

"A whole day, just to look something up on your computer?"

He was told the office received numerous requests each day.

"What if I pay ten dollars, can I get it rushed?"

The answer was no, but if he drove to Sacramento, the office there could look it up immediately.

"How come they can look it up on their computer *right away,* while you take a *whole day* to look it up on your computer?"

The woman didn't take kindly to his yelling and hung up.

Salman had searched several news databases, the SEC registration filings, and the Dun & Bradstreet corporate reports for an Everyware, but turned up nothing. "It's probably a new company," he guessed.

Sacramento was 110 miles away, a two-hour drive. Andy could make it before closing. It seemed a total waste of four hours, but he didn't care—he didn't know what else to do and it wouldn't feel right just to sit there waiting for lawyers to return their calls or forms to get processed. Without giving himself a chance to second-guess his action, he picked up his yellow corporate three-ring binder with all of Universe's documents and went down to his car.

He tried not to think of anything, just listen to music, but everything on the radio bothered him. Helplessness was the worst sensation. The team had been through a lot together, and they had been up against long odds, but at every juncture there was always something they could do, even if it was just coding. They couldn't code themselves out of this jam. The whole thing with Conrad seemed like an illusion. It had lasted less than ten minutes, and as Andy drove and stared at the passing landscape it was easy to pretend it *hadn't* happened—it was just a dream or a joke. The transaction was just on paper! It seemed ridiculous that a piece of paper could rule their lives. Some people signed a paper and expected everyone else to follow along. It's just a piece of paper! It can't *change* things, the world isn't any different because some ink got rolled onto a piece of paper. *I am Andy Caspar, and nobody can take that from me.* We live by rules printed on paper. What is a society unless everyone agrees to the rules? *But I do not agree. You cannot take this. We made it. We. It is not for sale.* We all agree to drive on the right-hand side of the road, but it just as easily could be the left. We all agree to drive sixty-five, but this car will go ninety with a touch of pressure. We agree our work can be taken from us by a piece of paper. *But I do not agree.*

Andy got off the freeway when he saw the state capitol building and pulled into a gas station to call for directions. Instead, the telephone book had a map of the state offices, and he made it to the front counter at the secretary of state by 4:30. He filled out a request for a copy of the annual registration filing for Everyware and stood in line. When he got to the counter they told him he needed Everyware's corporate identification number.

"I don't have it. Can't you look it up alphabetically?"

They referred him to a computer terminal across the room, where he could look it up himself. After he had done so, he turned the form in again. The clerk took his five dollars and disappeared through a door behind the counter. Andy had to wait only a few minutes. The clerk came back and slid across the counter a legal-sized photocopy from a microfiche of the registration statement.

Andy looked at it. His hands trembled, but he wasn't surprised. By this point, he wouldn't be surprised by anything. Everyware's corporate officers were Francis Benoit and Lloyd Acheson. The address was somewhere in Hillsborough, probably Lloyd's home. Andy looked at the form again, at the style of the letters typed into the fields. He took the form to a back counter and opened up his yellow binder to the same form for Universe. The typeface was identical. The amount of space between lines was the same. Andy examined the date. He and Salman had signed their Universe filing statement on November 27, as had Conrad Goss. Everyware's filing statement had been signed by Lloyd Acheson, as president and secretary, and Francis Benoit, as vice-president, on November 28.

• • •

Two hours later, Francis Benoit was sitting at his desk in his office at La Honda, trying to calm himself by breathing deeply with his eyes closed, when Andy Caspar burst through his door. His hands were clenched at his side. He didn't look like he had anything left to lose, which is a most dangerous state to be in. For once his presence matched his height.

Francis said, "I kinda thought you might be paying me a visit right about now."

"You're a jerk, Francis. I'm not going to let you get away with this. I'm going to get a lawyer and I'm going to make you wish you'd never bothered with me."

"A *lawyer*? And what are you going to *tell* this lawyer, that you committed a felony by failing to disclose your Hypnotizer code? Yes, I know you deleted that code, and I know you've since tried to profit from it. You're lucky you're not in court right now, Caspar, defending yourself. And don't think you couldn't be there in a flash, if I wanted you there."

"I'll bet you never even told Hank about the code! I'll bet you took it yourself and used it for your own advantage, and despite ten years here you don't give a fuck about La Honda—you're going to leave it to wither without you."

Francis chuckled at Andy's false sympathy for Hank. "Hank knows all I want him to know. But do you think Hank would have understood the ramifications if I *had* shown him the code?"

"You're not getting away that easy! I'll chase down journalists and tell them the whole story, and you'll be ridiculed when everyone learns you've committed the lowest crime of all—plagiarism. That was *our* work, *we* wrote it, *we* fought for it, *we* endured, not you, not *you*."

"Yeah, well, Caspar, you think you've been fucked, then get in line. I built a chip for Omega that was wasted, and for thanks I got to build another. Now you've built a computer that would have been a total waste, too, and you know why? Because you don't have the *weight* to make a deal. You're too small-time. Universe would have died on the vine in the commercial world. You need Lloyd Acheson to make a deal, just as I need him. People don't do deals with technology, and they don't do deals with companies— they do deals with *people*. This may be a new medium and a new economy and a brave new world, but the oldest human patterns still apply: it takes money to make money, same as always."

"What do *you* know about the real world? When have you ever been out in it? You've been here for ten years, insulated, thinking what you want to think."

"Oh, if you could see the look on your face right now, Caspar, just beautiful . . . So you got beat, so you got screwed, so you got cheated, so you got burned. . . . Don't look so surprised to see the primal forces of nature, Caspar. Where's your *history*? You live in a fantasy world, Caspar, where you believe what you want to believe. *Start-ups*—you're dreaming. *Entrepreneurs*—you're dreaming. What is the nature of power, Caspar? Power is like water on a plate of glass. You think you can stick your finger on there and pull away your own little droplet, just your own little undisturbed oasis, and you think you've done it, but then your droplet finds this tiny dry rivulet you missed, and through that travels home to the big droplet, it *crawls* back. That's its *nature,* Caspar, and maybe you can build a fountain and inscribe your name on the base and get the water to squirt from the top for a while, but you can't change its *nature,* which is to crawl back where it came from."

Andy blocked the doorway, his feet spread to the jambs, his arms overhead, grabbing at the molding. "All your rigamarole about the way of the world, the forces of nature, that's just psychological justification to reduce the guilt that will keep you up at night for having taken something that wasn't yours to take. . . . Let me ask you something, Francis. What does it say about a man that he would steal another man's ideas? Think about it. What does it say about a man that he would plagiarize another man's ideas? It says he doesn't have ideas of his own. It says he doesn't have the *mind,* doesn't have the brainpower, and so he has to steal from others. It says he's too tired or too lazy or too old or too uncreative. It says he doesn't have the stuff—"

"These accusations of plagiarism, Caspar . . . if I remember correctly, the Hypnotizer code was on Tiny's computer, so I assume that *he* wrote the code, but now you're here in front of me saying '*we*' wrote it, which is as much plagiarism as anything I've done. No one person *ever* deserves credit, but we give it to them anyway. Tiny's written some code, Salman has written some code, *you've* written some code, but *I've* written some code, too, Caspar—oh, yes, I've been designing a chip that will optimize its performance, oh yes, *wake-up call,* huh? Your motherboards were okay, but I can do better . . . so it's my work too, Caspar. You thought you could *own* it, but you only own anything in this industry by proving yourself on it every day."

"How—how long ago was it? How long ago did you set me up? When did you know? When you got the call from Travis Grissom? When you saw the Hypnotizer code?"

"Hah! Are you kidding? You're kidding, right? Travis Grissom, my ass. You're *kidding,* right?"

"No."

"Christ, Andy, I set the *whole thing* up. I've been looking for a chance to work on the three-hundred-dollar computer for a couple years. I *put* you on that project."

"Sure, to humiliate me. Because I would fail, because I had no money."

"*No*. Because it would *look like* that to you. And to Hank and Lloyd, it would look like a prank. Lloyd would never allow an ironman to work on the three-hundred-dollar computer—I knew that all along—least of all *me*. But if I made it look like just a prank, just a little tit-for-tat power play, than he would let it slide long enough for you to get some work done. You think I didn't do my research on you? In our very first meeting—Hank's office, re-member?—you said just enough to tip me off that you might be right for this. So I looked you up in Omega's employee records—I could tell you would hold a grudge against Omega, I could tell you would fight any heat that came from Hank or Lloyd. I never ex-pected you to bring in three other guys, but for that I tip my hat to you."

Andy couldn't believe it. "It was just supposed to *look* like a prank?"

Francis couldn't resist flashing a big smile. He'd always wanted it to come down to this. "Everything was going perfectly . . . you were supposed to run out of money, and then switch over to some other project. I was going to take a look at what work you had done, see if there really was anything there, like I thought there would be."

"And what would you have done?"

"It depends on the results. Maybe find a sponsor myself, maybe move to another lab less dominated by big iron, sell it—who knows? I was going to cross that bridge when I came to it. But then, you guys got a reporter all excited, and then you took your work with you. I had to improvise. It was all legal, mind you. Not moral, maybe, but legal. So don't use the word *stealing* around me—"

"How did you get our code?"

"It wasn't *your* code. It was *La Honda's* code . . . we gave you nonexclusive rights."

"But how did you get it?"

"It was on Tiny's computer, and then it wasn't. So I asked myself, 'Why would they bother to delete something the day before they leave? Gee, it must be *important*.' "

"What is it like to look yourself in the mirror every day, Francis?"

"Oh, don't give me that again. It doesn't work on me. I'm not thirty years old anymore. Every successful person in this town is just as ruthless as I am. And in five more years you probably will be too. You've done a good job, a bang-up job. And now I'm giving your code a chance to live. If it weren't for me and it weren't for me bringing in Lloyd, you would suffer a far worse humiliation than what's going on here. You'd have built a superior product that got no more attention than some undergraduate's senior thesis. I'm going to take your work and make it famous, and I'm going to give it a chance, and for that you should be goddamned thankful."

"Don't expect to get a Hallmark anytime soon."

"Getting screwed is part of the ritual, Andy. At least I'm not going to dumb down your technology. I'm going to make it better. I promise you that. When *I* was screwed, I designed a Falcon chip that was saddled with sixteen-bit software that made my chip design look slow. Wall Street analysts who used to look up to me stopped doing so—from their point of view I had delivered a chip that was faster, but not *exponentially* faster. They didn't care it was the software holding it back. I promise you that nobody will ever think of you that way. I promise you I will serve your work with respect, and if you can't recognize the importance of that, engineer to engineer, then you're not the man I thought you were."

Andy didn't say anything for a long, long time. Then he said, "I don't like you, Francis. I know you want me to like you, I know you want me to respect the incredible savvy of your plan, I know you want me to think highly of you for not dumbing down our work . . . but I don't. I don't like you. I don't have any appreciation for what you've done. I'm not going to give that to you, Francis. Taking my business is not enough, you want my respect, too?" Andy stepped forward, grabbed the doorknob, and as he stepped back again slammed the door closed.

9

What's in a Name?

At a quarter to six on Wednesday, Francis Benoit was with Lloyd Acheson in the Pacific suite at the Westin St. Francis hotel, sharing a drink and relaxing before the press conference.

On the second floor of the hotel, there was a party going on. Lloyd had hired a public relations firm to phone the media, and they had done an admirable job of prodding a decent number of stringers and editors to promise to show up at the announcement, but by two o'clock that afternoon the PR firm hadn't managed to cajole a single television station into sending a van over to the hotel. So Lloyd had gotten on the horn to a local cable outfit that covered stories for CNBC, the all-business channel, and passing himself off to the producer as a PR man, promised them a video exclusive—"you'll be the only one with video of Lloyd Acheson's big announcement," he said. Not wanting to miss an exclusive, the producer scheduled a van to head over there later. Then Lloyd called the CNN affiliate in Oakland, got a producer on the line, and again posing as a PR man convinced this guy that he didn't want to be scooped by a mere CNBC rigger on such an important story. So CNN found room in their hectic schedule to get a team at the scene. Then Lloyd called the local CBS station, and they weren't convinced they needed a *camera* to record just a mere *an-*

nouncement, but Lloyd told them how CNBC and CNN were covering it—they didn't want to be left out, did they? And in this manner, by six o'clock that evening, it was hard to maneuver through the crowd because of all the cords and battery packs making an obstacle course of the floor. Once he'd had a commitment from so many television stations, Lloyd called the local branch of the Look modeling agency, which was only across Union Square from the Westin, and mentioned how there would be all these television cameras on the second floor, so a gaggle of these pouty waifs tromped up Geary Street just as the place started to get busy. Lloyd also had sent a fax to all the local PR firms, and the word got out quickly. Every middling celebrity in town who needed to increase their television exposure—authors and politicians running for district attorney and old sports stars looking for more endorsement deals—had heard that if they showed up at six that evening at the Westin, they might get their mug on the evening news. This was no ordinary press conference, where the audience is the media and as soon as the speaker stops speaking everyone runs for the phones. This was an *event.* This was a *party.* Young women in white blouses and black skirts walked around carrying trays filled with flutes of champagne, while young men in black satin shirts and white trousers walked around carrying platters of scallops wrapped in prosciutto. Yet for all of this, nobody had any idea what Lloyd Acheson was going to announce! Lloyd was legally bound to make no statements until six. All they knew downstairs was that one of the kings of big iron was making an announcement about his new venture, and that this new venture had something or other to do with the legendary Francis Benoit. As the audience walked in, they were handed floppy disks slapped with an Everyware sticker; there were enough journalists in the crowd carrying laptops that pretty soon they were encouraged to insert the floppy and see what happened, what the heck. So they did, and their screen went blank and then reappeared with the slogan "If it's not Everyware, it'll soon be nowhere." But that was all! It just added to their curiosity.

Upstairs in the suite, Lloyd said, "Okay, let's go over it again. I'll talk about the general concept, the market, then you talk about our specific products. If we get off track, if reporters' questions lead us astray, just remember—me, general; you, specific. Don't be afraid to defer to me, rather than find yourself at the end of a long sentence with nothing to nail it down but hot air."

Francis was standing at the window, watching a wall of fog whip past. The city was far down below. He was wearing just a T-shirt and blue jeans. He was drinking a beer from the bottle. He didn't say anything to Lloyd.

Lloyd continued, "Now, if anyone asks you how much we intend to charge for the software, I don't want you to comment. Refer them to me."

"Why don't we just say that I'm a deaf-mute programmer?"

"Hey, what gives? You should be excited. This is your moment to be on top of the heap."

"It's just been a long haul. . . . It's taken a lot out of me. I thought I would be excited, but feel my pulse—it's like I just woke up. You know what I really want to do right now? I want to order a burger from room service and see if there's a game on television. Or maybe go down to the bar and flirt with the German tourists. I could take this or leave it. I can't understand it. I cheat, bully, and lie to get what I want, only to find all the pleasure's already been squeezed out."

"You're not the only one who feels this way," Lloyd said.

"I figured this is when you shine brightest."

"No, that's just the lights reflecting off my face. Look, Francis, you can't go down there with that sour look on your face. The press is going to want a story, a good story. They're gonna want to know about that moment of creation when you said, 'I got it!' They're gonna want to know where you were standing or sitting, what triggered it, did you look at your niece one day and it just popped into your head? Have you been thinking about it for a long time, waiting for the right moment? They're just doing their job. They don't adore you, they don't really care—they just want a story. *It doesn't matter what you say,* they'll write it down and think it's the coolest thing in the world."

"All I ever wanted was to stay at La Honda, but I couldn't pretend any longer. The industry kept intruding." Francis threw himself backward onto the bed. He stared at the ceiling.

"All right, but can you make that into more of a story?"

"The story is that Omega software dumbed down my chip."

"I don't know if this is the appropriate time for you to make negative statements."

"Hmmm. Then maybe someone else should make them."

"What's that supposed to mean?"

"Nothing."

"Hey, this is no time to get idealistic all of a sudden, Francis. Don't start pretending I'm the corrupter of your innocence—don't try to wash your hands of what we've created, not at this point. You're not twenty-five anymore, you *need* the glory, just like I do. We get older and we start wanting it both ways; we can't stand to see others get the attention we're just as deserving of."

Francis thought about that and saw the wisdom in it. Ten years ago, nothing mattered to him but his work. That wasn't quite true anymore. "There's something I've wanted to ask you for a long time. That legend about you, everybody's heard it. Now I gotta know. About the two broken legs, you hiking five miles, your life turning around."

"What about it?"

"Is it true? Or was it just something you said back when you thought it didn't really matter what you said?"

"Broken *ankles*. There's a big difference between a broken ankle and a broken leg. The story's accurate, but it's not the whole story. I've been trying to tell the whole story for years, but nobody wants to hear it. See, we never should have climbed that butte in the first place—it wasn't safe. But I insisted we could do it. I was stubborn and way out of my league but wouldn't admit it. Everybody thinks that was the day in my life I learned how to be a fighter—walked five miles with broken ankles. But the opposite was true; it was the day I stopped being so goddamned stubborn and bullheaded. Everybody's got a story like that. Nobody's been good their whole life. Some people, their crime is neglect, but there it is. Stubbornness, see? Refusal to see one's own limits. Everybody can see into the future. But not so many people can see the end of the present."

Francis listened to this and liked what he heard and wanted more. It was not that long ago—maybe eight months—that he considered Lloyd Acheson the enemy. But it wasn't Lloyd after all. It was the CEO of Omega who was his enemy. Lloyd Acheson was just a guy doing his job. Francis no longer had any hard feelings.

It's going to be okay. He went over to a laptop computer that he'd left running on the desk, its screen closed down. He opened it. "Check this out," he said. "Today I was fiddling with the way the operating system addresses RAM, and I came up with this thing called the Anticipator. It anticipates what you're going to do next and begins downloading into RAM even before you ask. . . ."

Lloyd came up behind him. "What do you say we go downstairs?"

. . .

The press conference was a blur, not worth the brain cells to record it. Francis Benoit watched Lloyd talk and watched himself talk and put a grin in at appropriate places and then wandered around in the lobby outside, partly repulsed by what he had created and partly amused. If it was a game, he wanted to play it. If it counted as real life, he wanted to disavow it. To make a game of it, he studied everybody's shoes. Like an anthropologist, he created categories and kept track of them in his head. There were inorganic shoes: polyurethane, vinyl, synthetic rubber, leatherette. There were organic shoes: canvas, calf, snakeskin, denim. There were shoes that took both hands to get on—shank boots, oxfords, buckled T-strap heels—and shoes your feet found their own way into— sandals, clogs, loafers, pumps, and moccasins. There were demure shoes and attention-grabbing shoes.

When he ran out of categories, Francis escaped back upstairs, locked his door, put the do-not-disturb light on his telephone, and drank a couple of beers from the stocked bar. "Welcome to the life of everything being taken care of by invisible people," he said aloud to the image of himself in the mirror. A few minutes later he was walking up and down the streets, staring at bright lights and the jutty sway of the shoulders of the women standing on street corners and realizing the thing that scared him most about himself was his desire to be alone for great periods of time. He could listen to his own thoughts and his own running commentary and never be bored, and one day he would wake up and nobody would want a piece of him anymore. His defenses would have ruined him—he would have neither friends nor the ability to make them. He went back to his hotel room. He got into bed and stared at the ceiling, and after a while he went over to his desk and opened the screen of the laptop and began to review his work.

In the morning, he got up and had room service coffee and looked at pictures of himself in the newspaper, which meant nothing to him, strangely. He didn't know if it was because he felt he deserved it, so *of course* his picture would be in the paper, or just because having his picture in the paper was only exciting if he had somebody to share it with. He didn't trust that anybody understood the Everyware concept, he didn't believe that they "got it," and headlines on the business page didn't change that. *They never get it.* Francis stepped back into the same clothes he had worn the day before and walked down the street toward the financial district, where he and Lloyd would be meeting this morning with their investment bankers.

He rode the elevator to one of the upper floors of the BankAmerica building, where his friend and portfolio manager Quentin Black was waiting for him in his office. They shook hands. Quentin had the slicked-back, gleaming look of a mallard. People walking by in the lush carpeted hallways stared at Francis as if he were a bicycle messenger who'd gotten lost. Quentin took Francis upstairs on an interior circular staircase. There was a conference room with the same view as from his hotel room, and about ten people in suits sitting around a table, chatting with Lloyd Acheson as though he were a celebrity, which, in a way, he was. *Crisp* suits. Quentin and Francis walked in, and Lloyd stood up immediately to introduce Francis as the "man with the big brain." Everybody seemed jovial. They didn't all try to break his wrist giving him a handshake. Quentin and Francis took seats in the back of the room against the wall.

One of the men said, "This deal's so hot I could cook bacon on the prospectus."

Another concurred. "I'm hearing so much buzz in the markets this morning that you'd think the killer bees have finally arrived. Lloyd, your name is gold. It's a *currency*. I say 'Lloyd Acheson' and my customers listen for once."

Somebody said, "Maybe Lloyd could sell off one of his *l*.'s, raise some cash."

"The uppercase *L* or the lowercase *l*?"

"Oh, definitely the uppercase. The uppercase-lowercase spread has never been greater. Carpe diem."

Even Francis got a chuckle out of that.

In the front of the room, a televideo screen snapped on, showing two men in chairs. These were the managing directors of the bank's high technology research unit and the capital markets syndicate. Francis assumed, but did not know for certain, that they were in New York. They began to outline a plan for Everyware. They recommended skipping the conventional second- and third-round financings from venture capital and other companies, and gunning straight for a public offering in six weeks. The market was hot, demand was high, and they didn't want to miss their window. They felt Everyware should offer only 25 percent of its shares to the public, using the remaining shares to trade for the stock of other start-ups. They suggested Everyware could grow by acquisition far faster than it could grow through its own sales. This was a "portfolio company" strategy—the market trusted Lloyd to purchase the right internet companies for them. Everyware would be more like a mutual fund than a manufacturing company.

A stack of comb-bound brochures went around the room slowly. The stack eventually got to Francis, and he took one and flipped through it. "Everyware, Inc." was embossed on the shiny plastic cover. The contents seemed to describe many of the points made by the man on the televideo screen. The high quality of the brochure conveyed a sense to Francis that this proposed plan was *the* plan, and that this meeting was less a brainstorming session than a review of decisions that had already been made.

Francis stood up. "Lloyd?" he said. "I need to talk to you."

Lloyd turned to the back of the room. "Let's finish the conference call."

"*Now,* Lloyd."

"This call—" Lloyd stopped, resigning himself to placating Francis. He pointed outside the conference room and went the other way around the table to get there. Francis met him and closed the door. They stood in the hallway.

"What's going on?" Lloyd said.

"This is happening faster than I thought."

"If you think this is fast, then you just wait."

"No . . . I thought there would be a time to give some input—this *brochure,* look at it . . . you've already made these decisions."

Lloyd stood with his hands on his hips, his back military straight. "I thought you didn't want anything to do with the financing or management."

"I didn't, but—"

"Don't worry. You're going to have your own research division, you're going to be worth twenty million bucks, nobody can touch you."

"La Honda, Hank, he needs our help—"

"Just let me take care of this."

"No, now wait, hold on, stop rushing me. I thought there was going to be a time to say this, but I want us to sell La Honda five percent of the company. Maybe you know it or maybe you don't, but Hank's had a little trouble down there this last year and he needs to be bailed out. This will take care of it five times over. I don't know if I owe it to him or if you owe it to him, but it's something I want to do anyway."

"What *for?* It's just money out of our pocket."

"I don't care."

Lloyd glanced back into the conference room. He didn't want to keep them waiting. "Can't we talk about this later?"

"What's to talk about?"

Lloyd sighed. It seemed a resigned sigh. "Am I going to have to come to you for every decision now?"

Francis didn't answer that one. He just sashayed back into the conference room and took his seat. Lloyd followed him.

Lloyd cleared his throat. He had a knack for doing it just right, not making it sound unnatural. "There's going to be some amendments to this plan," he said. "There's going to be a small second-round transaction, but it shouldn't cause us any delay. I'll give you the details later."

Lloyd and the two guys in New York began discussing how much of the Everyware shares should be reserved for employees. Lloyd seemed to think it was customary to set a big percentage aside, but the two guys in New York seemed amused by that idea.

"This isn't 1986 anymore," one said.

The other added, "Don't give away the farm unless you have to."

Francis turned to Quentin Black and whispered, "I thought most employees *always* got shares."

"Top managers, sure. But the days of secretaries retiring at age thirty-five are over. Give 'em a set of steak knives at Christmas, they'll be happy."

Francis stood up again. "Excuse me," he said. "Excuse me, hold on here." He walked forward to stand beside Lloyd. "Maybe you all are right about what we can get away with if we want to, but *I don't want to*. I want shares for the employees. I want to be able to hire people, engineers out of college, and say to them, 'Here's a piece of the action.' "

Lloyd looked up over his shoulder and said softly, "Let me handle this, Francis."

"No, no, you're not going to handle this. This is what I want and this is what I'm going to get and you're all going to give it to me without an argument. You guys here draw up the numbers and the papers and make sure the page numbers are in order and you'll get your commission, but don't try to sneak one past me. You want the deal fast? Fine, then don't drag your heels arguing with me or hope I'm going to change my mind. And I'm not going to sit through this meeting now waiting for the time you want me to sign a commitment letter. You got something for me to sign, you can messenger it to my house this afternoon."

Without giving anyone a chance to retort, Francis walked from the room. He walked out of the building and turned south. Across the road, something caught his eye.

A forty-foot-wide billboard was displayed for the oncoming Kearny Street traffic. In black type against a white background, it read:

> High tech insiders
> wear Lo-Tech
> on the outside.
> Lo-Tech Workware.
> When business is pleasure.

In smaller print, on the right-hand side, was "Modeled by high-tech insider Hank Menzinger." But the picture was not of Hank Menzinger. It was Andy Caspar, wearing a V-neck sport shirt with a tab-ring zipped collar. Andy's head extended two feet above the normal rectangle of the billboard. He was laughing, or something like it. The look suggested, *I'm having a better time than you.*

Oh, my! This was unbelievable! How had Caspar done it? What an incredible prank! Francis felt a rush of pride. He stood there looking up. He had the urge to stop one of these many people marching past, to grab their shoulder and point across the street and say, "Hey! Hey! I *know* that guy."

. . .

Nell Kirkham's hands hovered above her keyboard, waiting for the words to come. She was mad and anxious and excited and bitter and suffering too many feelings at once to calm down. She felt the kind of fluttering in her chest she got when she drank too much coffee. Her screen was blank. Her phone rang again but she wouldn't answer it. She had to write this story. When she came into work that morning and saw the lead story on Everyware, she saw her chance at revenge for Hank's having cut off her access to La Honda: Everyware was without a doubt an evolution of the VWPC—the device that Andy Caspar had been looking to get sponsored. The device that Hank Menzinger had laughed off five months ago. He had called it "not worthy." She looked down at her notes—"not worthy of sponsorship, not worthy of my time, not worthy of yours," he had said. Now Francis Benoit was letting the world believe he had invented it. He hadn't said so, exactly, but it was the conclusion anyone would draw from that morning's story. She wasn't going to let them get away with it. Hank had known she would write this story: he had said he would talk today, Thursday, and this morning he had left four messages in her voice mail, but she wasn't going to let him put his spin on it.

She felt a tap on her shoulder. It was one of her coworkers, pointing to the entrance of the newsroom. Walking down the aisle in her direction, taking large, leisurely strides, grinning at everybody who looked his way, was Hank Menzinger.

Hank was chuckling at how every reporter was wearing a telephone headset. This looked more like Mission Control than a newsroom. If not for the dictionary and thesaurus on every desk, there would be nothing to distinguish the newsroom from any back-office paper-processing division of some insurance company.

"I suppose you're writing about Andy Caspar," he said, coming up to Nell Kirkham. She looked frazzled. On some women that look is endearing. She wasn't one of them.

She said, "What I'm writing about isn't any of your business."

"I've got a better story for you. The inside scoop on why Lloyd Acheson left Omega. I'll give you the story if you lay off the Andy Caspar history."

Her eyes narrowed. "You're trying to cover up his involvement."

"This isn't the scandal you think it is, Nell. Technology is always a team effort, but the teams never get the credit. That story's below-the-fold, at best. More like page three."

"You're trying to keep me from pointing out that four months ago you thought the VWPC was a joke. 'Unworthy,' you said. You're trying to preserve your reputation as a visionary. That's all you care about."

She wasn't wrong about that. But she wasn't going to write it. He said, "Lloyd left Omega because of the six eighty-six. The story was right under your nose the whole time, but you never paid attention to the technology to see the obvious. If someone else gets this story, you're going to look foolish for having missed it."

That caught her without a comeback.

Hank went on, "Let me tell you the story off the record. If you use it—and I think you will—then you have to swear off the Andy Caspar story. Deal?"

"Let's go in the conference room and talk it over."

"I need to know we have a deal first."

"All right. Deal." It hurt her to say that.

They walked down the aisle to an empty inner room without any windows. He took a seat beside a small card table. She leaned her back against the closed door.

She said, "So I suppose the six eighty-six is in trouble, and Lloyd took the fall for it?"

Hank chuckled. "Hardly. It's right on schedule, going smoothly."

"Then what's the story?"

"Stop me if this gets too technical, Nell. A little history, first. Francis Benoit's Falcon chip was capable of running thirty-two-bit and sixty-four-bit software. Instead, Omega installed sixteen-bit Windows software, wasting the design. When it came time for the six eighty-six, Francis wasn't going to let it happen again. The six eighty-six is not only *capable* of sixty-four-bit software, it's *optimized* for it. It's a technologically excellent design. But here's the catch: when you try to run sixteen-bit software on it, it actually *runs slower.*"

"The six eighty-six is slower than the Falcon?" This seemed hard for her to believe.

"Only when running *old* software," Hank clarified.

"Like all those Windows apps."

"Right."

She was interested. "Okay, keep going. Walk me through this."

"So here's the consequences. A chip's got to run Windows applications to be a mass-market item. If it's not a mass-market item, then Omega will never get the unit volume out of it to bring the price down into consumer range. This means that although the six eighty-six is technologically superior, it will never be a desktop PC chip."

She picked up on it. "Then Omega's plans to build the future of their company on the chip have to be rethought."

"Exactly."

"It's not a consumer chip," she said, repeating it to make sure she had it right.

Hank said, "It's more of a workstation chip."

"Did Omega just find out about this?"

"No, they've known the whole time. Francis never made it a secret. They just never wanted to confront the consequences. They let it slide. Lloyd saw it all coming. He knew they needed a new game plan. Last Friday he went to the board and gave them an ultimatum. He forced the issue."

Hank could see that this was getting through to her. Her head was nodding slowly. She looked down at him. She said, "Okay. Let me go get my tape recorder and tell my editor. Stay here. I'm going to need all the details."

. . .

In the late afternoon light, Andy had convinced Tiny to get out of the office and go for a walk. They headed for the tree-lined residential streets of Menlo Park.

"Where's Salman today?" Tiny asked. Salman hadn't shown up at all.

"I sent him on a research mission."

"What, legal stuff?"

Andy said, "There's not really any point talking about it unless he discovers an opportunity."

Andy and Tiny were wearing their tartan golf pants. Tiny's body was making all sorts of sounds. His thighs rubbed together, generating a *vrup* sound with each stride. His sneakers scuffed the pavement. As his arms swung past his hips, his watch buckle was catching some material, letting out a click. Also, his breathing was slightly strained and heavy.

Andy said, "You're like a one-man band there."

"Huh?"

"You're making a lot of noise."

"I'm just walking."

"Did you watch too many Jerry Lewis movies when you were a kid? Look at your stride, look at your motion."

Tiny looked down. "I always walk this way."

"Tiny, what is sound?"

"Sound? It's a very long wavelength."

"Sound is *energy*. Listen to you—that's energy being released that could go into your stride."

"What am I doing wrong?"

"You're dragging your toes. Stop for a second. Stop."

They did.

Andy bent down and pointed to Tiny's sneakers. Below the toes, the soles were nearly worn through. "Take off your shoes," Andy instructed.

"Why?"

"If you're going to start working out more, you've got to go easier on your shoes or you'll be buying a new pair every week."

Tiny took his shoes off.

"Socks too," Andy said. Then Andy fished a Swiss army knife out of his pocket. With the large blade he cut the first inch of the rubber sole from Tiny's sneakers. "Okay, put 'em back on, but without your socks."

"But my toes will be sticking through!"

That was exactly the point. When they started walking again, Tiny was careful now not to scuff his toes. The sound from his feet disappeared.

After a while, Tiny said, "You're a good friend, Andy."

"Thanks."

"Did you read the paper this morning?"

"How could I not?"

"Did you see that story from Romania?"

"What? No, I—I just read about Everyware. Some political thing going on there?"

"Huh? No, about the tree bear they discovered."

"They discovered a bear that lives in trees?"

"Yeah. So do you know what that means?"

Andy thought out loud. "Well, a bear that climbs trees, it would probably have to have long toes rather than a padded foot, as other bears do. . . ."

"You're getting there."

"And it would probably have to be able to reach up, so its neck vertebral structure would be different . . ."

"Go on."

"And the tracks it would leave, with those toes, would probably be very odd, more like a very large humanoid . . . so—Oh! They think this is the explanation for Bigfoot or something?"

"Bingo! See, Andy, you don't even have to read the newspaper. You can just read the headlines and the rest can be deduced when you need it. Save brain cells."

"Well, it's good to hear you're reading *something* other than *The Guns of Navarone.*"

"Don't knock it."

"I'm not *knocking* it," Andy said. "I'm just glad you're taking an interest in what's going on in the world."

"Yeah, well, we're going to have a lot of time to do that now. Did you talk to any lawyers?"

"A couple. Sounds like it would cost us three hundred an hour, and none of them seems to think we have an easy case."

• • •

When they got back to the office, Francis Benoit was in the parking lot, leaned up against his fancy car, waiting.

Andy and Tiny stopped.

"What are you doing here?" Andy said.

"I came to talk to you two."

"We don't want to talk. So go—get out of here."

"Let me say something first."

"I said *get out of here*."

Tiny said, "Let's hear what he has to say. Why not?"

Francis said, "I want you to come work for me. Your whole team."

"You're lying," Andy said. "This is another setup."

"I'm not lying. What makes you think I'm such a bad guy? Maybe ten years from now—or five years from now, when you've seen this industry rebuild itself a few times—you'll understand I'm not all that different from you."

"I would like you to leave *now*."

"I need good people. You guys have proven yourselves. You'd get stock options. You'd make more money than you ever would have made had this still been your company. Money is freedom."

"I'm sorry, I'm not going to spend my life pretending *you* invented the PowerStation. I'm not going to let you pretend that, either."

"I didn't ask you to. I'm not trying to hide anything. They'd be good jobs, unlimited opportunity. And your team could stay together."

"I'll never take a job from you."

"Yes, you will. You will because you believe in what you built and you don't want to see it fail in lesser hands. You don't want to see it ruined. I may have taken your ownership, but I haven't taken your pride in your work. You're not the kind of person who can walk away from what you've started. If you were, this project would have been dead a long time ago. Maybe by now you hate yourself for being so goddamned dedicated, but even your own self-hatred won't stop you. Here's my home phone number. I want any or all of you—you set your salary. There's a lot of work to do and I know you and I know there's nothing you'd like more right now than to get back to work." Francis handed Tiny a slip of paper with a number written on it in pen. "I'm going now but I'll be at that number the rest of the afternoon and all of tomorrow, and if you don't call me, I'll call you."

"I'll be sure to turn the answering machine on . . ." Andy said.

"He said we could set our own *salaries*," Tiny said.

"Forget it. There's some things we don't do."

Francis opened the door to his car. "You don't have any reason not to work for me. I've never had any dislike for you, I've just been working my own angle, watching out for my own ass. Maybe you don't like me, but you've seen all my tricks, you know my moves, I'll never catch you by surprise again. And believe me, there's a lot worse out there. You guys talk it over."

"There's nothing for us to talk about," Andy said, "but if you and Lloyd want something to talk about, you might want to search the web for Everyware and see what's going on out there."

"We haven't got a web site yet," Francis said.

"I know you don't."

Tiny said, "What's going on, Andy?"

"Let him find out."

. . .

Up at La Honda, David Kim received an e-mail from Hank Menzinger. David Kim had spent the previous nine months on the 686 team, and he figured Hank's message would be some form of generic thank you for all the work he'd put in. David clicked on Hank's message. There was something odd about the message's display—and then David recognized it wasn't internal e-mail. It had been sent from Hank_Menzinger@Modnet.com—probably from Hank's home computer.

David,
Nell Kirkham will be coming by at 12:30 this afternoon to pick up a
photocopy of the 686 manual—at whatever stage the manual is in.
Please include ALL technical specifications, design notes, etc. Can
you make a copy and put it in her in box in the mailroom? thanks,
Hank

David thought that was a little strange—Nell Kirkham never
seemed interested in the technical specifications. But he wasn't going to question Hank Menzinger, no way. Last August, David had
made the mistake of trying to design the error-parity unit of the
686 differently than Francis had recommended. That would have
been fine if David's idea had worked, but it hadn't. Francis made a
little comic speech at lunch one day, commending David for his
assertiveness, and as a "merit prize" put him in charge of compiling the 686 manual, which would assist Omega developers in writing code that took special advantage of the 686's features.

At 12:20, Salman drove into the La Honda parking lot. He
waited in his car while some other ironmen came out of the north
building and walked across the quad. The cafeteria was in the
south building. Lunch was served from noon to one o'clock only;
Salman was hoping the north building would be less occupied for
that reason.

He climbed from his car and walked into the north building. The
mailroom was down the hall to the right. He poked his head in,
saw a guy, and backed out to the drinking fountain. Above the
drinking fountain a handwritten sign read, DO NOT WASH DISHES IN
FOUNTAIN. The guy left the mailroom. Every person at La Honda
had a box. It took Salman a while to locate Kirkham's. An inch-
thick stack of paper stuck out from her box. Salman couldn't believe how easy this was—just create a new user with Hank's name
as a pseudonym. No way was David going to question a request
from Hank.

• • •

Francis Benoit drove the Fiat hard, up into the hills, through chap-
arral and redwoods and open grassland. On the way, he tele-
phoned Lloyd, but got a message from Lloyd's cellular company

that his phone was not turned on. So Francis dialed Lloyd's pager, punching in his home number.

Francis left his car in his driveway, not bothering with the garage. He ran indoors to his study, booted his computer. So slow! Booted his web-browser software. Waiting, waiting. Francis couldn't sit down. Finally, his screen came up. He clicked on a search engine, one that was reliably up-to-the-minute, and typed "Everyware" as the search string.

So many news articles had been written about Everyware in the last twenty-four hours that the search found dozens of entries. In addition, the search listed every newsgroup conversation about Everyware that had been posted to the internet bulletin boards, and there were about a hundred of those. It seemed Everyware had created a storm of excitement overnight, and entrepreneurially minded programmers were abuzz with the news that there might be a way to undermine Microsoft's lock on the operating systems market—and if there was, they wanted in on it.

The search engine ranked its results, and one of the criteria for ranking was whether the word "Everyware" occurred in the very first line of a web page. There was only one page that met this criterion, and so this page was at the top of Francis's search rankings. It would also be at the top of any searches done by those entrepreneurial programmers who went searching for more info about this cool new software they were hearing about.

Francis clicked on the link to the page.

While the page loaded, the first line came up.

Demo the precursor to Everyware . . .

And then the second line.

Universe Corp.'s *Hypnotizer.*

It was a page that Andy Caspar must have put up. It offered free downloads of the Hypnotizer and several software utilities that the team had written. There was a paragraph explaining the obvious benefits to programmers of writing internet-deliverable programs that could run regardless of operating system. And then there was a live count of how many users had downloaded the program in the past twenty-four hours: fourteen hundred people.

Fourteen hundred people wasn't a huge number, no, but it freaked Francis out. Because the way these things tended to steamroll, each of those fourteen hundred might tell two or three others. And why not? If they had gone through all the trouble to search for Everyware and download the system, they would surely mention it to a few friends. And tomorrow there would be three thousand downloads. And the day after that, six thousand. It would grow exponentially. These wouldn't be casual users; these would be the diehards. Every programmer who had ever been pissed off by some brand manager, every programmer who had ever felt trapped inside a corporate bureaucracy, every programmer who had ever been cajoled into making compromises—they would all grow giddy from the possibility that they no longer had to work for anyone but themselves. They could just write programs to run on the Hypnotizer and distribute them over the internet—completely getting rid of diskettes and manuals and retailer margins and all the *middlemen*—wow! They could write programs the way *they* wanted, and for *whom* they wanted, and nobody could tell them otherwise. This was exactly the scenario that Francis had planned for Everyware, but nobody was going to wait for Everyware when the Hypnotizer was already available—and for *free!* Andy was giving it away!

"Fuck!" Francis howled into his empty home.

His phone rang.

"Lloyd!"

"I got your page. What's up?"

"Andy Caspar put up a web site. Thousands of people are downloading the Universe system for free." Even as he said this, Francis watched the live count of downloads increase.

There was a pause. "That's a crime. He's giving away our property. *We* own Universe. I'll sue that kid for every penny he'll ever earn. I'll get the lawyers working on it. Can you tell where the site is located?"

Francis took a moment to browse through some linked pages. "It appears to be on a server run by a game company up in Seattle. Oh, shit."

"What?"

"I've heard of these guys. They've got something like twenty thousand regular users. If all of *them* already have it, and that was *before* yesterday, this thing may be more widely dispersed than I thought."

"All right. We'll meet at my home first thing tomorrow with the lawyers. They'll line up a judge for a temporary restraining order. Find out everything you can, bring it in."

. . .

Lloyd Acheson had recently paid an architectural firm to install a freshwater stream on the grounds of his home. Stocked with minnows, the stream not only meandered along the driveway and crossed the patio, it actually went into one side of the house and came out the other. Indoors, it babbled through the entryway and living room. One of the unfortunate effects was that every morning the windows dripped with condensation, and Lloyd's million-dollar view of the bay was perpetually fogged over.

Francis was in Lloyd's study, continuing to examine the files posted by Andy for download. Lloyd was with three lawyers in his living room. It was 7:30 A.M., and all the lawyers were clean shaven. Lloyd was in gym shorts and T-shirt, but there was a Rolex on his wrist.

Lloyd turned to one lawyer and said, "Do you have a judge?"

"I know who to go to. You can get an order for copyright violations pretty easily. But, partly because of how easy it is to get the order, they keep plaintiffs from abusing it by imposing stiff fines if it's later proven there's no copyright violation."

"I don't care about fines," Lloyd said. "So let's do it. When's the judge get to work?"

"Well, there's one other thing. The judge won't give us the order unless we've first asked this game company in Seattle to take the material down voluntarily."

Lloyd shook his head. "That will take too long. We'll call at nine, and what will they do? They'll just call their lawyers, who will be in some meeting. They won't get back to us before lunch, and then won't make a decision until the end of the day, maybe tomorrow."

"Still, the judge is going to require that we attempt to resolve this ourselves before using the courts."

"All right. We'll make the call at nine. But let's have some ammo so this doesn't get dragged out." Lloyd turned to another lawyer. "We know Andy Caspar doesn't have many assets to forfeit. How about this game company? If it's on their server, can we go after them?"

"Only if we can prove that they *knew* all along that the material was not Andy Caspar's to post."

"How do we prove that?"

"The standard is all over the place. In some districts, they've got to exercise reasonable review of the material to *avoid* liability. In other districts, the very opposite is true. If they exercise any review at all it makes them fully liable, so they scrupulously avoid reviewing anything that gets posted."

"Well, that's enough confusion to scare anybody, which is what we need to do here. And they've got assets, right?"

One of the lawyers had been digging through credit reports overnight. "Kinda. Not much cash, per D and B. Operating income is from a contract, and all they've got is some computer equipment. No liabilities, and since the equity's not traded, it's not valued. They don't have much more to go after than Andy Caspar does."

One of the other lawyers cleared his throat. "I'm not making a recommendation here, I'm just asking the question. Is it smart for Everyware's first item of business to be a *lawsuit* against some engineers? From a PR angle, I'm saying."

Lloyd said, "I'm not paying you three hundred an hour to give me PR advice. There's something you've got to understand. These *programs* which are being downloaded are *small*. All of them fit on a single floppy. They can be copied and passed around easily. It's what *we* were going to do. But if everyone has them already, they won't bother paying for ours unless ours is *substantially* better. It raises the bar. Which could lead to a delay in our product release. A delay in the product release undermines investor confidence in the IPO. Do you get what I'm saying? I'm paid to worry about those possibilities. The sooner we can put this in court, the more minuscule the chance that any of what I have just described plays out. I would like to get a better night's sleep tonight than I got last night."

"Don't count on it." It was Francis. He was standing in the doorway of Lloyd's living room.

"Why?" Lloyd asked.

"I started looking at the code itself."

"Yeah?"

"And it's different. It's not quite the code that Universe sold us."

"Different?"

Francis nodded. "It looks like a different version. . . ."

"An earlier version?"

"Maybe. The original Hypnotizer that I saw was about ten thousand lines. The code off the web page is eleven thousand lines, as opposed to the most recent eighty-five hundred lines. My guess is that they built onto the old code for a while, then they wrote a more efficient version from scratch. What's on the web page is what they had right before they did the rewrite."

Lloyd turned to one of the lawyers. "That doesn't matter, does it? When we bought Universe, all of their intellectual property became ours, not just the most recent versions, right?"

The lawyer confirmed this. "Absolutely."

Francis didn't seem encouraged by this. He was rubbing his chin with one hand, thinking. His other hand was behind his back. He brought this hand forward, offering a piece of paper to Lloyd.

"This message is embedded in the code of every program. I printed it out. He protected himself about a month ago."

In front of each line, there was a special character which made the program ignore the line. After the special character, the rest was in English. It read:

This program copyrighted by Universe Corporation, February 2, 1996—Library of Congress file registration #917702449-03. On February 3, 1996, the copyright was placed in the public domain by corporate resolution. A notarized copy of the resolution is also on file with the Library of Congress.

• • •

Lloyd showed it to the lawyers. "Can he do that? If the Hypno-tizer's in the public domain, what does that mean—that anybody and everybody can use it?"

"It's not uncommon," Francis said. "Universities do this often, give their intellectual property to the public for the good of sci-ence."

When the lawyers didn't say anything, Lloyd began firing off questions. "How different does the code have to be? It's twenty-five hundred lines different, right? So if there's eighty-five hundred lines that are the *same*, doesn't that still mean he's violating our copyright?"

"It's tricky with software," one of the lawyers said. "If eighty-five hundred lines were the exact same, sure, that would be a viola-tion. But if the lines are different—if they get to the same place in a more efficient manner—well, it would just *depend* very specifically on how much was rewritten and how much wasn't."

Lloyd said, "But even if any sequence of one hundred lines were the same . . . wouldn't that violate our copyright?"

"Not necessarily. It's a gray area. If there's one logical way to get from *A* to *B*, that portion can't be copyrighted. For instance, you can't copyright a recipe for how to boil spaghetti. It has functional intent, not artistic intent. Functional intent isn't copyrightable."

Lloyd grew animated. "Gray areas are perfect! Gray areas are what scare people when we're suing for big bucks!"

"Remember, the *fines*—they can be very steep fines."

"How steep?" Lloyd asked.

"They're punitive, so whatever it takes to hurt us where it counts. And it will only be worse if the judge realizes we asked for an injunction without doing our homework on the code. Several million dollars, conceivably."

"So we'd better do our homework. Francis?"

Francis looked Lloyd in the eye. "Give me an hour." He turned and strode back to Lloyd's library.

Francis brought the two versions of code up side by side on the screen. Most computer code is "compiled," meaning it's translated from the cryptic-English language it was written in, such as C++, to the language of the chip's instruction set, a machine language that is entirely unreadable. But the Hypnotizer was different; since it was so small, it could be translated on the fly and didn't have to be compiled in advance. It was interpreted as it ran. For this reason, the code was still in its cryptic-English programming language. To Francis, as readable as a mystery novel.

Though ten thousand lines took up some three hundred pages, the code was broken up into functions, or components. Francis didn't even have to read the code. He could glance between the similar functions of each version and get a sense of whether the code was exactly the same, a little bit different, or fully rewritten. He had expected that some functions would be exactly the same, some would be slightly revised, and a few would be cut entirely.

But that wasn't what he was finding.

Every module was different. It was like comparing the look of pages from two novels, one with a lot of dialogue, one with a lot of dense description. Every function looked shorter, the logic slightly tighter.

Someone had entirely rewritten the Hypnotizer during the last month. A shiver went up Francis's spine. The original Hypnotizer had already been a brilliant piece of coding. Tenure-worthy code. Retirement-worthy code. From October's invention through early February, it remained relatively unchanged, got only a thousand lines fatter. Then, for no apparent reason, someone had thought it not quite worthy enough. Tiny? That just didn't make sense. Engineers will only rewrite their own code if there's a bug, and Tiny's original Hypnotizer was almost bug-free.

• • •

Andy looked at his watch. He had to be there in thirty minutes. Unless 101 was uncharacteristically free of traffic, it would take him at least that long to get there. He went and stood over Salman's shoulder.

"Well?" he said.

Salman was staring at the 686 manual. "I just haven't had enough time, Andy. *One day* is not enough. I need a week with this at least."

"My meeting's *now*."

Salman's eyelids were heavy. His breath was terrible. "I don't want to mislead you, Andy. Ask me a question that I can answer yes to honestly."

"Will it work for our purposes?"

"Of course, it would *work*. Just about any chip will *work*. The question is, how well?"

"I know that. I gave you a question you could answer yes to, didn't I?"

"Give me another."

"Can you take special advantage of its features?"

"I can't answer that. Who knows what bugs might arise."

"Okay, how about this. Do you have some good ideas to test out that might take special advantage of its features?"

"Yes."

"Yes?"

"Absolutely."

. . .

For Gordon Papa Lewis, it had been one hell of a scattered, manic, exhausting week, and he hadn't had this much fun in years. With the company in crisis mode, he didn't have to make a big deal out of hearing everyone's opinion before making a decision. He didn't have to schmooze, he didn't have to win people over to his side, he didn't have to placate the marketing division and pander to the product division. He could just make his decisions and throw caution to the wind, because the most important thing in a time of crisis was to look decisive, to look like a knowing hand was on the tiller. That's what investors wanted to see. Confidence. Papa Lewis had confidence coming out of his ears.

He'd been to Texas to talk with his parts manufacturers, he'd been to Boston to interview a CEO candidate, he'd been to New York to reject a buyout offer, he'd been to Chicago to reassure a big customer, and he'd been to Utah to reject a merger offer. Meetings, meetings, meetings. Two more today.

Research analysts from many of the investment banks and mutual funds had gathered in the conference room. Papa had chosen the executive conference room over the press room downstairs because it felt more communal, less antagonistic. Papa was just one of the guys, sitting around the table, talking straight.

Papa gave a rundown of his week. He circulated letters of support from all of Omega's twenty largest buyers. He assured them the 686 would begin testing in Singapore by the end of the month. He gave a preliminary estimate of third-quarter profits. In short, nothing to worry about. Lloyd Acheson had resigned, but there were sixteen hundred other valuable employees at Omega who hadn't quit. Replacing Lloyd wasn't an emergency. Papa wasn't going to be rushed into a bad decision on replacing Lloyd just to buoy the stock price when none of the fundamentals had changed.

They still had plenty of questions to ask. Papa didn't mind. He loved Q&A. Because he could always make whoever did the asking look silly.

"Did you read Nell Kirkham's most recent report on the six eighty-six?" they all wanted to know. Her article had been the lead on that morning's business page, with the headline, CHIP WITHOUT A CAUSE?

"I read it," Papa said. "So what? The six eighty-six has more power, more speed, than Microsoft knows what to do with. That's all she reported. So why are you asking me about it? Why don't you ask Bill Gates? He's the one who can't keep up. Why take it out on my stock? Every other chip manufacturer has the same problem. Why don't you take it out on Microsoft?"

"Let me be more direct," one of the analysts said. "Will you put the six eighty-six in the desktop computers you ship? And if you do, what software will you preinstall?"

Papa didn't flinch. "I'll install whatever consumers want installed. I can sign a deal with just about anybody. If users want Windows, they'll get it. They want thirty-two-bit Windows NT, that's fine, too. They want UNIX, no problem. You guys are seeing ghosts. The problem you're talking about doesn't exist. Omega customers will get every available software option. What more could they want?"

"If it's not a problem, then why did Lloyd Acheson resign?"

Papa scoffed. "Don't be naïve. Lloyd made a lot of money during his years at Omega, but he stands to make a killing at Everyware. You know how nobody in Silicon Valley likes to admit they're doing it for the money. Contradicts their view of themselves as moral people. So Lloyd cooks up some mishmash that sounds like a crisis, then hits the road."

"What about the rumor that Lloyd gave Omega a chance to purchase Everyware's technology before he resigned?"

"Absolutely not true. Why would he do that, when he could go public with the technology for a lot more money?"

"Still, since Lloyd Acheson and Francis Benoit are the brains behind Everyware, it *looks* like you must have had many chances in the last six months to bring their project under your umbrella."

"Really? Like when? Name one of the chances."

This caught the analyst off guard. "*Theoretically,* I'm saying. If they had been developing their plan for a while, it's natural to theorize that it could have been an Omega project."

"I would have appreciated Lloyd showing us the Everyware code, but he didn't. I would have expected Francis Benoit to offer us the Everyware code he had written, but he didn't. I never even saw their software until this morning, when we pulled a preliminary version off some web page." None of that was untrue. Papa was careful about the distinction, since these kinds of statements could come back to haunt him. Lloyd had proposed a new division to build small web computers, sure, but he'd never mentioned Everyware. How was Papa supposed to know how far along Lloyd was in development? Now Papa would go down in history as "the man who let Everyware go." He would be as infamous as the execs at IBM who let Bill Gates keep the rights to DOS for clone computers.

Papa saw his secretary standing at the glass door to the conference room. She was holding up a yellow slip of paper. Papa had developed a signaling system with her, to let him know how he was doing on time. The yellow paper meant that his next appointment had arrived downstairs and was on his way up. Red meant the appointment was already in his office, waiting. Papa didn't want to offend this guy by making him wait.

"Okay," Papa said to the analysts. "I've got time for only one more question."

. . .

Andy Caspar's attire was a little heavy on the plaid for Papa's taste. Papa studied him. "You golf?" he asked. Before waiting for an answer, Papa said, "You know who's good at golf? People who can control their emotions. I'm not one of them. What's your handicap?"

"I've never played enough times to have one."

"Good answer. Golf is a salesman's sport, a schmoozer's sport. You're not a salesman, are you?"

"I used to work here as one."

"You did? Christ, how'd that not make it in my brief? Oh, well. When?"

"Ninety-one, ninety-two."

Papa whistled loudly. "Growth years. All the work and none of the fun. Listen. You can tell I'm not the kind of guy who likes the rigamarole. I want to talk straight with you. You used to work here, you know who we were, what we did. I'm not holding any cards, you follow me?"

"So far."

"Our engineers took a look at the software you guys are giving away. We're interested in going in this direction, establishing a division—small at first, bigger if it warrants. Whichever way Lloyd Acheson's going to make money on it, we will match them. I know how Lloyd Acheson thinks. You know how Francis Benoit thinks. You've already beaten them to market, you got the lead. Six thousand downloads is only a few days' lead, but it's a lead. If we can keep that lead, it could be worth a lot of money."

"They've got better code."

"How do you know?"

"Because I wrote it."

"Huh." Well, there goes the lead. "Can you do it again?"

Andy Caspar was chewing on his lip. His eyes squinted. "Maybe . . . if I can see the outcome. That it won't get stolen from me again. You're not the only company that's contacted me. I'm very interested in finding the right strategic fit—how we might fit into Omega's overall plans."

Papa clucked his tongue. "Overall plans? I won't lie to you, Andy. My plan is simple: invest in what's growing and take profits from whatever's matured."

"Will you build the PowerStation?"

"I'll build whatever we can sell. We'll put the PowerStation in the pipeline. Marketing and sales will beat it up, tell us what our customers really want. Is it X for five hundred dollars? Is it Y for seven hundred dollars? If it sings, we mike it. You get the picture."

"All too clearly."

"That's what we hire those yo-yos for. They gotta have something to do, huh? Look, this works for us either way. If the software takes off but not the box, fine. If the box takes off but the market swings to Everyware software, fine."

"That's not a very visionary attitude."

"But it's a realistic one. I don't want to fight the market on this one. You want to understand what we're up against? Microsoft dominates the operating-systems market for desktop computers, and they're gaining in the race to control big iron. They've become the gatekeeper, and it's nearly impossible to compete with them. Maybe the only way to break their stranglehold is to invent a new box, a box that makes the operating system irrelevant. That's what I want your technology for. I don't care what price the box sells for. That's not *important*. We'll sell it for whatever consumers want to pay for it. What's *important* is that the box, at whatever price, doesn't have to kiss Microsoft's ass. So you want vision? That's my vision. I want to stop kissing Microsoft's ass, I want to return this industry to a level playing field, I want to smash the gatekeeper. How's that for *vision*? Huh? What do you want, Andy? Let's talk terms, huh? What do you want?"

"You know, just ten days ago I could barely get anybody to pay attention to our work. Now I'm sitting with the chairman of Omega."

"That was before Lloyd Acheson and Francis Benoit attracted all the attention to the kind of work you do."

"Is it really that easy?"

"Don't be cynical, Andy. If your guys' code wasn't any good . . . if your idea wasn't any good, you wouldn't be sitting here. Now, what do you say?"

He didn't hesitate. "I want a pledge to build the PowerStation and sell it for three hundred dollars."

Papa shook his head. "I can't make you that promise. Even if I could, it wouldn't be smart. There's not enough profit in it at that price. Without profit, it's unsustainable. You've come so close, don't be stubborn at this point."

"What are you going to do with the six eighty-six?"

"What does that matter?"

"I'm just asking."

"We're getting out of the desktop market and into the workstation market now, whether we like it or not."

Andy said, "The businesses that need workstations are not the same businesses that need desktop computers. You're going to have to retool your sales force, build up a new client base."

"Tell me something I don't already know," Papa said.

"All right. How's this? We can use the six eighty-six in your existing sales channel."

"Is that right?"

"The six eighty-six has some special features that make it an ideal server for the PowerStation. In a corporate environment, a single six eighty-six server can be the mother computer for up to sixteen PowerStations simultaneously. Maybe there's not much profit margin in the PowerStation, but it will help you move the six eighty-six, which I'm sure will have a high margin. And you've already got the sales force to sell it."

"Wow." Papa Lewis stood up and paced behind his desk. He said it again. "Wow." He turned to Andy. "What kind of special features?"

"Not so fast. You don't get any more details until we have a letter of agreement."

"How do I know you're telling the truth? Our engineers have to check it out."

Andy considered this. "Will you promise that if what I'm saying checks out, then you will build the PowerStation?"

"Only if it checks out."

"I want the promise. The promise is dependent on its checking out."

Papa Lewis squirmed. If what Andy said checked out, then Papa would build a million PowerStations—because it made sense, not because he was fulfilling a promise. He hated making promises. He loved opportunity, but once you made a promise the opportunity became an obligation. "Okay," Papa said finally. Andy had him. "I give."

"I'm going to want it in the letter of agreement."

"Signed in blood, no doubt."

"As long as it's indelible."

. . .

Andy wanted to tell Alisa before he told anyone else.

She wasn't in her room. Andy poked his head in and glanced around for clues. Her shoulder bag was on her bed. She might be out for a run . . . but then he saw one of her running shoes sticking out from under her bed.

Andy walked down the hill toward campus.

The barn doors of the design studio were unlocked.

He found her at one of the computer stations. She was wearing headphones and listening to music as she worked. He stood there a moment until she noticed him.

"How did you know I was here?" she asked.

"Just a good guess."

"You know me better than I know you. That's not fair."

"Only because you know yourself better than I know myself."

"Good point." She gave a coy smile. "But why know yourself when you can be rich instead, right?"

"What are you talking about?"

"I talked to Tiny. You had a meeting with Omega today, right?"

"Yeah."

"Well, I'm happy for you. Congratulations. You won't have any time to *enjoy it,* mind you, but at least you'll know it's there in your brokerage account, and when you come home at night you can cuddle up with your bank statement."

"Jeez, thanks."

"You did sign the deal, right?"

"I signed a letter of agreement."

"Same dif. Heads you win, tails I lose."

Andy put his hand into Alisa's hair and brushed it away from her face. He looked her in the eyes, very seriously. "Alisa . . ."

"What?" Her eyes were wet.

"What are you afraid of?"

"What am I afraid of? You're going to start wearing sport coats and ties to work . . . and you're going to get a nice house in Los Altos Hills, which you will rarely visit because you're always in Tokyo or Austin working a deal . . . and you'll start saying things like 'Jeez, a Mercedes is a very functional car' . . . and you'll start golfing with your broker on weekends. . . ."

"Your imagination is running wild."

"Andy, there are certain kinds of women who look perfectly at ease in a black dress, sitting at a linen-covered table in the middle of a fifty-dollar-a-plate restaurant . . . but I am not one of them."

"Who says any of that is going to happen to me?"

"Don't underestimate the cumulative effect of your environment. You're going to be running a new division for a very, very, very big corporation."

"Hah! Who told you that?"

"Tiny."

"Where did he get that idea?"

"He said he thought that's what—I guess he— What, did he have it wrong?"

"I didn't tell Tiny what I would be negotiating for because I had no idea what I would get. I didn't even tell Tiny what I wanted."

"What did you want?"

"I wanted to form a new company. Omega would give us a few million dollars in capital for thirty percent of the shares. In exchange, they would get an exclusive license to our work and pay us royalties."

"And what did you get?"

"I got what I wanted."

"Andy, that's wonderful!"

Andy said, "We'll go back to our office on El Camino. We might grow out of it soon, but I'm not moving to Los Altos just yet."

"I really don't have anything against Los Altos, other than whenever I drive through I'm stabbed with jealousy."

"Um, look, there's more you and I have to talk about."

"Not now, Andy, I'm in a good mood. We don't want to fight, do we?"

Andy smiled. "Not talk about *us*. No, it's . . . your design, and your name. . . . We have to pay you for that."

"I gave that to you."

Andy shook his head. "No, you didn't. You gave it to us to get us through the venture-capital meeting—"

"No, really, I meant you could have it."

"Alisa!"

"What?"

"I'm trying to help you out here. Now put on your negotiating hat and try to make a little money, will you?"

"I don't have a negotiating hat."

"It's a *metaphor*."

"I know that. Oh, wait. I have a negotiating scarf." She pulled her orange paisley bandanna from her pocket and tied it around her head. The untied corner stood up like a crown. Alisa crossed her arms and pursed her lips. "Okay, I'm ready."

Andy pulled a chair over and sat down in front of her. Their legs were intertwined.

"Okay," he said. "What do you want?"

"Make me an offer."

Andy thought about it. "How about we go out to dinner?"

"I could use some wine."

"Alisa, don't give in so easily!"

"What did I do?" she asked.

"You agreed to a meal. A meal creates an obligation. It means you can't get up and leave if the terms aren't good enough."

"Hey, you tricked me!" She pushed his hand off her leg.

"That's why *you* want to make the first move. That 'make me an offer' line is for novices. It suggests you don't know your own price. It marks you as a pushover."

"Can I bring you to my design-proposal meetings?"

"You can do this stuff. If you really care about your work, you'll learn. In order to protect it."

Alisa's mouth twisted as she thought. "Okay. A million."

"A million dollars! Now *I'm* going to get up and leave."

"A million kisses," she said quickly.

"Nice save."

"You can work them off . . . you know—over time. A thousand a month. We'll have to look hard at your schedule, see what you can fit in."

"That's still a thousand months! That's over eighty years!"

"Well, I drive a hard bargain."

Andy said, "I hope you don't do this with all your customers."

"I try it, but it rarely works."

"But seriously, okay? I'd like to pay you ten thousand for the design, and we'll probably need some more work on it, which you can bill at your regular rate. For the PowerStation name, I'll pay you a thousand-dollar option to reserve it; if we actually use the name, we'll give you another five thousand."

Alisa gave a poker face. Then it collapsed. "Is that a good offer?"

Andy admitted, "I don't really know. I've never done this before."

"It came out of your mouth like a pro. I like that option thing. Very suave."

"So what do you think?"

"I'd like to try to give you some wine, see if there's any room in that offer."

"Are you buying?"

She reached up and pulled off her bandanna. "Sure. I gotta spend money to make money, huh?"

. . .

A mere two blocks away from the headquarters of Omega Logic, Lloyd Acheson had leased six thousand square feet of office space. There was no view of the marsh, though—just the roar of the freeway. As office space in Silicon Valley goes, it was unremarkable: cord-woven industrial carpet and fluorescent lights, the large open rooms yet unbroken by five-foot-high cubicles. The lack of charm didn't offend Francis Benoit, but the idiocy did: the company was soon to raise a war chest of some two hundred million dollars, but Lloyd Acheson had spent the morning saving the thirty-dollar labor fee from Office Depot by assembling their conference room table by himself. On top of that, Lloyd wasn't any good at assembly. He kept insisting there weren't enough of certain screws, and then that some washers were missing, and then he had taken apart the whole thing again as he realized he needed to assemble it from the top down rather than from the legs up. The meeting that Francis had been called in for was delayed an hour, then another, and finally Francis had cajoled Lloyd into having the meeting without the goddamn conference table.

They sat around in chairs. There were some new faces, including a lady from the PR firm Lloyd hired, and there were some old faces, including some people Lloyd had brought with him from Omega.

Lloyd said, "All right, we need to decide whether to go out now with the software we've already got, or to stick to our old schedule. Francis?"

Francis said, "In eight weeks I will have a full upgrade from the existing version. It'll be worth the wait. It will blow the Hypnotizer out of the water. Encryption security built in. Two-to-one real-time compression. Filters both in and out of all prominent word processing apps."

Lloyd nodded firmly. Then he said, "Can we wait eight weeks?"

A marketing guy spoke up—the guy had been hired just *yesterday*—"Let me get this straight. Is the system we have available today *better* than the Hypnotizer package?"

Lloyd said that it was. "It's better."

"But not a full *upgrade* better," Francis added. "It's better code, but doesn't offer very different features."

"So what?" the guy said. "As long as it's not any worse, we should get it out there. Full bore. Grab the market share. Upgrade in twelve weeks."

Francis let out an anguished sigh. "First impressions matter. The market's going to look at what we have and say, 'This is the same as the Hypnotizer. Why pay for what I can get for free?' "

Francis's new marketing nemesis shook his head. "No they won't. We're a name brand. Users will flock to our product because of credibility. We sell it in. The Hypnotizer's got some word of mouth, but that doesn't compare to a well-placed story in *Business Week*."

Francis couldn't believe it. He was arguing with some guy *who had just been hired yesterday!* Who hadn't even *heard* of the Hypnotizer until last week! Whose only experience with the software was a ten-minute demo two days ago!

The lady from the PR firm that Lloyd had hired spoke up. "I've gotten some calls," she said.

"Press calls?" Lloyd asked.

She nodded. "They want to know how we look upon this competition from the Hypnotizer crew."

"It's not competition!" Francis sighed. "In three months, nobody will even remember them. Just the word *competition* makes us sound on the defensive!"

She seemed to ignore him. "So, how should I describe it? A setback?"

Lloyd shook his head.

The marketing guy said, "*Setback*'s too strong. How about a *wrinkle?*"

"A *kink,*" Lloyd said. "Let's just say we haven't got all the kinks worked out of our system. Characterize the Hypnotizer as just a kink that we're working out. You know the drill."

Francis put his head in his hands. "I can't believe we're arguing about whether something is a kink or a wrinkle." He stood up. "You don't need me for this. You guys do whatever you're going to do. Do me a favor, huh? Next time, if you're not going to listen to what I have to say—if the point of the meeting is just to let me vent an opinion that you've already discounted—don't waste my time." Francis left the room.

• • •

Andy stopped working and sat up and took a deep breath. For a moment, he stopped worrying about the next curve this business would throw him, and in that lull he felt an explosion of confidence that made him tap his feet with excitement. He had accomplished something he never even would have let himself wish for. He wasn't exhausted or dying for a vacation. He was here doing the thing he loved doing.

"Hey, Andy! Andy!" It was Salman. They were back in their office, sitting at their copper-pipe desks, hard at work.

"What?"

"What's my title?"

"Huh?"

"My title. My job title. What is it?"

Andy rolled his eyes. "Whatever you want it to be."

The excitement drained out of Salman's face. He walked over to Andy's desk.

"What's the matter?" Andy asked.

"A job title doesn't mean anything if I don't earn it. I want to be *given* the title by my boss."

"All right." Andy thought about it. "Okay, Salman, your job title is now chief technical engineer, networks. And you deserve every word. There, does that make you happy?"

"Depends."

Andy groaned. "Depends on what?"

"What's *Tiny's* title?"

"What does that matter!?"

Salman coolly explained. "Maybe there's nothing great about being chief technical engineer, networks, if Tiny is the senior president of the entire product division."

Andy couldn't avoid a chuckle. "Tiny is a chief technical engineer, too."

"Of networks?"

"No, of hardware."

"Cool."

Salman went back to his desk. He sat there for a while, tapping his pen rapidly and staring out the window. Andy counted to five. By the count of four, Salman was back at Andy's desk.

"Hey, Andy?"

"What?"

"What's *your* title?"

"I don't know. I have to be *given* the title by somebody other than myself, don't I?"

Salman apparently hadn't considered this. "Yeah."

"Why don't *you* give it to me?"

"Me? All right." His eyes rolled off to the side as he thought about it. He bit his lip. "What would you *like* it to be?"

Andy wasn't going to bail him out. "Whatever you want."

Salman blushed with anguish. "Okay, maybe *you* should be senior president of the entire product division."

"You sure?" Andy cracked a smile.

Salman smiled with him. "Somebody's got to do it. And I just don't think Tiny's quite ready for the responsibility."

Salman went back to his desk again. Andy waited for Salman's head to turn back to his screen. When it did, he counted to five, and Salman didn't move. That seemed to be the end of it. For a while.